Anatomy of a Park

Anatomy of a Park

The Essentials of Recreation Area Planning and Design

Second Edition

Donald J. Molnar, ASLA

Professor, Department of Horticulture
Purdue University
West Lafayette, Indiana

With

Albert J. Rutledge, ASLA

Professor and Chair, Department of Landscape Architecture
Iowa State University
Ames, Iowa

Illustrations by Donald J. Molnar

WAVELAND

PRESS, INC.

Prospect Heights, Illinois

For information about this book, write or call:
Waveland Press, Inc.
P.O. Box 400
Prospect Heights, Illinois 60070
(708) 634-0081

Contents

Introduction to the First Edition   vii
Introduction to the Second Edition   xi

1. Context: Past and Present   1
2. The Umbrella Considerations   15
3. The Aesthetic Considerations   35
4. The Functional Considerations   49
5. Plan Interpretation   83
6. Site Design Process   91
7. Plan Evaluation   107
    Et Cetera   149

Appendix 1   Selected Park and Activity Size
             and Facility Standards   153
Appendix 2   Recreation Needs Survey   155
Appendix 3   Recreation Needs Survey of
             Community Leaders   163
Appendix 4   Selected Game Area Size Standards   172
Appendix 5   Selected Game Area Layout Diagrams   173
Appendix 6   Responses of Selected Trees to Recreation Use   174
Appendix 7   Responses of Selected Soil Types to Recreation Use   175

Bibliography   183
Index   187

Introduction to the First Edition

*T*his book lays bare the essentials of park design. It is not written primarily for designers, although it may serve them as a refresher or a catalyst for discussion. Rather, this volume is addressed to nondesigners: lay members of park boards, park directors and superintendents, recreation leaders, faculty and students in university park management programs, the citizenry at large. To all those, in fact, who have this in common: You are the ones directly affected by what a designer proposes for the development of your parklands; you have a stake in the results; you live with them.

To weigh the potential impact of such results upon you as a park user or agency person, consider simply that all recreation activities need a physical facility. Here is where the bulk of your money is tied up, surfacing first as bond revenue used for either land acquisition or construction. For such large expenditures, should you not expect highest quality? Yet, how often have you accepted dull playgrounds, unsafe swimming pools, or forested areas which have the intrigue trampled out of them the week they are opened? How much of this can be traced to poor design or lack of any design at all?

Most of your operating budget goes into maintenance. Yet, could not such common problems as erosion, poor drainage, endless trimming of little corners and overgrown areas, and other repairs which take so much maintenance time have been avoided altogether if they had been dealt with through design before the development was actually constructed?

What can design do to minimize vandalism, discourage lurking undesirables, cut down conflict between autos and pedestrians, and remedy a host of additional problems associated with the public use of land? Many of these questions are answered herein through an introduction to *site design,* which we will define as *a thought process that proposes to anticipate problems of land usage and provide a physical solution that ensures that the problems never occur.*

There is poor site design as well as good. Needless to say, you would prefer the latter. But can you recognize its essentials? Especially in the paper stage when the cost of making modifications is small compared to the complications and expense of making adjustments after the work has been constructed? Can you judge what is the best possible development for your site and circumstances?

Sure you can. At least you possess the primary ingredient which will enable you to ensure that your park agency exploits design potential. You have common sense. What is perhaps needed in addition to this is some basic briefing on what constitutes design substance. You do not need to become a proficient designer, for just as you rely on your attorney to establish your legal bounds and your business manager to strike the best bargain, you may expect a professional designer to offer solutions to your facility layout and construction problems.

What you need is the knowledge that will qualify you as a critic of the professional designer's proposal, for you all have the opportunity to play that screening role, spurring park agency staffs toward installing quality works or upgrading subpar developments. If you are an administrator, the designer's plans will come across your desk for signature. If you are an elected member of a lay board or an appointee on an advisory council, plans will be formally presented for your review. Even if you are a citizen without official portfolio—a park user—your voice can be raised in public meetings or through written reactions to pictorial spreads in the news media.

The role of critic is often forfeited by the nondesigner with this rationalization: "Designers are experts. Who am I to question their efforts?" To repeat: You're the person most affected by the work. You live with the results. If you don't exercise your rights as a critic, you sign a blank check.

The designer should be considered the expert in putting pieces together into a whole. Hire one accordingly. For your own benefit, however, you can easily become the expert in breaking the whole into its contributing parts and evaluating the relative worth of each. And you need not be a master chef to become a discriminating gourmet. In the latter role, you can substantially participate in the decision-making process that leads to the development of your parklands.

If at this stage, you see some value in what I am proposing, perhaps you are asking, "Could you supply me with a list of publications on park design and development?" Well, there are many pamphlets and magazine articles dealing with single phases of the subject: technical writings on zoos, golf courses, amphitheaters, stadiums, tennis courts, or picnic areas; symposia proceedings on nature trail layouts, trash can design, or parking lot schemes; construction hints from a superintendent in Minnesota, a designer in Washington, a maintenance foreman at Yellowstone. It would take months of painful research, leafing through hundreds of magazines and soliciting from dozens of agencies, to compile such scatterings. Even if a full listing were available, the question would still remain: "Which one should I read first?"

There are several books either totally or partially devoted to park design, but most of these also focus on such special aspects of development as playground design, marina planning, or forest recreation construction. Many of these volumes, along with the few which attempt to be comprehensive, are noted in the bibliography. But despite all the writing that has been done on the subject, one element is missing: a basic manual on park design which ties the fragments together and helps make advanced reading meaningful. Without such understanding, where do you begin?

This volume tries to answer that question, for one of its purposes is to provide a framework to which the details of more specific readings can be related. It is proposed as a "nontechnical technical book," hopefully within the digestive capabilities of the nondesigner, yet providing a substantial introduction to the field. Further, this book reflects this designer's attempt to supply collaborating professionals with a sense of his objectives and the issues he considers relevant. More specifically, by prying beneath the surface — the grand tour and the fancy rendering — to get at what actually makes design succeed or fail, these pages provide information and procedural suggestions which will assist those evaluating both completed works and works still in the paper stage.

Emphasis is on evaluating plan drawings, since this is the form in which most solutions are presented by designers. The relationship to the evaluation of constructed works is strong, however; if you can understand what to look for in the drawings, your focus will be sharpened when you are confronted with a physical work. In turn, acute perception of what causes a completed work to fail or succeed hones your ability to critique the plan drawing.

Anatomy of a Park might also serve as a textbook. Augmented by tales from experience, slides, plans, and field trips, this book could serve as an outline guide for a presentation of the essentials of park design to majors in the fields of park management and recreation programming. It could also provide organizational material for the preparation of short-course seminars for professional administrators and other agency personnel.

This book, then, is meant as a foundation. For a basic briefing on park design and development, this is where you might begin.

Albert J. Rutledge

Introduction to the Second Edition

*T*his book has made a lot of people happy. The publisher has been pleased by good sales and the authors have been gratified by positive reviews from professional colleagues. Most importantly, the readership for whom the book was intended seems to have been served well. Because the need for a starter volume on the topic continues to exist, this edition again proposes to serve as a basic reference and teaching text on the fundamentals of park design.

Most writings on park planning by others remain technically oriented, or focused in depth on special issues, specific project types, or historic movements. Or they have been so comprehensively addressed to everything associated with park development from activity programming to regional system management that only a few pages can be spared for discussing the basic principles of design. Other writings have therefore tended to complement rather than compete with *Anatomy of a Park*. Since one favor deserves another, the first decision reached in approaching this edition was to retain the original elementary, nontechnical, and single-purpose concept, and hence not to compete with other works. The strength of a spare format, avoiding a ponderous tone, is still the target.

Most of the new material is authored by Don Molnar, but the source from which it is drawn is the shared involvement and experiences of both Rutledge and Molnar in constantly widening areas of practice in park design. Since design fundamentals have remained remarkably stable over the last decade and a half, most of the original material has been retained. With no major surgery required, concentration was directed at strengthening the book's delivery in two significant ways.

The first was to redirect emphasis to reflect some new priorities in the field. Specifically, the original book was keyed to the need for wise land-use judgments because of the *fast disappearance of land* suited for recreation purposes as well as a need to upgrade the visual appearance of the built landscape. While these typical 1960s environmental goals remain important, current economic pressures have mandated increased attention to the *fast disappearance of funds* for land acquisition, development, and management. Accordingly, we have heightened the prominence of those segments which best speak to ways of gaining *increased productivity* from the dollars spent for park development.

We have also given further attention to the integration of drawings and text, especially at the ends of Chapters 1, 2, 3, and 4, where most of the redirected emphasis occurs. The increased productivity theme is also reflected in a major case study and a design-evaluation exercise which we have added to Chapter 7.

As with the first edition, we have tried to provide here as "timeless" a piece as possible on the subjects which concern designers who plan lands for recreational use. We hope it will continue to be found useful for years to come. For a basic briefing on park design and development, this is still where you might begin.

Donald J. Molnar with Albert J. Rutledge

chapter one

Context: Past and Present

We live in an age of specialists. This is good, for it allows subject matter to be probed and applied in depth. But specialization has its drawbacks as well, since many disciplines have become *so* specialized that their implications frequently cannot be understood by people in related fields. As a result, experts are often isolated from the potential contributions of others.

In today's complex society, no single discipline can pretend to solve substantial problems without collaborative assistance from allied fields. Accordingly, this book proposes to foster an understanding of design and designers among park administrators, recreation leaders, and others responsible for park development. All of us must perform as a team if quality works are to become widespread.

While it may seem reasonable that a team relationship should exist, it is missing in too many cases. To some extent, lack of collaboration is due to the professional isolationism brought about by the specialization phenomenon. Much of it can also be traced to what can be described as a historic hangover. Therefore, the history of the field warrants review and evaluation with an eye to its contemporary relevance.

FROM OLMSTED TO TODAY

It should be no surprise that park and recreation policymakers and landscape architects are often allied when one realizes that we have the same parent: Frederick Law Olmsted (1822–1903). It was Olmsted who, in describing his role as designer-superintendent of New York City's Central Park, conceived the title *landscape architect* and applied it for the first time in the mid-nineteenth century to those who organized land and objects upon it for human use and enjoyment. It was also Olmsted, with the development of Central Park, who initiated the first real park and recreation movement in the United States. (See Figure 1-1.)

Out of these beginnings emerged three related phenomena: an American design style suited to nature-oriented parks; a split of recreation authorities into two opposing camps, passive recreation enthusiasts and active recreation advocates; and a situation in which landscape architecture schools provided many park authority leaders.

In part, these traditions were rooted in a revolution which occurred in England preceding the development of Central Park. Nineteenth-century industrialized England was laced with dirty, vice-ridden poverty-stricken, run-down cities. As a psychological counterthrust, England moved into its Romantic period, its people escaping from their oppressive environment through songs and poems that expressed nostalgia for idyllic nature and had a strong component of fantasy.

The well-to-do, utilizing their financial advantage, escaped physically, fleeing with their families and belongings to the countryside. There they called upon designers to plan their country estates. Sensing a desire for relief from every reminder of the city, designers strove to

Figure 1-1   Frederick Law Olmsted (right), the nation's first landscape architect, designed Central Park (left) and supervised the early stages of its construction.

create patterns which excluded the axes, circles, squares, and other geometrical patterns which visibly organized the city. They discovered the alternative in nature and began to lay out roads, walks, and other use areas in the "loose" organizational systems associated with nature, rather than with the regimented forms produced by the mathematically oriented minds of their predecessors. Sweeping lawns and meadows appeared. Human works were fitted to existing land configurations. Plants were allowed to exhibit their natural forms. As shown in Figure 1-2, the acreage took on a relatively undisturbed "natural" appearance despite the inclusion of constructed necessities.

Figure 1-2   The English Romantic style of landscape design.

Olmsted found himself in a situation somewhat parallel to that in England. In the 1850s, New York City was also industrialized and highly overcrowded. While Olmsted was sensitive to the "English solution," he was equally concerned with the plight of the common person. Reasoning that the entire population could not flee to the countryside, he proposed that, within the heart of the city, there should be rural landscape where a person could go quickly to "put the city behind him and out of his sight and go where he will be under the undisturbed influence of pleasing natural scenery."[1] Working with this principle in mind, he collaborated with English architect Calvert Vaux in a competition to design Central Park. The Olmsted-Vaux plan won, and Olmsted stayed on to oversee the construction.

Olmsted was an extraordinary man, Central Park (the first planned park in this country) being but the first of his contributions to open-space planning and development in the United States. Subsequently Yosemite Valley in California was set aside as the first state park. Its preservation was brought about as a result of a report Olmsted compiled in 1865 on the natural wealth of the region. Shortly thereafter, Olmsted conceived the idea that municipalities should link a series of parks into a working complex, thereby evolving the concept of a park system. His influence in this regard is still evident in such cities as New York, Buffalo, Philadelphia, Boston, and Washington, D.C., the lands proposed by him for acquisition being the backbone of their park systems today. He was also the creator of the parkway concept, having advanced the idea of this type of roadway to connect Riverside (which he designed as the country's first residential subdivision) with Chicago in 1869.

Olmsted's superior ability to blend roads, buildings, walks, and other construction into the existing landscape without visible disturbance led to emulation by other outdoor-area designers, now called landscape architects. Although they provided a legacy we enjoy today, many became trapped by the style that had proved so successful for Central Park. While such naturalized developments were well suited to passive and semiactive types of recreation, they were decidedly more difficult to justify for facilities for active sports, especially when these were located in little corners of the urban scene where segments of unassuming nature might appear strangely out of place, if it was possible to install them at all. It was also argued that active sports and related activities hardly needed to be surrounded by rustic

[1] Charles E. Doell and Gerald B. Fitzgerald, *Brief History of Parks and Recreation in the United States,* The Athletic Institute, Chicago, 1954, p. 33.

trappings. Accordingly, the landscape architects of that time and many into the twentieth century either shunned the design of active-sport facilities or attempted to stuff them into a rural mold.

On the recreation side of the ledger, Olmsted was a persuasive champion of his cause. Olmsted was convinced that the essential recreational need was for rural retreats in the heart of the city. This conviction became the primary tenet of *the* park and recreation movement of the times. As the movement grew in acceptance, another came along. Physical education enthusiasts proclaimed that recreational pleasure could also come from planned exercise, skill development, and the excitement of competition. Rather than cooperate, Olmstedian naturalists and active recreationists became wrapped up in the virtues of their own causes and formed poles not only of thought but of administrative authority as well.

Parks were defined as naturalized passive retreats. *Park departments* became solely concerned with parks as just defined. Landscape architects (schooled in the Olmstedian tradition) turned their energies to park development and, in their enthusiasm, included options in park management in their university programs. Such background led landscape architects not only to the design of park areas in the early part of this century, but to roles as park administrators and policymakers as well.

Concurrently, *recreation areas* were defined as active-sport–oriented facilities—they included playgrounds, hard-surface court areas, and team sport fields. Municipal *recreation departments*, separate from park departments, were formed to handle only recreation areas and were staffed on the policy level by administrators with a physical education background. As a result, *parks* received much design attention, *recreation areas* very little. Unfortunately, one can only conclude that such separation and lack of interdisciplinary collaboration resulted from nothing more significant than professional pique.

This situation remained relatively stable until after World War II when new demands pushed aside the old conflict. Population upsurge and unparalleled economic expansion focused eyes upon the question of land use in its broadest sense. Accordingly, landscape architecture education expanded its horizon in order to cope with the contemporary complexities of any type of land use problem: subdivision, campus, industrial complex, active *and* passive park, plans for whole cities and regions. To make room for new design programs, many schools dropped park management as an option for their landscape architecture students.

At the same time, population pressures and increases in leisure time raised serious questions about the depth and scope of the recreational experience. The same population upsurge hastened purchases of public park land to the point that heretofore sleepy park agencies awoke abruptly to find that they had become complex managerial concerns. In reaction, university programs in park administration and recreation research were expanded and many more were formalized as recognized entities with highly sophisticated missions.

Today we are left with vestiges of the historic hangover; some park departments are still not speaking to recreation departments. But these situations have become increasingly rare, for one happy result of the post-World War II trends was the unstoppable movement toward combining all leisure-time services under one administrative roof. This process was finally to force recognition of what should have been self-evident from the onset. Leisure-time needs can be satisfied through both active and passive means as was implied midstage in the movement by Charles Doell in a few simple definitions. Doell, superintendent of parks emeritus of the Minneapolis park system, set forth *recreation* simply as "refreshment of the mind or body through some means which is in itself pleasureful"[2] and defined *park* in its broadest sense as a "piece of land or water set aside for recreation of the people."[3]

Agencies have also witnessed an influx of university-trained administrators who have inherited the roles formerly filled by landscape architects, engineers, horticulturists, and others who once moved from their related interests to management posts. The intensive background in management which the new administrators possess has been gained at the expense of technical prowess in some areas, thereby increasing their reliance on on-the-job advice from others in such fields as design, construction, and maintenance. While much technical problem solving must now go the collaborative route, what remains as before in the hands of the administrators by virtue of their continuing positions at the top of the organization chart is final approval of and the ultimate responsibility for the acts of their consultants and staff.

Meanwhile, in recognition of the contemporary philosophy, landscape architects are paying equal attention to facilities for passive and active recreation pursuits. In the past few decades, mainstream designers have acquired the habit of designing land-use units on their own merits, having purged from their thinking the preconceptions which previously led many to stuff design elements into nonconforming molds. This sensitivity to the need for responsible land use was not the result of an accidental discovery.

During the 1960s and 1970s, the public visibility of both recreators and landscape architects increased. Generous federal funding became available for land acquisition and development, and agencies multiplied their holdings at an unprecedented rate. Unparalleled demands were heard for increased quality of service; these came from a vocal and politically alert citizenry sensitive to the use of federal funds (their tax dollars) and anxious to participate in decisions about spending those funds. The voices of environmentalists and behavioral scientists were especially heard and came to influence decisions about the provision of places which could have a salubrious effect upon the human condition.

Environmentalists, for instance, focused on the ugliness of both the city (Figure 1-3) and the countryside wrought by building booms with back-to-back developments characterized by blank reaches of asphalt, blaring signs, unpalatable forms, and choked roadways tangled around walking routes — all like dirty dishes in the sink (Figure 1-4). This raised a demand for visual refreshment as not only a basic need

[2] Charles E. Doell, *Elements of Park and Recreation Administration,* Burgess Publishing Company, Minneapolis, 1963, p. 3.

[3] Ibid., p.5.

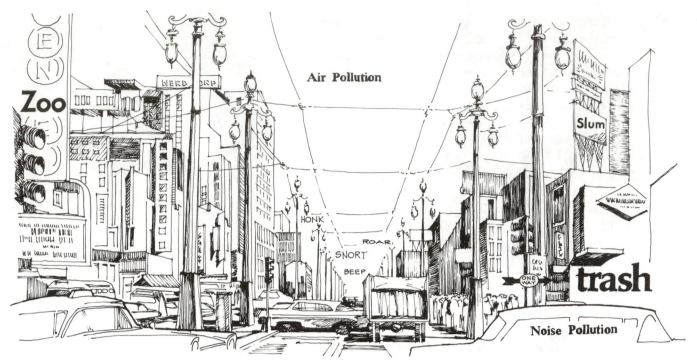

Figure 1-3   Blight in the city.

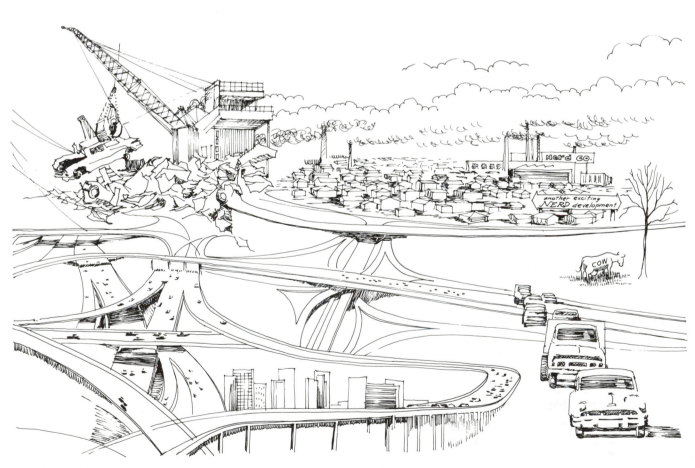

Figure 1-4   Chaos in the countryside.

but a fundamental human right. Behaviorists reinforced this notion with the supposition that physical surroundings consciously or subconsciously shape human attitudes, breeding tranquility or tension, pleasure or dissatisfaction. And they surmised that the chaotic physical environment was adding tension to tension and thus exacerbating the already unbalancing stresses of job, home, and everyday existence.

It was noted that Olmsted's parks were for escape. But was escape entirely possible in an age when unlimited mobility took us past so much shoddiness on a daily basis? How lasting was the momentary relief of a park experience if one had to return to face that which drove one to escape in the first place—when what drove one to escape comprised by far the greatest proportion of one's environment? The prognosis was discouraging. Accordingly, parks were given a larger assignment than to be vehicles for escape. Rather, it was postulated, they should be developed as exemplars of what is possible in terms of soul-satisfying environment not only for those who engage in an activity within, but for those who pass by daily as well. Parks were also to be catalysts for promoting higher standards in other types of development, helping to move us toward the day when everything human beings build will contribute to positive physical surroundings.

Mental exercise was, it was also argued, another need of the times. Mass production systems which provided a wealth of goods had at the same time produced an environment of repetition. Uninterrupted monotony dulls the brain and creates mental lethargy. On the other hand, mental capacities may increase when the mind is continuously called upon to act. When brains are subjected to difference, comparisons are made, capacities to distinguish are exercised, curiosities are developed. To counter the phenomenon of creeping boredom, designers were called upon to provide environmental diversity by ensuring that each development was distinctive and unique.

Mass-produced products were additionally seen as contributing to identity loss, for they were tailored to the "average" person, a "person" constructed of hypothetical responses such as that of the person with head in the oven and feet in the refrigerator who concludes that "on the average, I feel comfortable." The average person does not exist. Thus, products created for that person are created for no one in particular.

Pride, pushing aside the hollow feeling of anonymity, can result from being surrounded with things that have personal associations. This notion gave urgency to the need for activity-preference surveys and other forms of citizen expression to ensure that parks were developed according to the actual needs of user populations rather than those of mythical average people. It also mandated designers to attempt to give developments "personalities" with which their users could identify—truly something "mine" as differentiated from "yours."

The development explosion of recent decades also generated an unparalleled competition for land: land for housing, factory, school, regional shopping center, campground, golf course, athletic complex, and an infinite number of other needs. In the search for acreage, vested interests militantly strove to outfox others in order to gain

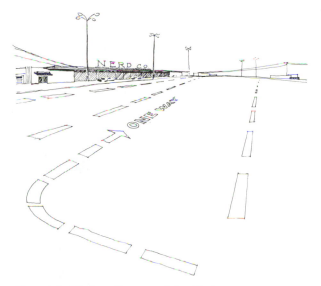

Figure 1-5 *Bleak and barren and devoid of compassion for the human condition.*

possession of the land they required. Others be damned. Too often this blind competition led to improper use. Facilities were ending up on sites more suited for other uses and those uses were being left with no appropriate sites. In the rush, sight was lost of the fact that land is limited and that its unbuilt-on reaches were diminishing rapidly. Leisure-service agencies were particularly affected. In countless cases, prime forest went under for industrial development while park districts were left with naught but flat and barren fields.

One million acres, an area approximately equivalent to that of the state of Rhode Island, were being bulldozed each year (Figure 1-6). Wise land-use judgments were critically needed and land analysis strategies were devised to ensure that each interest could be satisfied, but only on parcels appropriate for its use.

FACING THE PRESENT

In contemporary thinking, appropriate design is design that meets objectives considered particularly relevant for the individual park site. This is not to say that broad goals common to many park situations do not exist. Such requirements as good drainage and efficient circulation must be satisfied in all solutions. What is implied is that design criteria should be developed through analysis of each situation rather than through reflection upon what has been found to be applicable to other circumstances. From this it follows that, even where some objectives

Figure 1-6 "The good Lord is makin' more people, but he ain't makin' no more land."
— Will Rogers

repeat themselves often enough to be considered common to all developments, the manner in which they are best satisfied is most likely to be unique to each case. Each park has differences in site character at least. Hence, since what may be appropriate in one situation may not suffice for another, suspect the design solution which appears to be a rubber stamp etched from a prior scheme.

The unique requirements of a particular circumstance can only be discussed with information related to that job in front of us. Before dealing with such specifics, however, it would be useful to set forth those objectives which have been found to be common to most developments. To do so, let us first examine some conditions that portend to influence park design in the present decade of the twentieth century. By doing so, we merely acknowledge what history has taught. Recalling that the movement from geometric to nature-oriented design arose out of a desire to disassociate with the city, it may be concluded that meaningful work is done in response to the times.

Even though the environmental rhetoric of the recent past has subsided somewhat, the issues raised in that era remain ripe for attention today. Too much of our present surroundings continues to breed tension, monotony, and anonymity. The production of visually refreshing, mentally stimulating, and pride-stimulating parks as environmental exemplars is as important today as at any time in the past. The making of wise land-use judgments is an equally valid contemporary goal. Land is a finite resource. Errors in assigning uses to land are a luxury of bygone times. Mistakes cannot be easily abandoned. Day by day it becomes clearer that there are no similar sites down the road.

It is also evident that today's work must be accomplished without the generous outlay of public funds that distinguished the immediate past. Inflationary times, cycles of recession, and changes in political attitudes have collectively created this condition. The immediate results have been a slowdown in land acquisition as well as a cutback in leisure-agency services. Public recreational needs have not diminished, however. How can those needs be met with static, ofttimes shrinking, budgets? That is the fundamental present challenge; the answer may possibly serve as a cornerstone for a more permanent and productive philosophy.

The first response to the challenge has been a search for sources to augment public moneys, since a basic level of funding must be maintained if anything is to be accomplished at all. For land acquisition, philanthropic foundations are being courted with increased fervor, and for development funds, joint private-public ventures are beginning to be discussed. Such operations, where private entrepreneurs might invest in the construction of profit-making enterprises (say, skateboarding complexes or aquatic playgrounds) on public lands, are argued by some to be the saving direction of the future. Indeed, a number of astute planning consultants, as part of their ordinary services, are starting to offer assistance in obtaining foundation grants and putting together funding packages with the private sector. Substantial attention is also being paid to the acquisition and recreational development of depleted mining sites, exhausted landfills, abandoned railroad rights-of-way, and other properties which no longer serve their original purposes (or are, for the owner, a liability, needing care but not producing a profit) and as such are often less expensive to obtain than untouched lands.

Heightened attention must also be given to increasing the productivity of the land agencies already have. Multiple-use concepts are being explored with renewed vigor. These include ideas for multiseason use of spaces to broaden their active life (adjusting the summer baseball field for soccer in the fall). Another strategy has been to give recreational assignments to minimally used parts of the park which originally had exclusively a service function (rooftops might thus become sun decks or tennis courts). The challenge is to look at a familiar scene but see it in an unfamiliar way: from the height of a 3-year-old; through the bifocals of an elder citizen; in three other seasons — wet, dry, snow-covered; filled with people celebrating a special ethnic occasion, eating, drinking, listening. What else could it be? (See Figure 1-7.)

A trend toward the rehabilitation of old parks as opposed to the development of new sites entirely from scratch is also presently being witnessed. This is due in part to the funding crunch — fewer new sites are being purchased. But it also results from new activity demands of changing urban neighborhood populations and the pressures the new populations put on old places designed to serve bygone needs. As with other multiple-use questions, creative thinking about adapting original facilities is very much a part of the rehabilitation routine. The "flatten everything to the ground" urban renewal mentality of the 1950s cannot be afforded. Since it is essential to get the most from limited funds, the more that can be recycled into the new scheme, the better the plan.

The need to get the most from scarce dollars also gives new prominence to those traditional design objectives which affect energy consumption. Buildings oriented to reduce solar gain in the summer and exploit it in the winter, planning actions which reduce maintenance cost of outdoor areas — these are now more than agreeable goals. They are musts.

The contemporary mandate for increased productivity brings a new imperative for research that can lend greater certainty to design and management decision making. Information about the life span and usefulness of materials is especially needed. Surfaces: What materials last longest under various conditions of recreational impact? Plants: Which ones draw least on critical water supplies yet perform well functionally and aesthetically? Land itself: What are the least expensive, most effective materials and methods for stabilizing and upgrading sanitary landfills and similarly spoiled lands? Typically, answers to these and like questions have been pursued in academic or materials-industry settings. It is worth pondering whether results could be hastened with more direct involvement on the part of park agencies, which might put aside experimental areas in the parks themselves where tests could be run under actual conditions of use. Industry as a potential partner in this quest has much to gain in personnel services and much to offer in land and financial resources.

Findings from both general and specific research about people and their needs provide information that can make the outcome of planning and management actions more predictable, thus increasing pro-

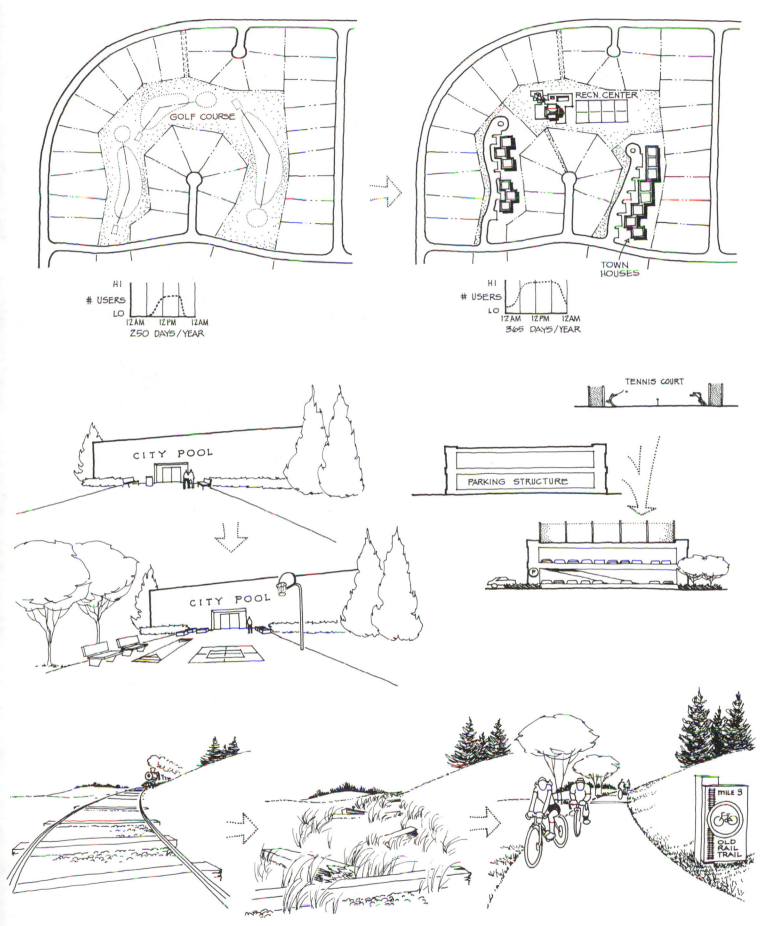

GOLF COURSE

HI
USERS
LO
12AM 12PM 12AM
250 DAYS/YEAR

REC'N CENTER

TOWN HOUSES

HI
USERS
LO
12AM 12PM 12AM
365 DAYS/YEAR

CITY POOL

CITY POOL

TENNIS COURT

PARKING STRUCTURE

P

MILE 3

OLD RAIL TRAIL

Figure 1-7   What else could it be?

ductivity and gaining the best return possible from each dollar spent. To minimize errors in planning, broad assumptions about recreational usage are no longer enough. Responses from the specific populations to be served must be gathered and analyzed. Before the fact, surveys, formal or informal, must be made to determine what the future users of the park want to do, see, hear, enjoy. After the fact, observations must be made and objective conclusions drawn concerning successes and failures in user satisfaction. Are people doing what they said they wanted to do in the park? Are they sitting, playing, watching, picnicking where the design directed those activities?

The data must be gathered. The records need to be kept. The core of increased productivity is information, information like how much, how long, how many, when, where. These questions must be asked about whatever cost money, time, or commitment of assets. These records of performance — of both products and people — are vital to any conclusions drawn and directions taken. The problem with adequate data has historically been the sheer bulk of material that must be stored, accompanied by the difficulty of trying to evaluate all of it to successfully determine a direction.

But the handwriting is on the disk. The computer in its incredible advance toward integration into every aspect of our lives has already become the means of drawing conclusions from previously unfathomable masses of information. In common use already are programs that use matrix forms to allow manipulation of many types of data bases to produce statistical answers in the form of charts, graphs, and spread-sheeted schedules. A computer is only a tool, not an end in itself. As a tool it carries with it the obligation of every user to use it well. The putting of the best possible effort into filling data banks in order to properly feed the computer is justified by the computer's ability, unlike so many of its human partners, to remember everything it's told, cross-reference every scrap, and evaluate every alternative against all criteria.

As more information becomes available, central data banks must be developed and programs written which permit direct-response forecasting of the consequences of planning decisions. Data bases constructed from records kept and information stored will permit access to the real marvels of improved environment, increased user satisfaction, and expanded resources. At a time of watershed in the willingness to see value in minimum change and economy in maximum efficiency, the computer deserves a welcome as the means for knowing the best decision has been made.

CONTEMPORARY DESIGN GOALS

Every action begins with the identification of objectives. While no two design projects are ever alike, each having differences of site, facilities, users, and other parameters, there are several goals which remain constant for all projects.

In the most general sense, foremost is the provision of facilities which lend grace to the environment, provide mental stimulation, have pride-inducing personality, and make best use of the land. Of commanding priority, however, is the implementation of planning measures that increase the productivity of sites put to recreational use. These are traditional design goals, but they are singled out for special focus here in response to the unique demands of our times and our foundation-solid sense that these concerns should be part of any permanent philosophy.

Within this contemporary context, we can identify further common objectives to be met in the design of park properties. In the following chapters, these are offered as *principles* or broad guideline categories in which judgments must be made as the designer proceeds through the problem-solving process. The principles are equally applicable to sites for passive uses and those intended for active functions. They are addressed to the satisfaction of general contemporary needs as well as to the specifics of individual projects.

These principles are then broken down into subparts, called *matters of concern.* Each concern should be weighed when considering the variables of any project.

Principles and matters of concern are the *whats.* Illustrations are laced throughout to indicate a few *hows,* ways in which principles might be satisfied and ways in which the matters of concern might be treated. Since it is impossible to set down every possible circumstance, illustrations are meant merely to indicate the wide range of opportunities for principle satisfaction. In addition, the appropriateness of the *hows* must be considered on the merits of the cases in which they are presented. Quite reasonably, what satisfies for one instance might not work for another.

chapter two

The Umbrella Considerations

*T*his first set of considerations can be read as a broad overview of the principles that guide design decisions. It comprises the overarching framework to which all other goals must relate.

PRINCIPLE 1: EVERYTHING MUST HAVE A PURPOSE

If wise land use is essential, there is no room in site design for whimsical judgments, even though many design "moves" may come to the designer intuitively. Intuition is a means, a mental shortcut, to solution, but it is not a justification for results. Decisions can and should have convincing backup. They must be supported by sound and logical reasons.

Design elements, therefore, must have an identifiable purpose. One such purpose is to establish appropriate relationships between the various parts of the park complex. These parts include: *natural elements* (for example, land, water, plants); *use areas* (game courts, ball diamonds, parking lots, roads, walks, maintenance yards); *major structures* (buildings, dams); *minor structures* (drainage, electrical and other utilities, fences, benches, drinking fountains, signs); *people;* and other *animals.* In addition, all are affected by *forces of nature* (wind, sunlight, precipitation). (See Figure 2-1.)

While each part will present its singular demands, no part can work in isolation from another. Follow steps A – F in Figure 2-2 and note that, for instance, orientation to the sun affects the location of the amphitheater, for the sun must not shine directly in the eyes of the audience (A). The amphitheater siting directs the placement of the parking lot (B), which narrows down the possibilities for access routes

Figure 2-1 A park is a complex of many parts.

to the public streets (C). The amphitheater parking lot could serve the nearby marina, but the marina noise, in turn, must be neutralized before it reaches the amphitheater (D). The traffic invited to this amphitheater-marina complex must not raise havoc with surrounding land uses as it would if it proved a safety hazard for children crossing neighborhood streets (E). On the other hand, the smells, noise, and visuals emanating from surrounding facilities must not cause the enjoyment of theatergoing or boating to be lessened (F).

Interdependence among all the parts must be recognized and accommodated if any single part is to work. Consideration of such relationships extends from the broadest determination of the park's place in the city plan to the smallest decision about where to place the trash basket.

Matters of Concern

1A. *Relation of Park to Surroundings* Design focus must extend beyond the park's boundaries in order to answer such questions as: Will the proposed park development cause flooding in the valley below? Will it cause traffic to back up into residential streets? Will the arrangement of the new facilities replace the pleasant view of undeveloped land with an unpalatable distraction? Will the location of play areas encourage baseballs to fly into backyards?

The reverse, the impact of the surroundings on the park, is equally significant. Will adjacent land uses send stomach-churning odors across proposed picnic areas, create safety hazards, or destroy the

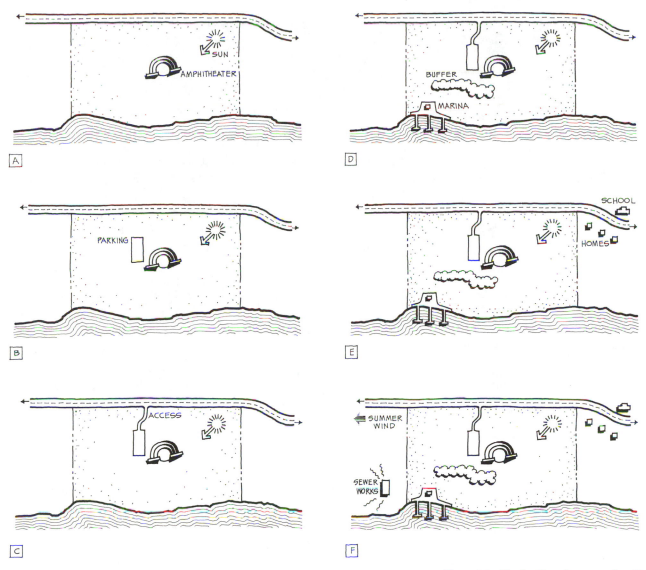

Figure 2-2 The location of every park unit affects the workability of another.

park's serenity? In a positive sense, do the surroundings offer potentials to be "borrowed"—a good view, a major access route, a utility source?

Through purposeful design measures, a sharp designer exploits the advantages of surroundings and overcomes the limitations posed by adjacent lands and their uses. The designer attempts also to see that the park remains the best of neighbors, never causing the usability of surroundings to be diminished.

1B. *Relation of Use Areas to Site*   Land cannot be wasted. Every corner of every site must be assigned a use. This does not necessarily mean active use. Lying fallow, land may serve as a buffer or a viewing panorama. It may be left as conservation acreage if it has been determined that active trespass would cause loss of wildlife cover or vegetation that holds back flood waters. Even an undisturbed swamp serves a valuable purpose, for its porous surface allows rainwater to pene-

Figure 2-3   Use areas may require different degrees of slope.

trate and refill underground reservoirs. Fill in or pave over the swamp, and the water supply for neighboring habitations diminishes.

Whether they be for active or passive uses, *facilities should be assigned only to portions of the site that are compatible with those uses.* As an example, consider the implications of a single site factor: degree, or steepness, of slope. As illustrated in Figure 2-3, tennis courts cannot function unless they are on flat land. Tobogganing must be matched to relatively steep pitches. While neither tennis nor tobogganing do well on precipitous slopes, these grades are ideal for separating two non-conforming activities such as a temperance meeting and a brewery company picnic.

All uses can be cataloged as to their demands for slope and much more: type of soil (stability, fertility, permeability), need for vegetative cover, nearness to water, utilities, and transportation, orientation to sun and wind, to name a few.

Therefore, it is essential in design to identify both the limitations of the site and its potentials, to overcome the former through the thoughtful location of facilities and exploit the latter. To bring this point home, see Figure 2-4 and consider the consequences if use areas are not located where site characteristics are compatible: Picnicking is designated for the sun-baked field, while nearby trees are cleared for the parking lot; buildings are constructed on shifting soil bases, while intermittent walking routes are laid out on adjacent stable surfaces; the amphitheater is situated in a howling wind tunnel, the winter roads where the snow loads are heaviest, and the ballfields in the marsh.

1C. *Relation of Use Areas to Use Areas*   Before being assigned to locations on the site, various uses should be analyzed in terms of compatibility with each other. Such an analysis unearths both common and disparate threads among the units. For instance, as illustrated in Figure 2-5, nature walks, canoe lagoons, and spooning nooks can be considered alike for they are quiet and soul-satisfying; tennis courts, handball surfaces, and basketball pavements are related because they are noisy and sweat-producing, and are therefore opposed to the quiet grouping.

By locating common units together and segregating them from non-compatible use areas, activity enjoyment is enhanced; such distractive battles as noise versus quiet are eliminated. In addition, movement patterns are simplified. Those with an interest in one type of activity need proceed to only one area to find a full range of sought-after

Figure 2-4   The results when use areas are located on unsuitable portions of the site.

pursuits. Area supervision is also made easier. A single supervisor can keep track of, say, preschoolers if all of their activity areas are grouped together, whereas more personnel would be required if such play zones were scattered all over the site. And maintenance procedures are simplified. Since like activities usually require similar maintenance chores, performance time can be minimized if maintenance equipment — trash trucks, horticultural equipment, infield draggers — are able to concentrate on clustered areas.

In weighing similarities among use areas, sometimes clear-cut decisions can be made. Most often, however, use areas are found to be interdependent for one reason, but incompatible for another. For instance, maintenance yards conflict visually with picnic sites, but movement between them must be easy; parking lot noise detracts from the concert, but the lot must be located nearby; playground complexes are for kids, but for supervisory purposes must be associated with adult areas. However conflicting, all such demands must be treated in the use-area organization proposal. Perhaps in the latter example, the playground could be physically separated from the adult station by a low barrier, yet, over the barrier, remain visually evident for supervision.

After relationships between use areas are decided on, the design task becomes one of finding sites which fit the desired pattern; for example, for picnicking a well-drained sector with ample shade trees and stable soil lying next to a cleared patch suitable for parking but away from the school building situated just outside the park's limits. (See Figure 2-6.) Thereby an "ideal" relationship is struck in accordance with all three matters of concern discussed so far: relation of use areas to use areas, use areas to site, park to surroundings.

1D. *Relation of Major Structures to Use Areas* In a sense, a building may be thought of as a use area and decisions regarding its location made on that basis. Special attention should be paid to the relationship of various rooms to adjacent outdoor areas. This will raise such questions as: Is the gym entrance handy to the playfield? Can the children move from the kindergarten to the totlot without having to cross the parking area? Are classrooms buffered from noisy game facilities? Can non-swimmers move from the bathhouse to the wading area without having to walk along the edge of the deep pool?

1E. *Relation of Minor Structures to Minor Structures* Just as a park is a complex of related areas, each use area is a complex of interdependent physical elements. As secondary as these concerns might be when weighted against the other relationship questions, inattention creates rightful public irritation. Is the bench close to the refreshment stand? Or must a parent juggle a half-dozen ice cream cones for 100 yards before he or she is able to sit down among the brood? Is the seat near enough to the light fixture which is supposed to illuminate its surface? Is it the right distance from the trash basket, thereby accommodating the easy flip of the discarded newspaper? If the basket is in an inconvenient location, the paper is going to stay on the bench waiting for the wind to blow it all over the site.

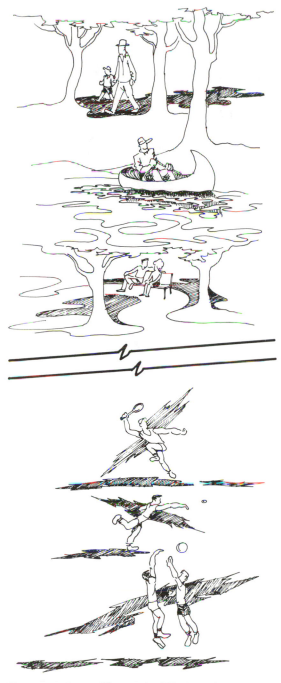

Figure 2-5 Compatible uses should be located together and should be separated from groups of disparate activities.

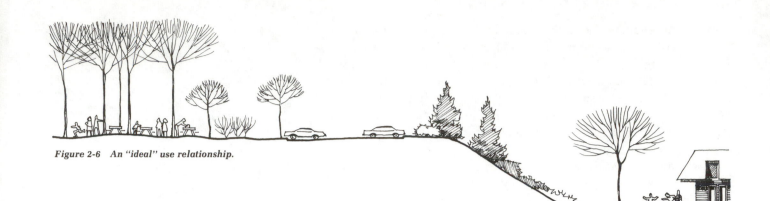

Figure 2-6 An "ideal" use relationship.

The Key Word

Establishing ideal relationships is only one purpose of design. Other purposes will be articulated later. For now, consider that this introduction to relationships has been set forth to illustrate the broader point that every design move must be made for a logical reason. To ferret out purposes that may be at odds with your own and to guard against arbitrary judgments and half-baked conclusions, the simple question to ask of a designer is: "Why? What is your purpose?"

From the broadest concern ("Does this facility belong in this part of town?") to the most incidental detail ("What underlies the selection of that material, color, shape, height, width?"), expect "Why?" to be answered to your fullest satisfaction.

PRINCIPLE 2: DESIGN MUST BE FOR PEOPLE

People are the benefactors of any park development. Right? Then why is development success so often measured entirely by how well it meets the demands of machines and equipment, how it simplifies administrative paperwork, and how it fits an unyielding formula of quantitative standards? Perhaps it is because some minds have become immune to the knowledge that these impersonal requirements are merely means to serve people, not ends in themselves.

The elevation of impersonal requirements to prime measures of development success can lead to the creation of an uncomfortable mold into which people must then be forced. This conflicts with design purpose, which in park design is to develop an environment which fits people.

Matter of Concern

2A. *Balance of Impersonal and Personal Needs* While it is essential to meet the requirements of machinery, that is not enough. For instance, in the design of roads and parking lots, it must be recognized that the automobile demands a certain road alignment, gradient, roadbed structure, and curb height, as well as a 10- by 20-foot paved slab for storage. It must be remembered at the same time, however, that the *people inside the auto* seek visual refreshment and mental exercise. As exemplified in Figure 2-7, these could be provided for them by roads

Figure 2-7   Roadway design should meet both the demands of the auto and the needs of the people inside.

rhythmically curving between softly rounded earth shoulders, revealing appetizing views, with peripheral distractions screened and oppressive natural elements shaded out — as the motorists wheel over proper alignment, up and down appropriate gradient, between suitable curb heights, and into the parking lot.

The demands of the auto, the gang mower, and the utility network must not overshadow the needs of the people whom these inanimate objects propose to serve. Both sets of requirements must be given substantial due.

Administrative efficiency is likewise an essential in park agency operation, and it is often met through the purchase of standardized equipment. Certainly, it is simpler to fill out an order blank for 100 standardized items than to requisition the same number of custom-tailored units, and it is economical to purchase mass-produced equipment. But what happens when the result is that everything looks alike, looks alike, looks alike? Mental stimulation is suppressed. Individual identity is smothered in anonymity.

When can the economic benefits of standardization and mass production be realized without cheating the prime benefactor — the user? Consider dovetailing the previous principle into this one by applying the key word, *why*. Ask: "What is its purpose?" If park benches are primarily for sitting, they might reasonably be mass produced if they prove comfortable, and look-alike items distributed about the park if the visual effect of their sameness is submerged in an overall uniqueness about the development. This is another reason why rubber-stamp layouts should be avoided; if the design is unique, the standardized parts of the scheme will be only incidental portions of a refreshingly individual whole.

In addition, for a purpose such as the communication of information, standardization can actually benefit people. Since repetition creates familiarity, similar styles for all signs and waste receptacles, for example, provide immediate signals for users in the time of need. Because one has seen the object and identified it with a particular function before, one knows what to look for. This familiarity helps the user to spy it quickly (Figure 2-8).

Yet, "typically" standardized playground apparatus, always the same swings, the same teeter-totters, the same slides, fails when measured against purpose. As a major unit in the park, the play complex is

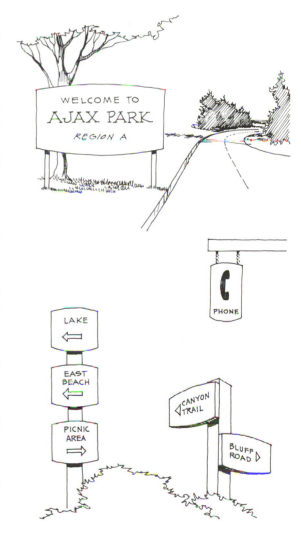

Figure 2-8   Similarity among sign styles helps the traveler in search of a message.

likely to have significant perceptual impact. Sameness here can lead to the dulling of visual appetites, especially among the adults who are there to supervise their kids or who pass alongside every day. Another kind of sameness about traditional apparatus frustrates one of the purposes of play. Such stock items can only be used in one fashion, and therefore stifle a child's discovery mechanisms. This deficit is compounded by the fact that even from the start, the kids have no say in the way in which each piece can be used, for a single way has been dictated by the item's design.

As a result of unmindful inertia, standardized equipment quite often continues to be purchased long after it has outlived its reason for being. Traditional playground apparatus is a classic example. Coincidentally, the question of this equipment's usefulness brings us back to the question of purpose — which at its root is still this question: Why? In this case: Why do children play? The comfortable old theory came with the primary title of *surplus energy* (kids have these poisonous humors within that get pumped out only by working like crazy on equipment type X), followed by the subheadings *motor exercise needs* (in which the upper torso, lower back, upper arm, and other body parts have to have developmental support through specific activity on equipment type Y), and *social skills* (the innate craving for social order and equity is brought out and polished by the opportunity of taking turns waiting to use equipment type Z).

That's the theory. Sorry. Turns out that play is, well, it's *just for fun.* In Mike Ellis's book *Why People Play* his more specific answer is that they play *for the stimulation they receive.* In *A Visual Approach to Park Design* Al Rutledge points out that after actually *observing* what was going on in a playground, without prejudice of a filtering theory, it became obvious to him that the kids weren't staying on *any* equipment long enough to burn energy, develop motor skills, or, saints preserve us, learn the kinds of social skills touted by the advertisements. Their target was purely the momentary stimulation offered by the equipment — one shot and on to the next piece. Yet this discredited theory is the basis for the play-equipment standard.

A discussion of standardization in park planning necessarily reaches further to consider use of the popular tables which propose quantitative standards as well as types of facilities and activities for typical park properties (see the sampling included in Appendix 1). Since full lists of these *quantity standards,* which express national or regional averages, are found in almost every book dealing with recreation-area development (as well as in many design-data manuals such as Hutmacher and Mertes's section in *Time-Saver Standards*) there is no need to present a complete tabulation here. However, it is relevant to this discussion to forewarn about their blanket application since to apply these standards uniformly to all properties is, at best, to depersonalize development.

A decision on the degree of attention to be given to any quantity standard should hinge upon some understanding of how the standard came into being. We have gone through that process with the play-facility standard. It evolved from an anachronistic theory. It deserves to be rejected out of hand. The play-facility standard also implies that children from tots to teens have the same play needs — a curious implication. This example raises the most fundamental question which must be asked of any model: To what degree does it suit the specific and varying demands of those who would use the works? As an example, let's take a serious look at standards for *activity areas*, specifically the widely printed suggestion that every neighborhood park should contain a softball diamond, playground equipment, multiple-use pavement, and a turf area. As with most standards, this is based on national averages without a pinch of allusion to the user groups whose needs the recommendation pretends to satisfy. Even where it could be argued that it reflects a majority trend, its usefulness as a planning guideline is marginal since in a given place any national minority can be the resident majority (Figure 2-9). And it is the specific place with which a designer must deal.

Figure 2-9 *The resident majority.*

Sadly enough, no matter how emphatically standards might be labeled *flexible,* the temptation to regard them as absolute is great. They appear to offer a substitute for thought and an easy path to solutions. *Facility and activity standards must be taken simply as points of departure which deserve to be modified according to the unique demands of each and every circumstance.* Clearly, parks for the economically deprived may require different elements than parks serving the more secure middle class. Surely, conclusions about a Chicago neighborhood are not equally valid in East Podunk. And likewise, parks in neighborhoods with substantial teen populations should have facilities which are different from sites in neighborhoods which are overflowing with tots or unmarried young adults or senior citizens.

Obviously, any development responsive to people provides activities and facilities tailored to the clientele at hand. Ideas for these are more likely to come from recreators with a finger on the pulse of the locale and on-the-spot research than from impersonal generalists far removed from the scene drawing up lists in their rocking chairs. Suffice it to say that first and foremost is the gathering and analysis of data on leisure-time needs as expressed by the potential park users themselves. These *demand studies* are typically accomplished through questionnaires, interviews, and public meetings called when a park is due for capital improvements.

But while demand studies do help bring the local people into the development process, a nagging worry remains; demand studies do not reveal every facet of need. Whatever people say they want springs from a need and should therefore receive substantial attention. However, rare are the people who possess enough insight to identify every condition which could benefit them. Accordingly, it is incumbent upon professionals to take up where public articulation falters, folding into their work human satisfaction factors seldom expressed in public proclamations. Realistically, the science of sorting out little-understood human needs is inexact at best, and its application is often checked by the ever-present fear of becoming a self-righteous moralizer rather than a servicing prophet by mistaking a purely subjective conclusion for one which indeed does contribute to the common good. However, questions raised by physiologists, psychologists, sociologists, anthropologists, ethologists, and others attempting to understand human behavior point to areas in which leisure-time experts can operate, translating reasonable hypotheses and theories into activity

Figure 2-10 Organizing play pieces to provide experience continuity conforms with an observable play pattern among children.

Figure 2-11 Where playground devices are isolated from one another, the potential for continuous play experiences is diminished.

Figure 2-12 Planning sessions with a special clientele require special preparation.

programs. The ideal effort is a collaborative interplay among researchers and appliers.

Park users themselves are a primary source for the information on leisure-time needs which they may be unable or unwilling to articulate under direct questioning. In our book, *A Visual Approach to Park Design*, we demonstrated how both planners and recreators may unearth design-relevant insights through the simple process of casual but sustained observation of parks in use. Those insights can lead to generalizable ideas about how to produce satisfying environments as in the case of the designer who noted children placing planks between play devices and enthusiastically crawling, jumping, swinging, and wrapping themselves around them while continuously moving from one piece to another, innovating all the way. From this he concluded that for optimum play fulfillment, all playground pieces should be connected rather than spotted about as was (and continues to be in many places) the most common practice (see Figures 2-10 and 2-11).

This attractive hypothesis led the designer into a sequence that demonstrates the concept of park as design laboratory. Before creating a new playground, the designer gathered data by observing existing play facilities and objectively evaluating the observed activity as real expressions of need by the children (rather than "incorrect" behavior because it wasn't what would have been expected). The speculative conclusion drawn from the observation then became the basis for a physical design experiment testing satisfaction of those needs. Continuing observations *after* the fact provided the confirmation of the speculation: Observed needs were real needs, satisfied as play followed the patterns predicted by the design, supported rather than impeded by the equipment.

Observation alone may not enable a designer to identify the needs of special populations. Where the population of "watchees" differs significantly from the "watchor," all action may cease when deliberate observation begins. The target population either may disappear or become observers of the observer. Confronted with this situation, some designers may reduce their observation to a minimum and increase their speculation to a maximum. If they see that derelicts disappear once a park has been cleared to permit viewing from the street, they might speculate that the most comfortable environment for the derelict is one that is screened from the world of the affluent. The more likely reason for disappearance of the derelict population would be the loss of the comfortably separated setting for watching the passing parade rather than the need for screening. Who is screened from whom? But this remains speculation without local site-specific research.

Recognizing the hazard in this kind of speculation, designer Ron Izumita of POD Inc. determined to go beyond the observation stage and cursory laundry list of ideas when he developed the nationally recognized "Skid Row Park" in Los Angeles. The clientele, definitely a special population, were actually participants in planning sessions concerning the design program for a park space in their territory (Figure 2-12). With three-dimensional apparatus as basic as paper cups and sticks, ideas were exchanged and tested, and needs were identified; through the participation an interest was achieved that has sustained the constructed park as an environment that the users enjoy and that the city can live with.

Izumita acknowledges that the first level of participation would never have been achieved without some incentive. In this situation it was the offer of $5 and a free meal—*after* the planning session. Special populations may justify special methods as in this case. The wisdom of the method is confirmed by the after-the-fact support of the park by its special population.

Interestingly, in a similar setting with a similar population in another major city, a park design built on assumptions based on observations affected by considerable (unfortunately unrecognized) designer bias and completed without client participation was voted a loser by the local barrio population. They proceeded to disassemble it splinter by splinter in a matter of weeks. Failing the after-the-fact test, the park is confirmed as not acknowledging the needs of its special population. Neither the designer nor the district can afford practice shots. Observation interpreted to reveal real needs and augmented by participation of a special population is design insurance and a designer's responsibility.

In other economic and cultural settings—for instance, upper-middle-income singles in condominiums, senior citizens in their retirement enclaves—participation may be as difficult to achieve. Residents may say, "Good heavens, we can't decide—you're the professional," placing the same kind of reliance on the designer's expert opinion as on a lawyer's or a doctor's. In this case the skill of the observer, effort devoted to observation, and background knowledge of parallel situations are critically important. The designer must put what little is said together with much that is seen and derive needs that are valid. The client vote on a completed project in this situation may not be as violent to the physical setting as in the down-and-out arena. In fact, as a negative, it may simply be the no-touch–no-talk treatment. The damage that results, which is professionally more deadly, is to the reputation of the designer.

In order to bridge the dangerous chasm between park as plan and park as product, the designer, knowing that users may have difficulty interpreting the plan drawings, needs to find practical ways to help them "get their minds around" the plan. The designer might use the Izumita method, or employ sketches, built models, or computer simulations. User representatives might visit other parks with similar facilities which can serve as demonstration labs for their park development. The bridging, however accomplished, is very important.

The perception of the park as laboratory offers designers and recreators a potential so far only partially tapped for evaluating the overall success of design work. Besides unveiling hidden aspects of recreational need, observation of newly constructed parks in use can also reveal much about how well the planning dollars have been spent. This type of evaluation requires that all design objectives for a project be treated as hypotheses or hunches about how people will use or otherwise react to specified aspects of the work. Postconstruction evaluation findings provide evidence of what worked and what didn't. And such evaluations go a long way toward pinpointing where adjustments are deserved or preventing the duplication of mistakes in the next job.

Sadly, postconstruction evaluations of park properties are rarely if ever conducted. Conceded, the process imposes an additional burden on the staff. Yet that seems a short-sighted argument when the purpose of the test is the proof of maximum productivity per dollar spent. Steps to ensure that design work gives the highest return in user satisfaction can ill afford to be treated as niceties. They are necessities. To heighten human-satisfaction returns, we must also pay closer attention to what the social and behavioral sciences have to say about human needs and incorporate the best of those offerings more thoroughly and consistently into the planning of physical works.

The often expressed hope of designers for factual support of behavioral theory is being met as more useful publications are hitting the stands. William H. Whyte's studies of people in urban spaces are an example of the knitting of threads of theory into the fabric of fact; Whyte's theories are supported by documentation of people observation in plazas, squares, mini- and maxi-parks, and all types of urban areas where leisure time is spent. The appearance of his *The Social Life of Small Urban Spaces* as book and subsequent film was an event of critical importance to anyone involved in urban-area recreation design. Whyte's work includes examples of techniques used in gathering data from and about human subjects who inevitably seem to be ham exaggerationists in the presence of movie or video equipment. Whyte's techniques as discussed in the book include simple people-mapping procedures as well as more elaborate but very effective time-lapse filmmaking techniques.

The authors' *A Visual Approach to Park Design* is another useful reference; it conducts a search-and-distill mission through the rapidly expanding literature concerning people observation, presenting a compendium of the knowledge of territoriality, personal space, and interactive social behavior related to park and recreation activities and exploring the design implications. The essence of the literature, which should hardly be surprising, is again the critical importance of observing people to understand their needs. An important emphasis is on how to train one's own eyes to really *see* what one looks at. Many generalizable data are offered, but the reader is cautioned that behind any generalization is the *exception,* the particular issue or characteristic that necessitates direct observation and knowledge of *that* situation: the physical setting, the reaction of the people to its potential, the people in the setting of their own current lifestyles, the people as seen by themselves—what they think they are, like, and do. People watching becomes the central and critical requirement for the designer, but, *and this may be surprising to some designers,* it is also the most desirable *activity* for people. Seeing and being seen. This is a need that includes and transcends all other activities, and encompasses all categories of people regardless of age, sex, and interests.

Consequently activities *plus their settings* get to be successful people-pleasing elements very much to the extent that they permit and promote the visibility of the action; no matter that it ranges from almost passive nonaction like talking to extremely hectic superaction like a pickup game of basketball (Figure 2-13).

Figure 2-13 Orientation of sitting places toward activity spots encourages human interaction.

The "two's company" of interaction and meeting people is another all-ages need basic to society; it ranks just below seeing and being seen. Where interaction is to be encouraged, benches should be grouped to face each other (Figure 2-14), never placed back to back or in isolation. In addition, distances between benches are important to conversation making, as indicated by Robert T. Hall in his book *The Silent Language.* Anthropologist Hall points out that members of different cultures automatically assume unique distances when conversing, and he lists what he has found to be the most comfortable talking distances for Americans. In his book *Personal Space: The Behavioral Basis of Design,* psychologist Robert Sommer reports that back-to-back and far apart placement of seats is a technique used in airline terminals to drive people from the waiting areas into bars and coffee shops where the atmosphere is more conducive to conversation. (Not coincidentally, this is where the terminal can make a buck as well.) Therefore, if you see park benches arranged like those in transportation terminals — and most of them are — you may conclude that the designers wanted to discourage interaction, or drive visitors into bars, or didn't know what they were doing when they ordered the benches set out (Figure 2-15).

Figure 2-14 Grouping of benches fosters conversation and silent inspection of others.

Freedom to be unencumbered by domineering authority and chart one's own course has been identified by some behaviorists as another human need. As we will see in the section dealing with circulation, landscape architects can meet this requirement by organizing facilities and traffic ways so as to guide visitors into use patterns which they might have chosen for themselves, rather than force them to move about only as others demand. *Freedom* also suggests a need for space which is not allocated to predetermined activities. As exemplified in Figure 2-16 these would be arenas for satisfying whim, "do as you damn well please," areas, places to throw a ball, lie on the grass, chase a greased pig, or do whatever suits your fancy at the moment.

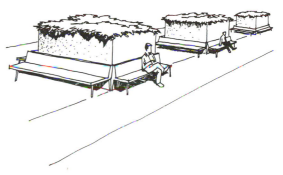

Figure 2-15 Isolation of benches hinders being with others.

The designer's understanding of these needs and others unique to a population is distilled from the process of looking and listening. Getting to know the user is the most important step toward the goal of creating a design to satisfy that user. No formula is offered or available for satisfying these needs. Realizing that the needs can be identified and that the means for doing so is improved and expanded people-watching doesn't make the process of satisfying them simpler. But at least designers should not ignore clues thrown down in front of them. In a conversation, a landscape architect marveled at the panoply of bright colors displayed in the dress and other physical symbols of an ethnic gathering. Yet, the brightest color found in a major renewal development which he designed for their neighborhood was a tepid grey. The designer admitted two things: The people identified with bright colors; they hated the new development.

The burden returns to the back of the designer. The people contact has to be made and its depth and duration is a direct correlative to success in learning their needs and creating a good design for them. Spinoffs like improved security, reduced vandalism, and user satisfaction are the frequent and sometimes unexpected coincident results.

Figure 2-16 *Simple open space should be set aside to satisfy the leisure-time whim of the moment.*

At the risk of allowing reemphasis to become overemphasis (a risk worth taking in this case): Two professional pitfalls must be rigorously avoided.

The first, the rubber-stamp replication of standard facilities, entails danger because it transfers a conclusion from one source to another setting. Each situation must be met on its own merits. Standards are only starting points.

The second, the imposition of a personal view, no matter how well intended, is a destructive disservice if it crushes what the designer should regard as a blossom—the user's need. The parallel to a tender plant is appropriate. The need expressed may be an unrecognizable, even feeble sprout, needing the water and care of a creative design response, not to be choked out by a weedlike standard that "will work because it's worked everyplace else." Under the pressure of budget and time constraints plus users' admitted dearth of knowledge of their own needs, the designer is still obligated to remain objective and nurture the needs expressed or discovered in the park-laboratory. Before time and money are spent constructing a hunch, observations made with eyes wide open will definitely be informative and probably fun to make. The effort to look at people, before and after they have a park, and *see* what they do is an effort that must be made.

The question is that of professional responsibility. The professional with a balanced view of responsibility to and for the client-user will focus on the creation of order from the apparently chaotic, occasionally conflicting elements of human needs and site characteristics. The designer's view of a site as an array of understandable, usable systems is the result of knowledge and experience—the traditional academic foundation.

Both client's needs and the users' needs must likewise be understood as systems — political, economic, and personal. The designer's experience with and knowledge of these human systems is equally as important as a knowledge of site systems. It has to be obtained from people, the users of the work. Knowledge may be obtained in a case-specific, time-compressed way, through data solicitation and compilation. Limiting the time spent in people contact has some obvious liabilities; the depth of disclosed information may be meager. As mentioned previously, people don't necessarily know themselves very well. Or knowledge may be a deeper, cumulative sort gained by long-term observation and contact with the users. The benefit of this extended contact is obviously the corroboration of things said with things seen. The pity is it cannot be hurried to meet a typical schedule.

The designer's responsibility and most important service is to offer the best professional advice based on complete consideration and synthesis of site and human factors: the fiscal, the physical, the aesthetic, the functional, the political. The designer must see the consequences of proposed actions. Decisions may not be the designer's responsibility, but supporting those decisions by appraisal of the outcome is professionally central.

This may not seem like a very definitive set of instructions. It isn't definitive — just as standards aren't. Process is our most important product. The most important part of the process is bringing people into it; understanding people's actions, their environmental responses, and their needs, and guiding the physical design process to meet those needs. Later, in the discussion of the site design process, more will be said about blending people's needs (program) with physical resources (site). But, consider some checklist items reiterating some previous points to reinforce conclusions:

- Has information been gathered from all ages, sexes, races, groups represented (*really* — have you seen people on the street you're not sure about)? How about all economic levels?
- Is what you heard what you see?
- Is what you have concluded what *you alone* concluded?
- Are trends reasonably represented? Is future potential identified? Future decline?
- Are some trends (fads) *un*reasonably represented? How influential are status symbols?
- What is the relationship between budget capacity and user appetite? Has phasing (and ordering of priorities) been discussed?
- How much have you, the designer, unintentionally influenced the design? Has a direction taken been the result of trying to please? obey? avoid?
- Is there any joy in the apparent conclusions?

The Key Word

Where the limitations and requirements of mechanical devices are determinants, where economic and administrative efficiency is a consideration, where average standards are held out as the magic answer although the action is ostensibly taken to provide for people, the key word is simply *people.* Is the satisfaction of their needs *the* priority criterion in the development?

PRINCIPLE 3: BOTH FUNCTIONAL AND AESTHETIC REQUIREMENTS MUST BE SATISFIED

If we surround ourselves with specialists because we believe in their in-depth knowledge of their subjects, we should expect more from their efforts than quantity. Specialists' products must also have *quality.*

Site design quality can be evaluated on two bases. The first is highest dollar value, that which can be measured in terms of hard cash. Evaluation of highest dollar value is simple. Weigh the relative costs of alternative solutions. If the problem is surface drainage and blacktop will generate the necessary flow, it may be economically foolish to consider brick.

But highest human value—that which is judged in terms of human response—must also be measured. Human value, adding to or detracting from a person's well-being, is found in the intangible influences possessed by every tangible object: in a tantalizing view, the roll of swelling topography, the shade of a tree, or the intrigue of a paving pattern. While the value of human response cannot be price tagged, it is very real nonetheless.

Matter of Concern

3A. *Balance of Dollar and Human Values*   To arrive at a quality park design, both dollar and human-value aspects must be weighed. These aspects boil down to *functional* considerations (upon which the dollar sign can be placed) and those of *aesthetics* or beauty (from which pleasurable human response is gained). Therefore, our blacktop versus brick dilemma cannot be resolved solely by applying a cost factor.

Function and aesthetics may seem like polar opposites, but they are not irreconcilable. Progress is being made in attitudes toward the value of quality and its payback in human pride and consequent care. Technology continues to shoot forward, providing new materials and applications, and the means, through the computer, of looking at more and more data to test old assumptions and prevailing but unproven opinions. Paper models for "what-if" questions can be built from facts and figures and brought to life in cost-saving practices without compromising the quality of the original design.

Life-cost analysis is one of these forecasting techniques. Carrying cost estimation further than the fracas of the initial bid- and blood-letting, further than the initial cost of construction, life-costing examines the question, so easily lost sight of in the front office, of the cost of the creature throughout its useful life, not just its creation. In goes repair, rebuilding, replacement—many more than three R's. Some agencies have found first costs may be merely 10 percent of life cost (Figure 2-17).

Requiring appraisal of each design choice in terms of its performance potential imposes a proper responsibility on designer and user to stress unity and simplicity in the planning phase of a project. The

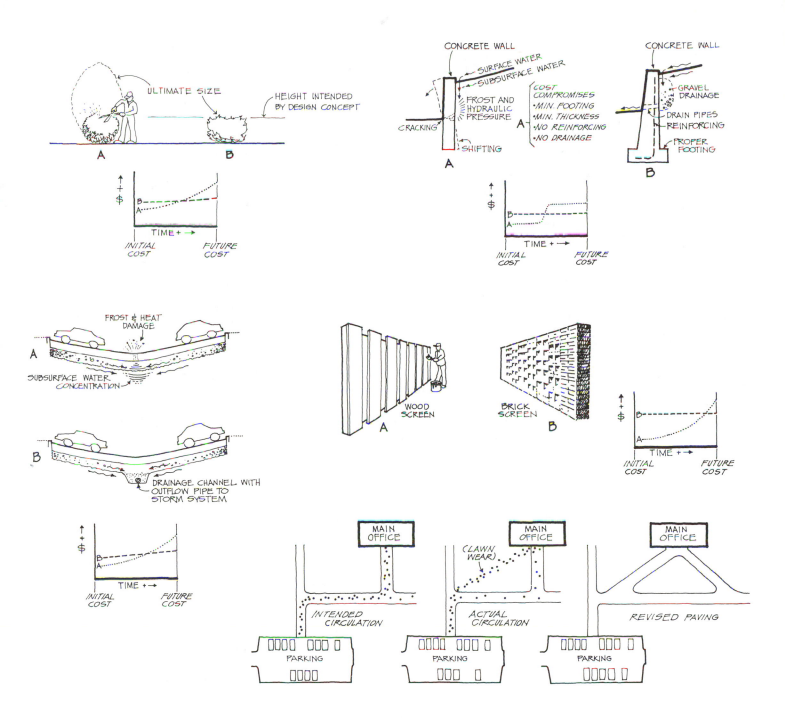

ULTIMATE SIZE

HEIGHT INTENDED BY DESIGN CONCEPT

A   B

CONCRETE WALL

SURFACE WATER
SUBSURFACE WATER

FROST AND HYDRAULIC PRESSURE

CRACKING

SHIFTING

A

COST COMPROMISES
• MIN. FOOTING
• MIN. THICKNESS
• NO REINFORCING
• NO DRAINAGE

CONCRETE WALL

GRAVEL DRAINAGE

DRAIN PIPES
REINFORCING

PROPER FOOTING

B

FROST & HEAT DAMAGE

A

SUBSURFACE WATER CONCENTRATION

B

DRAINAGE CHANNEL WITH OUTFLOW PIPE TO STORM SYSTEM

WOOD SCREEN
A

BRICK SCREEN
B

MAIN OFFICE

INTENDED CIRCULATION

PARKING

MAIN OFFICE

(LAWN WEAR)

ACTUAL CIRCULATION

PARKING

MAIN OFFICE

REVISED PAVING

PARKING

CENTRAL URBAN PARK

SUBURBAN PARK

RURAL PARK

HIGH

INTENSITY OF ACTIVITY

MAINTENANCE COST/SQ. FT.

SUITABILITY OF SELF-MAINTAINING NATURAL SYSTEMS

LOW

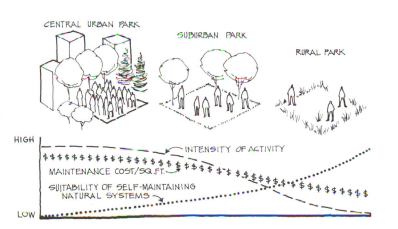

Figure 2-17 Life-cost considerations must reach beyond the cheapest installation. How much will it cost to keep it functional? Try your own charts of some problem areas.

Figure 2-18 *The land drains well and steps accommodate the grade change (function), while the paving patterns satisfy visual appetites (aesthetics).*

advantages of design with these virtues are in the impact of unified appearance on the beholder and in the economic benefits of simplicity of materials — fewer replacements to inventory, fewer processes to train for and track, and greater opportunities to concentrate operations and equipment.

It is important, in striking a balance among dollar and human values, that problems of function and of aesthetics be solved concurrently. Hand in hand. Never apart. (See Figure 2-18.) Aesthetics are never thought of as window dressing applied after function has been solved; function is never treated as an evil forced in after some pretty picture has been established. This "togetherness" in the design process will be illustrated in subsequent chapters as it will be shown that many moves which can be termed aesthetic actually strengthen the functional side of the solution. And, as design strives to balance dollar and human values, so too should evaluation. The relative success of a scheme should be measured in both contexts.

The Key Words

Every design solution must be workable. That is, every object and system of relationships proposed must function in the most efficient manner possible. Judgments regarding highest dollar value or degree of function can be wrapped around the term *efficiency*. In evaluation, this is the word which provides a test for every one of the site's working parts. At the same time, the word *experience*, in its cerebral sense, can be used to trigger critical thoughts about the aesthetic success of the same parts.

Aesthetic solutions address themselves to the refreshment of the mind as set forth in this definition of beauty: "An emotional response in the mind of the beholder that to him is pleasureful." When this definition is overlaid on Mr. Doell's idea of recreation, "refreshment of the mind or body or both through some means which is in itself pleasureful," the tie between aesthetics and park development becomes obvious, *and* it becomes obvious that the tie is a close one.

Aesthetic quality reaches you through your senses; that is, you must see, smell, hear, touch, or taste something before it can have influence upon you. Accordingly, that which is charged with aesthetic duty must capture the attention of your senses. It must not rely upon contrived intellectualizing for its essence to emerge; it must generate an impact that makes its presence unmistakably felt. On the other hand, if its perceptual message is so weak it remains unnoticed, you will come away from it without gain, the result being akin to the experience of sucking on a straw in an empty glass. Nothing.

Triggered by the word *experience*, measurement of the aesthetic success of any development begins with the asking of the following questions in turn: Is a sensory experience provided? Is it strong and influential? Is it pleasurable?

TO MORE SPECIFIC CONSIDERATIONS

Attention to purpose, people's needs, function, and aesthetics are the umbrella considerations which spread themselves over the entire period of design thinking. The key words: *why, people, efficiency,* and *experience* focus attention on basic issues with which the designer contends and, therefore, comprise the tests which must be passed by every development commitment.

Nestled under the umbrella are more detailed principles which also guide design decisions. In the ensuing chapters, these will be presented under the labels of *aesthetics* and *function,* for it is in the course of solving problems of experience and efficiency that actual project purposes, people's needs, and dollar and human requirements are identified.

Aesthetics and function are separated here for discussion purposes only. It must be remembered that in the design process they are interdependent.

chapter three

The Aesthetic Considerations

*T*o weave aesthetic quality into a development, a designer applies not only principles of artistic composition but powers of intuition. The possession of the latter is a must. For in such a complex field as aesthetics, there exist so many factors capable of modifying each other that it is impossible to set down, much less follow, rules that never vary. Yet, it is not necessary to possess this mysterious capacity in order to discriminate between the pleasing and the displeasing. Unschooled observers can readily gauge the aesthetic reasonableness of any development if they simply sharpen their powers of awareness.

The initial step in honing awareness is to establish extremes on a mental "excellence scale" as you go about the environment. Although beauty may be hard to describe, you certainly know when you are under its influence; for instance, you would probably not find it too difficult to rate the relative aesthetic merits of Frankenstein's monster and Michelangelo's *David*. It should be just as easy for you to judge a blank-paved, junk-filled playground against one with stimulating layout and imaginative equipment.

To know the best, you should also experience the worst. Thus, never at any stage of shopping for excellence should you feel you have seen all. Remain alert; always be on the lookout for something a notch below what you have previously considered poorest. But also continue to expect that which is above the best you have heretofore seen. Developments you are directly concerned with can then be appraised against the extremes in this mental catalog.

To establish degrees of excellence (or offensiveness) among those developments which lie between the extremes, provisions for *order* and *variety* should be measured. While "beauty is in the eye of the beholder," order and variety are psychological appetites which most

Figure 3-1   Too much uniformity results in monotony.

Figure 3-2   Excessive dissimilarity breeds chaos.

Figure 3-3   Order and variety in balance.

Figure 3-4   Invigorating: an expression inherent in nature.

behaviorists agree are common to all beholders. Regardless of its other attributes, an aesthetic composition must possess these if it is to generate a pleasurable response.

The need to perceive order or logical correctness about what is experienced stems from the human need to understand and find reason and regulation in human works. Under the influence of order, the mind experiences tranquility. All is right with the world. Everything fits into place. One can go about meaningful activities without being disturbed by the surroundings.

The desire to witness variety or contrast — a touch, but only a touch, of disorder, difference, or change from the expected — is rooted in the need to exercise one's senses. Variety provides excitement and stimulation. It is the spice that combats boredom, keeping the faculties alert, thereby honing them for other tasks of daily decision making.

Yet, overabundance of either in the environment is equally distressing. If regulation is too obvious or there is "too much of the same" as in Figure 3-1, the scheme becomes tiresome and monotonous. Conversely, if contrasts ricochet about in unending fashion as in Figure 3-2, the result is unnerving chaos which feeds mental distress.

In a successful design, both order and variety are present in fragile equilibrium. Note in Figure 3-3 that there is just enough order to suggest logic and stability, coupled with the right amount of dissimilarity among the parts to vitalize the situation. Primarily, it is the designer's intuition that points to the appropriate mix; one may state, "Designing is like preparing a fine stew by ear."

To measure provisions for order, the following criteria can be applied. Whether or not the proper amount of variety has been instilled, however, must be left to the critic's personal judgment. To help tune up your ability to make that judgment, comments regarding variety will be interjected wherever opportunities arise.

PRINCIPLE 4: ESTABLISH A SUBSTANTIAL EXPERIENCE

The first step toward understanding or sensing organization — perceiving order — in a work is the placing of a label upon it. It is answering the question: "What is it?" This is why you see titles on abstract paintings. They are the artist's concession to the general public.

Since it is impractical to hang labels on a park development, the development itself must have such strong character that it produces an impression capable of being identified. As illustrated in Figure 3-4 such impressions are distinctly etched in nature. Because of their distinctive characteristics, we have come to label natural units as, for example, prairie, desert, lake, plain, and are immediately able to distinguish one from another.

The same thing is possible among human works, as is pointed out in Figure 3-5. Each constructed unit is capable of evoking an emotional image whose influence could cause one immediately to label it *peaceful* or *exciting* or *awesome* or whatever else might appear to fit. If the radiating image is strong enough to be labeled upon first contact, it will quickly capture the viewer's attention, thereby maximizing the possibility that the development will provide the experience which the label implies. How do constructed works create such substantial expressions?

Matters of Concern

4A. *Effects of Lines, Forms, Textures, and Colors*   The raw materials of site design are not trees, land, and paving materials, but things whose presence is as real as those material objects (see Figure 3-6): *lines* (single edges indicating directional movement), *forms* (external appearances of objects defined by lines making closed circuits), *textures* (distribution of lights and darks over surfaces caused by inconsistencies in illumination), and *colors* (qualities of reflected light defracted by the eye's prism). These are the raw materials of any artist, as was inadvertently admitted by James McNeill Whistler when he insisted that we call the famous painting of his mother "Arrangement in Gray and Black." Whether found in Whistler's work or in the trees, land, and paving materials a landscape architect deals with, lines, forms, textures, and colors possess the potential for producing emotional effects.

Consider first the potential inherent in lines and forms. (Since a series of forms rhythmically leading the eye to and fro attain the directional tendencies of line, line and form can be investigated together.) Straight lines are bold and domineering; they move the eye forcefully (Figure 3-7). On the other hand, horizontal forms are peaceful, calm, and restful, for they lie comfortably on the ground at harmony with gravity (Figure 3-8). Ninety-degree verticals possess a dynamic quality as they move the eye upward; the more attenuated the form, the more forceful the movement, and hence the greater the uplifting sensation of soaring (Figure 3-9). Diagonal and zigzagging lines are active and spirited, for there is lots of erratic movement in many directions (Figure 3-10). Curved and undulating lines are not as dynamic as zigzags. Being slow and meandering, they are inclined to be gentle and tranquil (Figure 3-11). But if the curve changes direction rapidly, it can produce an animated or gracefully spirited feeling (Figure 3-12).

Pronounced rough textures are bold and domineering like straight lines and, in the extreme, ponderous and primitive (Figure 3-13). By contrast, fine textures are inclined to be sprightly and a bit fussy. Since fines are more subtle than rough textures, they can produce a more casual effect (Figure 3-14).

Bright and high-value colors are gay, lively, and spirited (Figure 3-15). Deep hues are somber and mellow (Figure 3-16). Neutrals (greys and browns) recede to the background and are therefore useful in separating clashing colors, toning down the potentially hectic effect of many unrelated hues. This is why stage designers often use neutral backdrops against which to play the bright costumes of many dancers. When applied to buildings and other dominant facades, this premise might be equally successful in separating out the conflicting hues of city neon.

Color any development cautiously. Since color appeals to the most primary instincts—consider the attraction of both children and sav-

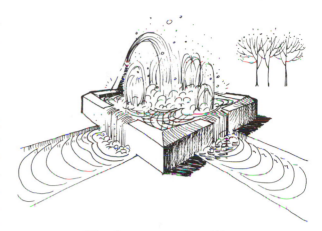

Figure 3-5   Exhilarating: an expression within the capabilities of a human being to produce.

Figure 3-6   The raw materials of design.

Figure 3-7   Straight lines.

Figure 3-8 Horizontal forms.

Figure 3-9 Vertical lines.

Figure 3-10 Zigzagging lines.

Figure 3-11 Gently curving lines.

ages to red cloth and bright beads—its sensational qualities are the first influences felt. Thus, where the reading of lines, forms, and textures is essential to the scheme, color must be used with some restraint, for if strewn about with heavy-handed abandon, it will overpower everything else at the scene.

Every material object, whether it be fence, shrub, trash can, piece of playground equipment, or body of water, has line, form, texture, and color. That is, through these elements, all ordinary things have aesthetic potential. It remains for the landscape architect to harness that potential in order to produce an emotional effect.

4B. *Effects of Dominance* To exploit their potential, the designer must act from an understanding that the aesthetic elements are never experienced alone, but in relation to one another. It is seldom that the pink bloom of a tree is felt as disturbingly garish, but it may be if it clashes with nearby blues and yellows. Accordingly, the designer must contend with the qualities of all objects seen from every viewpoint in the park.

One reason why you gain only marginal impressions from many developments is that, as you move through them, you do not contact enough objects which exhibit like qualities. For instance, in an outdoor restaurant, there may be a scattering of signboards with bright cheerful colors, but their impact might be watered down by the presence of an equal proportion of dumpy furnishings and somber-appearing material. Having equal visual importance, each quality neutralizes the other, and there ensues little emotional reaction to either.

But what happens when, through creative action, most objects within visual range are made to exhibit similar characteristics? Say, bright cheerful colors on the signboards and sun umbrellas, fine textures in the plantings, sprightly dappled areas of light and dark provided by grillwork, and pulsating water in the fountains. They all add up to an exhilarating atmosphere. Although contrasting qualities might be interspersed for variety's sake, they should occur in limited amounts and remain subservient to the one emotional feeling which has been allowed to *dominate.* As demonstrated in Figure 3-17, the development now has a coherent expression. It says essentially one thing. It can be labeled. And most important, because the lines, forms, textures, and colors are, each in their own way, making a similar statement, the development's expression stands a good chance of being felt.

However, because visual focus is never static—the eye continually swings about bringing new objects into view—additional moves to intensify the dominant effect are necessary in order to ensure that it does indeed capture the mind. Measures must be taken to see that the eye focuses only on objects which have the dominant qualities and does not stray to things which radiate other expressions.

In fact, of all the aesthetic criteria, dominance is and has historically been most important. If people, questioned about where their eye focuses in a designed complex, name a number of specific highlights, dominance has not been well considered. The unity of a place, its vital individuality, is traded for an exciting bench, a clever light, and impressively sculpted shrub, an intriguingly complex paving pattern—

all *things* and all *separate.* The more things achieve individual notice, the less compelling the dominant effect and the weaker the personality of the place. The things are remembered. The place is forgotten.

As an example, access ramps appended to a nonunified design may be lauded as a satisfactory solution because they are new and suddenly are more obvious than the other pieces in the collection. The result will be embarrassingly abundant attention. If, however, the design is the product of a clear conception, is an entity in which all parts are completely necessary, showing a dominance of unifying forms, materials, and colors, then a ramp incorporated with the same sensitivity that marked the original design will seem to have always been there as soon as it is complete. Its form, material, and color will immediately seem right. Simply, it won't stick out if it isn't stuck on (Figure 3-18).

4C. *Effects of Enclosure* The simplest aesthetic move is to wall out the irrelevancies. Consider, for example, the room in which you are reading this material. The walls screen out hallway distractions. You are, therefore, forced to address yourself only to what the room contains, receiving an impression that it is dreary, exciting, peaceful, or whatever.

Enclosure by walls, ceilings, and floors aids in putting the dominant effect across. It does much more. Beyond serving to assist the performance of lines, forms, textures, and colors, *enclosure itself* has a psychological influence on the confined person.

The effects of enclosure are hardly ever consciously appraised, but you are affected by being enclosed even though you may be absorbed in other pursuits. A parallel can be drawn by an allusion to music. It is not necessary to listen consciously to a tune in order to be caught up in it. Many supermarket managers know this well. Throughout the day, they pipe in dreamy melodies to encourage a slow shopping pace, thereby generating shelf browsing. But near closing time, they step up the tempo with such tunes as "Stars and Stripes Forever," because the help wants you out so they can go home.

Two basic aspects of enclosure play upon the subconscious of the confined. The first is *volume,* or the amount of "emptiness" which surrounds you. Picture the feeling that evolves from and between extremes. Feel yourself encased in plaster. Proceed to being shut up in a closet. Then move to the den of a "typical" home. The degree of comfort generated at these various stages is directly related to the surrounding volume. Arrive at a volume minimally comfortable for a single person, and you have a room suited to introspection: the den.

For contrast, associate yourself with maximum volume: an empty room twice the size of the Houston Astrodome. Consider sitting there, and it should be immediately apparent that this is not a volume suited to meditation. You may have an initial sensation of awe. But this will soon degenerate into discomfort as there arrives the sudden realization of your smallness in relation to the vast amount of volume which surrounds you.

The second influencing aspect is the *type,* or form, of the enclosure. While there are many variations, most enclosing forms can be placed in three basic categories. There is first of all static or complete enclo-

Figure 3-12   Spiritedly curving lines.

Figure 3-13   Rough textures.

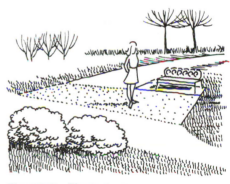

Figure 3-14   Fine textures.

Figure 3-15   Bright colors.

Figure 3-16   Dark colors.

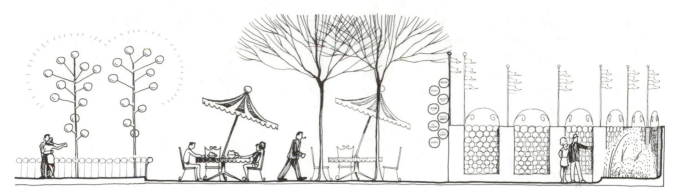

Figure 3-17 *A strong aesthetic statement is made when all objects within visual range are made to exhibit complementary qualities.*

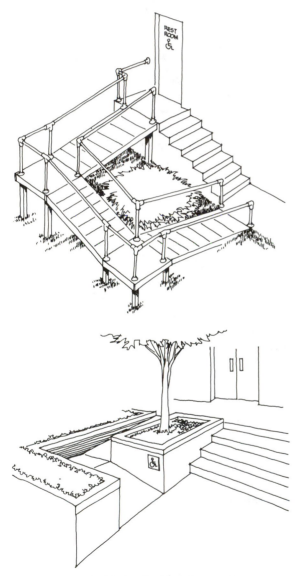

Figure 3-18 *Unified design doesn't stick out as if stuck on.*

sure. Usually square or circular, a static volume does not give a sense of motion. It is inactive. It just sits there. As such, it is well suited to functions which require isolation or attention to the center.

On the other hand, linear enclosures are elongated volumes that "move" in a definite direction and are open at both ends. Since the volume moves in a direction, so will the eye of the person contained in it, making it logical for him or her to proceed physically on the insinuated tack as well. Therefore, while a linear volume is not conducive to inward-oriented activities, since its motion might be distracting, it is well suited to movement or circulation: a hallway. At the end of its tunnellike form, you might find a static enclosure: a room. The completeness and lack of movement of the terminating volume signifies a definite end to the journey.

The third type, free enclosure, is a meandering volume which allows movement of the eye in any number of directions. It is suited to unregimented activities where individual choice is being encouraged. Free enclosure is seldom found in buildings although occasionally you may have come across free-flowing "roomless" houses which allow even the children to roam about at will, giving them the impression that all is theirs, too. A house laced with these uninhibited volumes is also a great place to throw parties.

However, the point is not to dwell upon architecture, but to use rooms and hallways as introductory examples of what is faced by landscape architects in the outdoors. Such a devious route to the issue appears necessary, for while everyone understands that interior rooms are enclosed, few recognize that the outdoor environment is as three-dimensional as the indoors. (See Figure 3-19.) A prime purpose of outdoor-area design is not simply to devise two-dimensional ground patterns, but to create three-dimensional volumes so that the aesthetic and functional advantages of enclosure can be gained.

In the jargon of the landscape architect, exterior rooms are called *spaces*. The floors of these exterior spaces are termed *base planes* and can be comprised of earth, water, low-growing vegetation, and all varieties of paving materials. Walls are called *vertical planes* and can be laid up with stone, concrete, fencing, trees, shrubs, and building facades. The ceilings are designated *overhead planes* and can be defined by overhanging tree branches, pergolas, constructed cantilevers, and even the sky.

In addition to containing their occupants and providing the various sensations of enclosure, the spatial planes serve necessary functions.

As illustrated in Figure 3-20, the base plane takes traffic. Where vertical planes are above 5 feet in height (eye level), they can be sight, noise, wind, and sun barriers. Below this height, vertical planes still form physical deterrents and thus can help to guide circulation. Overhead planes provide additional shelter from the elements.

Since the planes have both aesthetic and functional ramifications, the two objectives must be dealt with concurrently in the design process. Thus, a designer considering the location of a fence must not only be thinking about the size of the volume it will circumscribe and the visual effect to be achieved, but also about its relation to wind direction and about details regarding its construction and maintenance.

The wisdom underlying the concurrent handling of aesthetics and function is further supported by the fact that aesthetically pleasing spaces can serve to make functions more efficient. For instance, static spaces aid in maintaining solitude for passive forms of recreation which would otherwise be destroyed by outside distractions. Static qualities also help the functioning of activities complete unto themselves where inward attention is desired, assisting the concentration of participants as in lawn bowling or assisting the concentration of spectators as in an amphitheater.

Spatial types can also give information suggestive of an action. Static spaces provide a logical climax to a journey. The complete nature of the space halts the eye, dashes the urgency to continue forward, and provides the security of knowing that one has arrived. As demonstrated in Figure 3-21, the static space says "Stop." The linear space as shown in Figure 3-22 says "Go" and thus becomes a logical place for a roadway, bridle path, walkway, or similar construction. The free space as illustrated in Figure 3-23 suggests "Meander." Here the eye has many choices of direction. It is allowed to wander and frolic. Although free space is therefore unsuited to a function where explicit movement direction is required, it serves quite nicely for unregimented play activities where one can do as one pleases, where one is being encouraged to be in charge and chart one's own course.

It is as difficult to think in terms of outdoor volumes as it is to convey their emotional effects if you are not experiencing them at the time. Communication here is also hampered by the fact that the materials which lay up outdoor spaces are far less obvious than those with which a building architect works, and there are many subtle variations that often escape all but the searching eye. For example, in instances where opaque vertical planes are missing, the simple lowering of a tree canopy creates an intimate *sense* of enclosure. (See Figure 3-24.) While lacking sides, what is created is still for all essential purposes a container. Its form may not be consciously seen, except perhaps by a student of such things, but it is surely felt by those within.

Whether or not you can trace out a form is secondary to the degree to which you can feel the sensation that a space conveys. However, to reinforce the substance of this chapter in your mind, you may wish to seek out both. Accordingly, in any number of outdoor circumstances in which you find yourself, observe what materials make up the overhead, vertical, and base planes. Although comprised of earth and plants, you may find that the spaces are as hard and as defined as architectural spaces and can be readily categorized as purely static,

Figure 3-19   The outdoor environment is three-dimensional.

Figure 3-20   The planes which enclose outdoor spaces.

Figure 3-21   Static space.

Figure 3-22   Linear space.

Figure 3-23   Free space.

Figure 3-24   An intimate space secured by the low tree canopy.

Figure 3-25   The unrestricted overhead plane denies a sense of comfort to the space.

Figure 3-26   Strong vertical planes provide a message of movement to the eye.

Figure 3-27   Lack of a vertical definition creates mental ambivalence.

linear, or free. Or they may possess merely approximate form, which, if accompanied by sensation, served their aesthetic purposes as well as those of more obvious definition.

Appraise the impact of the sensations. Sit under the low-hanging branches of a crab apple tree in an enclosed courtyard (Figure 3-24). Is it comfortable for retreat, meditation, subdued conversation? Then place your chair in the middle of a football field or, even better, the Bonneville Salt Flats if it is handy (Figure 3-25). Feel any difference? Now walk down a road flanked by Lombardy poplars (Figure 3-26). Are you compelled to move forward? Afterwards, stroll into a flattened wheat field (Figure 3-27). Have you now lost the urgency to strike out in a definite direction? Finally, survey a panorama of rolling valleys laced with undulating brows of mature trees. Does a refreshing and uplifted feeling come upon you as your eye meanders through the animated volumes? Move down into the nearest glen. Are the initial sensations retained?

This gets us to another point. Just as the functional areas of the site must be considered one in relation to another, so too must the spatial experiences provided. Nobody is plopped into a space from above like a chess piece. A person moves through a space. Thus, the impact of a space seen prior to coming upon another must be considered, which means that what the designer strives for is a carefully conceived complex, a sequential organization of related views and sensations. Unless spaces are so connected, much of their impact can be lost in the intervening gaps. The fact that they are disconnected is another reason why many outdoor spaces go unnoticed.

These awareness tests should make it easier for you to understand why a site development plan cannot be adequately appraised as a two-dimensional pattern. In the critic's eye, the site should leap from the paper as an interlocking sequence of volumes, each space serving a function, each outside "room" conveying an emotional message, for this is the reality of the plan once it is built. (Compare Figure 3-28 with Figure 3-29.)

In the appraisal, however, remember that the full experience will not come from the quality of the spaces alone. As significant as their impact might be, the spatial planes form but the aesthetic skeleton of the site plan. They are only bare walls which remain to be adorned with lines, forms, textures, and colors. It is the grand sum of *all* the emotion-producing elements which produces the experience: the effects of enveloping space *coupled with* the characteristics of the lines, forms, textures, and colors of the defining planes and of the objects in the space. Substantial experience comes from this complementary contribution. Without enclosure, the effects of lines, forms, textures, and colors are watered down. But without the aesthetic elements, the spatial compartments will have a sterile look.

PRINCIPLE 5: ESTABLISH AN APPROPRIATE EXPERIENCE

While order may be advanced through a dominant effect, it is not ensured unless the effect can be sensed as appropriate. Stated in another way, it is not enough to simply feel an impact and know what it is. The answer to the question "Why is it?" must also be apparent.

One answer to "Why?" might be: to provide an experience which extends something the viewer already understands. Such a provision accommodates order by drawing upon a person's tendency to associate one thing with another that logically belongs with it: hotdogs and beans, Reggie Jackson and baseball, but certainly not ice cream and sauerkraut.

In site development, surmising that what exists is already understood and therefore accepted, the landscape architect strives to transfer the aesthetic qualities of that which is already present to that which is proposed for new construction. As will be discussed, the existing qualities from which the designer draws these clues of association may be something about the physical character of the site, the personal makeup of the user, or the atmosphere commonly associated with the function. If the landscape architect were to ignore such clues, he or she might produce a blatant sore thumb. The beholder then would not only be disinclined to embrace it, but, not understanding *why*, would be quite likely to hold it up to ridicule.

This in no way rules out the unique. Indeed, it has been stated that variety and new experiences are essential to everyone's well-being. It does suggest, however, that that which is foreign may be more readily accepted, hence more meaningful, if it is rooted in something which is familiar. This is quite in keeping with the point made earlier about dominance. To repeat: "While there might be contrasting qualities interspersed for variety's sake, they should occur in limited amounts so as to remain subservient to the one emotional feeling which has been allowed to dominate." In addition, while this principle is addressed to the provision of order, it will be shown that in its own ambivalent way, its application can also ensure variety.

Matters of Concern

5A. *Suited to Personality of Place*   Locations have personalities or pervasive moods which can be described as, for example, awesome, exhilarating, peaceful. Where these dominant effects are created by nature, everything contributes to the experience. Little seems out of place. When people interject their things amidst this order, there is disruption. But the fact that constructed inclusions are concrete, steel, and tailored beams hardly constitutes a license to dismember the prevailing influence. Rather, here is the opportunity, indeed the demand, in the interest of avoiding chaos, to wed human works to existing conditions. This is actually common sense, for it is easier to provide a substantial experience through an intensification of what already exists than to first water down a pervasive mood and then begin all over again with the insertion of a feeling created from scratch.

There are two basic ways in which human inclusions can be made compatible with their place. The first may be called *physical extension*. That is, new features can be positioned so as to appear to grow organically from the site. Structures may either be tucked into existing corners as indicated in Figure 3-30 or made to rise from crests as illustrated in Figure 3-31. The former is a rather passive acknowledg-

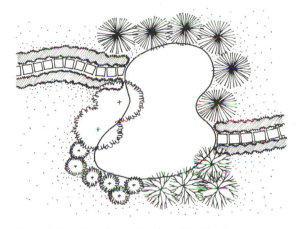

Figure 3-28   *A two-dimensional reading of a site plan is misleading.*

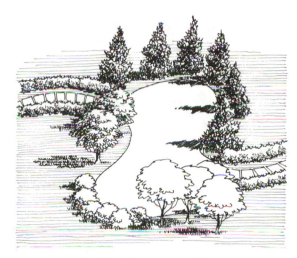

Figure 3-29   *The plan must be interpreted in terms of its three-dimensional reality.*

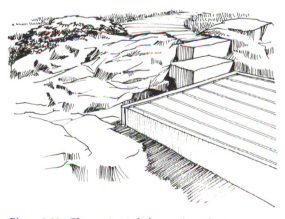

Figure 3-30   *The constructed element is made to grow out of its surroundings.*

Figure 3-31 The constructed element is sited so as to extend the drama of the existing topography.

Figure 3-32 Nature's textures are repeated in the material of the human structure.

Figure 3-33 The patterns of the old building are reflected in the new.

ment of prevailing mood, whereas, through exaggeration, the latter accents and hence intensifies an existing emphasis.

The second method works through an *awareness of the factors which give the place its personality:* our old friends, lines, forms, textures, and colors. As found in existing vegetation, soil, minerals, and other elements of the original landscape, these qualities may be repeated in the construction materials that go into the new one. Or dominant forms such as the horizontal sweep of the prairie or the sharp angles of mountain peaks can be reflected in related human structures.

This concern is as applicable to natural areas as it is to urban situations, for in both cases it boils down to a desire to achieve transition from the existing to the proposed. In the woods or wherever human structures are quantitatively minimal, the thrust is to make human works appear to be a part of their natural surroundings. Thus, where nature predominates as shown in Figure 3-32, the call is: *Blend people with nature.* Where buildings and pavements are abundant, there remains no less an opportunity to make developments compatible with the old, for lines, forms, textures, and colors of surrounding structures can readily be reflected in the details of the new works. Or the new may be made organic extensions of what exists through the creation of viewing channels to significant features outside the construction limits. Thereby, one is tied to another, making both seem related parts of a whole. Where people are responsible for both the existing and the proposed as illustrated in Figure 3-33, the parallel call might therefore be: *Blend the new with the old.*

This urge to effect a transition often directs the selection of locations for certain facilities, for it becomes easy to tuck a facility into the site if the proposed location approximates the form of the new structure. Existing hollows are ideal for amphitheaters; valleys are well suited for roadways; broad flats are perfect for playfields. The matching of function to existing site form also minimizes installation costs, for to effect the blending of the new with the old, all that is required is minor reshaping. (See Figure 3-34.)

5B. *Suited to Personality of User* In the transition from old to new, creativity can provide certain twists which will ensure that, at the same time, effects which reflect the personality of the user are interjected. This might be called for in private places where individual traits are easy to discern. For an individual of conservative bent, only clean, sharp, no-nonsense design devoid of excessive ornamentation might be desirable since it is likely that this individual is most comfortable in this type of environment. Yet the severity of such design would probably unnerve a more ebullient personality. Such personalizing is well in keeping with the desire to surround a user with the familiar, for what is dearer to a person than his or her own self? Success in this can foster a most intense sense of identity through which pride may be generated.

The premise can be equally well applied to public places (Figure 3-35) which are used by homogenous groups such as ethnic groups or those with strong regional traits. Flamboyant design seems reasonable for the public squares of the extroverted, and the daring and unorthodox are forms which the pioneer-minded might happily embrace.

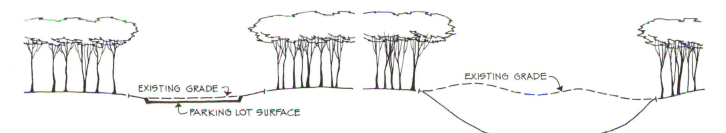

EXISTING GRADE

PARKING LOT SURFACE

EXISTING GRADE

PARKING LOT SURFACE

Personalizing areas with characteristics familiar and appropriate to the users creates a powerful base of identification with and pride in a development. This in turn can generate the caring attention essential to good maintenance of the area and respect for it. The landscape architect has to strive for this personalized quality yet not lose sight of function and efficiency.

Figure 3-34 New construction can be readily fitted to the form of the land if the original surface approximates the desired finished grade (left), but extensive disturbance occurs where there is a major disparity between the two surfaces (right).

5C. *Suited to Personality of Function* If we stretch definitions a bit, we will find that activities also have personalities which can be translated into physical development through design. Recognition of such a thesis is useful in situations where the personalities of users cannot be readily determined, for it can be assumed that users will go to a place in a frame of mind associated with the anticipated activity. It follows that meditation will be enhanced if it takes place in a peaceful environment (Figure 3-36), perhaps a static space with cool colors, fine textures, and placid waters, while playground action will be heightened in a free space with bright colors and other features which add up to spirited and active surroundings. This placing of function in an appropriate setting intensifies user enjoyment. By aesthetic suggestion, one is encouraged to engage in the activity more fully.

At the same time, however, recall the importance of mental exercise. The designer can enrich projects with unexpected variations, fascinating details, or exciting surprises: an unanticipated opening to a view, a gurgling pool appearing in an apparently tranquil setting, or a suddenly discovered richness of material in a hidden place—all potentially stimulating mental experiences because of the unexpected contrast they provide. These small touches of contrast are sometimes the toughest things to deal with in a design because to balance them requires great sensitivity. If they become too frequent, they slip from contrast to confusion, killing the dominant effect. Yet they are important. Without some contrast built into the design's personality, that personality may be so functionally correct it will be unforgivably dull.

5D. *Suited to Scale* Scale is a relative unit of measurement. As expressed in physical features and spaces, its appropriateness must also be sensed in a quality work. Designers of outdoor facilities concern themselves with two types of scale.

The first is *human scale.* To understand our world, people have a tendency to measure things in terms of that with which they are most familiar. The most basic "known," hence the most widely used unit of measurement, is one's own physical self. If one is to be comfortable, there must be things in a space which can be mentally measured in terms of one's own height, arm length, width of finger. If these are not provided as shown in Figure 3-37, people tend to become confused

Figure 3-35 A public place.

Figure 3-36 A place well suited for meditation.

Figure 3-37 Discomfort: things of human scale are missing.

Figure 3-38 Security: human scale is present.

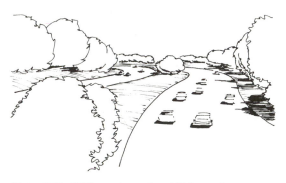

Figure 3-39 While one is moving at high speed, only masses can be experienced.

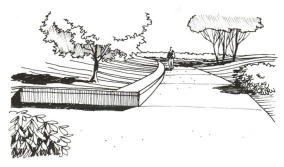

Figure 3-40 While one is moving at a walking pace, details can be comprehended.

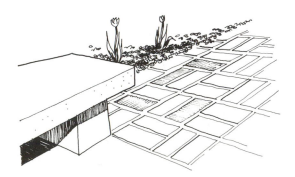

Figure 3-41 When one is sitting, detail intricacy may be demanded.

and cannot comprehend. They are overwhelmed. Set yourself in the midst of the Grand Canyon and you might be awed, but you will remain uneasy, for your sense of security will be affected. You will not be able to stand it for any duration. To stem this anguish and gain mental comfort, you need to be surrounded by things of human scale, elements which can be measured in relation to your own self. (See Figure 3-38.) This holds true for any place where a person is expected to linger.

Speed scale is also of design concern, for the swiftness with which you move affects your ability to experience. If you are going at 60 miles per hour in your auto, you can only distinguish the large shapes, sharply contrasting textures, and great masses of color illustrated in Figure 3-39. Details cannot be comprehended.

If you are walking, however, the slower pace enables you to experience the greater intricacy shown in Figure 3-40. And when you stop, you are able to investigate and understand all textural and color subtleties. In fact, when you sit, you may subconsciously demand such nuances as indicated in Figure 3-41, for in their absence you may become bored. Here is another example of aesthetic direction shaped by functional realities. The function, in this case the type of movement, supplies the purpose behind the aesthetic decision.

UNDERSTANDINGS AND HABITS

The tying of development to place, user, and function and the consideration of scale make design visibly logical, for the experience provided is sensed as appropriate. It fits. The preceding can also be used to illustrate other points in retrospect: with attention to these matters, design gains *purpose;* it is addressed to satisfying the senses of *people;* it interweaves *aesthetics* and *function,* for aesthetic direction is supplied by insights related to how the site will be used. In other words, all the tests posed by the umbrella principles are passed.

In addition, while instilling order, moves to ensure the appropriateness of experiences, especially those moves which seek to preserve the existing character of a site, serve variety as well. Just as people vary, so do pieces of land. Like a person's fingerprints, each site is unique. Therefore, measures taken to see that the new extends and intensifies present site qualities are steps which will guarantee that the site *remains* unique.

Too many people are blind to this simple device for maintaining what is left of environmental diversity. Those who dump hilltops into valleys or, even worse, obliterate forests with Coney Islands deserve no better than this upon their headstones: "What you have made may be found in many places; but what you have destroyed is found nowhere else in the world."

What might also be carried over from this chapter is awareness of some essential creative purposes. It is the designer's task to place functional areas in appropriate spaces on the site. If such enclosures are only vaguely defined, the landscape architect moves to reinforce their structure so that their experience-producing potential may be realized. Where outdoor rooms of desired type or form do not exist at all, the architect's charge is to create from scratch spaces to serve the functions. Once the spatial skeleton has been established, the task is to finish off the experience by providing a composition of lines, forms, textures, and colors appropriate for each spatial compartment.

In addition, as you appraise a designer's work, it will be useful to understand the implications of the aesthetic principles. Ask such questions as: Is an experience sensed immediately; does it come on as a definite impression? Is there variety; does the experience remain fresh after many journeys to the site; are new perspectives continually discovered? Give it the second- or third-journey test to ensure that intrigue remains after novelty has worn off.

Is experience appropriate to the function it serves? Or is it completely out of whack with what is going on: a honky-tonk frivolousness in the midst of passive pursuits or placid surroundings for hustle and bustle activities? Is there adequate transition between old and new? Is development sensed as an organic extension of its surroundings, or is it a comical sore thumb?

To sharpen your critical abilities so that you can spy the clues which will lead you to ask these and similarly penetrating questions, form some general habits. Compare experiences on your excellence scale. Are they perhaps akin to Figures 3-42 and 3-43? Negative or weak experience means that the designer has not done a good job, whereas positive experience is evidence of the landscape architect's ability to provide refreshment of the mind.

Look at things in aesthetic terms or in terms of the qualities that add up to experience. See that shrubs, just as much as fences, pavements, or earth, have texture. Note that a mass of trees can form defining vertical planes just as readily as walls can. Decide for yourself about the sensory potential of three-dimensional volumes in the outdoors. (See Figure 3-44.)

Search out these qualities. The development of awareness and critical sensitivity is what this chapter is all about, along with emphasis on the fact that aesthetics have purpose. These judgments are not frosting-on-the-cake afterthoughts. Ask: Why this color? Why this texture? Why that particular three-dimensional configuration? Why that opening in the space? Why such complete enclosure? Expect clear, logical, and convincing answers.

Figure 3-42   Rate this scene on your excellence gauge.

Figure 3-43   Where would you place this vignette on your experience scale?

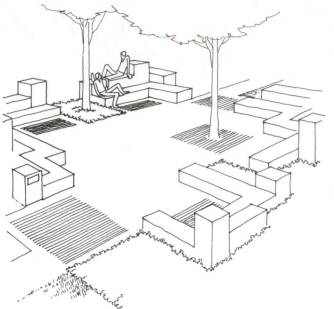

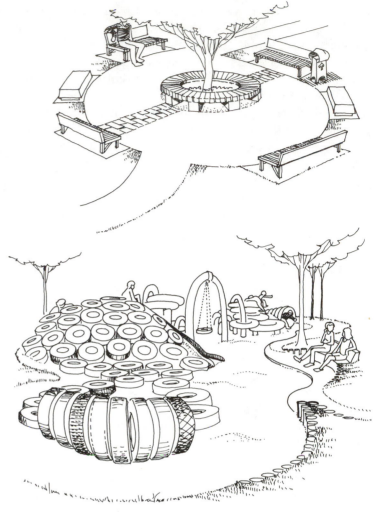

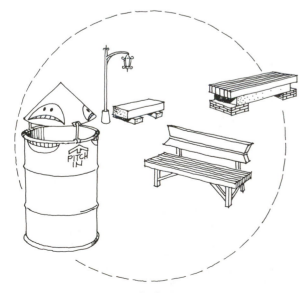

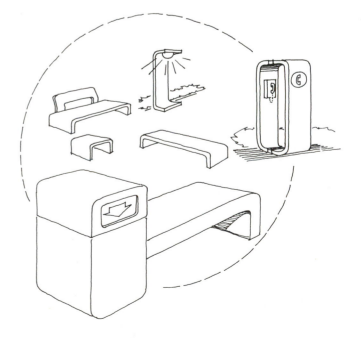

Figure 3-44   Some more examples for you to rate.

chapter four

The Functional Considerations

*U*nlike Whistler's art, landscape architecture must be used as well as experienced. Its beauty is irrelevant if it is not functional. Functional efficiency can be judged almost entirely on the basis of tangible evidence, for in contrast to aesthetics, where much analysis is qualitative and depends upon sensing the feel of the thing, the functional effect of design is predictable. You can focus on an issue of workability—say, the movement of autos from point A to point B—put yourself in the place of the user, maintenance worker, administrator, or whoever else is going to be affected, and go through all the possible motions of use to determine the functional reasonableness of the scheme.

What is best or highest quality is a product which has no weaknesses. While there should be no letup in pursuing this goal, it may not always be possible to achieve it. Weaknesses can stem from the unavoidable inability to satisfy conflicting requirements: a demand for a certain provision, but a budget unable to stand the expense; the need for a football field, but a site with precipitous topography. Compromises may have to be found; the critic must be able to distinguish these from questionable conclusions which have resulted from either mental laziness or lack of problem-solving ability on the part of the designer.

The knack which can enable you so to distinguish springs from a continually growing knowledge of what is possible. Thus, it is suggested that you constantly compare park developments and the workability of their parts with a view to developing a *functional* excellence scale to go along with the aesthetic measuring device already discussed. Extreme cases will be easy to ferret out: It works, or it cannot be used at all; it's the right size, or it is obviously too small for its purposes.

As useful tools in determining degrees of quality, the following issues deserve concentration. While each job will have its unique problems, these are the issues generally faced in all instances. As common concerns to which solutions must be found, these are the major points which a critic must chase down to conclusion in order to determine the functional quality of a plan.

PRINCIPLE 6: SATISFY TECHNICAL REQUIREMENTS

Let's start with the most elementary matters faced in design — those whose handling is the easiest to observe on the site or drawing paper. These are the minimal standards of quantity, structure, and performance which must be met if the product is to be at all usable.

Matters of Concern

6A. *Sizes* We have said that it makes sense to locate facilities on portions of the site where only slight remodeling of the topography will be necessary. This, along with the self-evident need to ensure adequate elbow room for all the functions, means that the landscape architect must test proposed locations against use-area sizes before he or she can proceed to satisfy more complex requirements. Size information comes from many sources including manuals developed by park agencies, university extension services, and recreation researchers. The sampling shown in Appendixes 1, 4, and 5 should give you an idea of the kinds of data which are available, while more extensive lists are found in many of the references cited in the bibliography.

Size recommendations for playing fields and court-game areas can be accepted with little question, for such measurements are determined by the rules of the game. However, size suggestions for many other use areas such as totlots and picnic areas can be modified as design purpose might require, for they are based on rather fragile precedents.

For instance, a widely used standard indicates that a totlot should have 2400 to 5000 square feet of surface. This standard has been arrived at by averaging out a sampling of lots in several cities across the country. As reasonable as it might prove to be, its adequacy should always be checked against the type of equipment, mode of circulation, need for buffer, and other demands of the specific lot to be dealt with before it is given a blanket acceptance.

Individual design requirements, then, become an understandable basis for deviating from a standard size suggestion. In addition, as will be demonstrated, existing *site characteristics, design moves* which may be employed, and *agency policies* can be equally valid reasons for departure. Consider the standard which suggests ten to fifteen picnic sites per acre (4356 to 3904 square feet each). If each picnic area is to be placed upon a base which is stabilized with blacktop or gravel or has privacy screening, more areas may be in order. However, if the site has erosion-prone soil, canopy trees which will suffer under concentrated foot traffic, or steep slopes susceptible to gullying, fewer picnic areas, if indeed any, would be advisable.

There are several dual-use concepts which can make areas smaller than standards suggest adequate for many uses. One is the school-park policy whereby play facilities used by schoolchildren during the day are released to the neighboring public in the afternoons, evenings, weekends, and summers. Since the same area is used by both school and park patrons, facility duplication is minimized. Thus, 40 acres of dual use, the school-park, does the same job as 60 acres divided between a school playground and a park. (Design organization which allows a school-park concept to succeed is illustrated in the chapter on plan evaluation.) Agencies can also put the same patch of ground to several uses where seasons of play differ; tennis courts can be flooded for winter skating, football fields can revert to softball diamonds in the spring, to give just a couple of examples.

Standards are therefore looked on by the designer as guides and points of departure. Whereas some might be relatively inviolate (a tennis court requires 6000 square feet), others may be modified in accordance with an analysis of the situation at hand. In addition, many use units, such as passive recreation retreats, cannot be standardized. For these, the amount of site best suited to the purpose usually dictates its eventual size. Caution: In considering deviations, understand that arbitrary adjustments can lead to poor quality. Have you ever seen campers jammed elbow to elbow in violation of the standard which proposes four to seven units (10,890 – 6223 square feet each) per acre? As seen in Figure 4-1, the attractiveness of the area which drew the camper in the first place has been wrecked.

In order to determine size adequacy, you might first check proposals against standards. Where manuals are unclear or where deviations exist, the application of the key word *why* becomes useful. It should precipitate an explanation of the designer's rationale, which you may accept or reject.

Figure 4-1 *Inadequate space between campsites subverts the camping experience.*

6B. Quantities Each park contains a number of things — use units and physical objects within each unit. Judgments regarding the appropriate type and number of units usually evolve from the demand studies mentioned when we discussed the umbrella considerations. Thus, if five tennis courts or one hundred boat slips are called for, it is because it has been determined that the demand for tennis or boating will cause that many to be used constantly. In most cases, such judgments are only best guesses and have to be reevaluated once actual participation is measured after installation. This is why it is always good practice to provide for expansion of those facilities whose popularity might be expected to increase in the foreseeable future.

The number of physical elements considered adequate for each park unit is usually obvious, such as two posts, a net, and nearness to a drinking fountain for a public tennis court. A few others have been identified for us in the ubiquitous standards. (See the Appendixes.) As we have pointed out, many standards can be accepted with little question: A family-sized picnic area might very well contain one table, a fireplace, and a trash basket shared by adjacent picnickers; a campground should reasonably have one toilet for every thirty campers. On the other hand, as discussed in Chapter 3, the suggestion that the preschool play area should have only the standard chair swings,

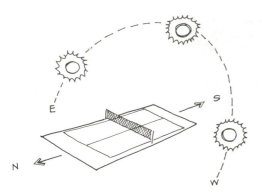

Figure 4-2 *Orient tennis courts perpendicular to the sun's course.*

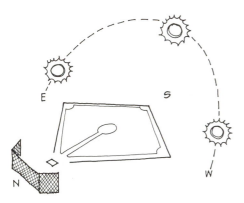

Figure 4-3 *Lay out baseball diamonds so that the sun is not in the eyes of the batter.*

Figure 4-4 *The sun should be at the viewers' backs.*

Figure 4-5 *Beaches should receive full solar exposure.*

Figure 4-6 *Eastern slopes are ideal for camping where morning dew and afternoon heat are undesirable factors.*

sandbox, small slide, and simple climbing device may be construed as lazy design.

In evaluating the adequacy of quantities, therefore, attention should be focused on the count of activity units in relation to anticipated use and the number of physical elements necessary to facilitate that use. But functional quality does not evolve merely from providing adequate room and the proper number of things, as the perpetrators of so many "asphalt jungle" playgrounds and other sterile developments would like us to believe. Even under a self-evident principle such as meeting technical requirements, there are additional matters to square away.

6C. *Orientation to Natural Forces* First of all, consider the effects of sun upon activity. To keep blinding rays out of participants' eyes, tennis courts and other play areas where a ball is sent back and forth should have their playing axes laid out at a 90-degree angle to the sun's daily course, or essentially on a north-south line. (See Figure 4-2.) For ball diamonds and other facilities where the missile's course cannot be predicted, priorities must be established since all players cannot be given equal protection. Taking baseball for example, a line from the plate through the mound to second base is the axis usually oriented perpendicular to the late afternoon sun (when the sun is lowest, hence its rays most hazardous) since this protects the batter, catcher, and pitcher. (See Figure 4-3.) A similar premise applies where spectators are of primary concern. As shown in Figure 4-4, a viewing station should be oriented so that the sun remains at visitors' backs during peak hours.

The sun can also be a useful force, and swimming beaches and garden plots should be oriented to either south or west in order to be given the advantage of maximum solar exposure. (See Figure 4-5.) An eastern orientation is ideal for most campgrounds, for as illustrated in Figure 4-6, the morning sun can quickly erase overnight dampness, yet its heat is replaced by cooling shade in the afternoon.

Wind is another natural force which can affect activity efficiency, as is only too obvious to the players who must lean into the gales and chase the frolicking fly balls in San Francisco's Candlestick Park. Ballparks, tennis courts, and other units where missiles are caused to fly about do not belong in the direct course of intensive wind currents. As demonstrated in Figure 4-7, the direction of wave-billowing winds should also determine the location of boat docks. However, wind blockage or lack of atmospheric motion can decrease camp and picnic ground usability, causing a pall of cooking smoke to hang continuously in the air as if to remind us all of Los Angeles, the ultimate example of inattention to the effects of natural forces in the location of human works. Therefore, as illustrated in Figure 4-8, every opportunity should be taken to orient such grounds to available breezes; this criterion should also be used to determine the placement of other activity areas in humid climates.

Park structures for permanent human habitation such as offices, concessions, rinks, gyms, and meeting spaces require heavy use of heat- or cold-producing energy to resist sun, wind, and winter cold. The site selected and developed for such structures can offer protection if orientation and landform are considered at the early planning stage. The proper combination of earth sheltering and solar design can open the building's interior to warming south sun in winter yet insulate against punishing summer heat with a cool earth jacket around the bottom, sides, and top of the structure (Figure 4-9). Even existing buildings, structurally unable to support soil piled on or over them, can be made at least less vulnerable to energy loss by creative use of plantings for wind buffering in winter and shade protection in summer (Figure 4-10).

The amount of annual rainfall and the periods of drought and downpour present clues as to the seasonal availability of water for wells, fluctuation in the level of water bodies, and flooding possibilities in the lowlands. The absence of underground reservoirs and presence of stream-bank instability and bottomland inundation can be decisive considerations in locating many facilities.

So, too, can conditions caused by snow, especially when coupled with other matters of orientation. For instance, because of its relation to wind and sunlight, the lee side of a hill and its north-facing slope are where snow loads will be greatest and remain for the longest period of time. Figure 4-11 therefore suggests the most appropriate location for ski and toboggan runs in temperate zones. It also indicates where roads which must be kept open in the winter should not be placed.

6D. Operating Needs Appropriately balanced by attention to personal needs, the requirements of cars, boats, and maintenance equipment must claim their share of the planning. The fact that the minimum turning radius of an auto is 20 feet will dictate facets of road and parking lot layout. The knowledge that the maximum grade for a launching ramp is 15 percent indicates what has to be done to the marina bank. The understanding that a power mower cannot negotiate slopes over 33 percent leads to decisions regarding the limits of grassy pitches. Information like that illustrated in Figures 4-12, 4-13, and 4-14 is gleaned from technical manuals and, where these are not available, from measurements taken while the machine is in operation.

As a focus for design concern, *operating needs* can also refer to administrative procedures considered essential to the efficiency of the recreation complex. This is especially germane to the operation of complicated special-use areas such as marinas and zoos where each administrator has strong ideas about how the complex should be run. If the zoo manager considers it most efficient to do most maintenance during those hours when the public is not allowed on the grounds, the designer can opt for a service circulation system which makes generous use of public walkways. However, a network of drives apart from pedestrian ways might be more advisable if heavy service is required when the public is present.

Most operational determinations are arrived at through personal interviews between the designer and those who will be running the facility after construction. A cooperative spirit benefits both parties here. Although an understanding of the operator's methods may point one way to efficiency, alternative and possibly more efficient modes of operation might be offered to the administrator by the landscape architect as design possibilities unfold.

Figure 4-7 *Boat docks should be located out of the path of water-churning wind.*

Figure 4-8 *Picnic areas require breezes to take away cooking smoke.*

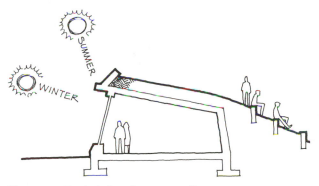

Figure 4-9 *Earth-sheltered structures offer natural insulation plus usable surface space.*

Figure 4-10 *Buffering structures from winter winds and trapping winter sun can reduce energy loss.*

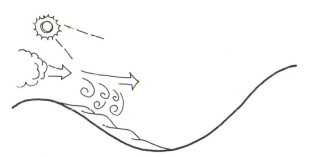

Figure 4-11 *Heaviest snow loads occur on the lee side of north-facing slopes.*

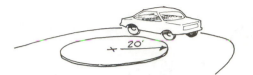

Figure 4-12　Tight turns are hard to negotiate.

Figure 4-13　Steep pitches are tough to manage.

Figure 4-14　Drastic slopes are difficult to mow.

Machines and facilities operate. Well, people also "operate." Their physical limitations must be appreciated in design especially where *comfort* can be affected, as demonstrated in Figure 4-15. Does the edge of the seat catch your leg at mid-calf or mid-thigh, or does seat height allow your knee joint to curve comfortably? Does the slant of the seat cause your bottom parts to slide unceremoniously into the gap at the base of the back slats? Are the back slats spaced so that each digs into your spinal column? Comfort also decides the question of whether to have a back or not to have one. A backless bench may suffice for transient sitting like waiting a few minutes for a bus. But comfortable back support is essential for a long lunch break or for reading *The New York Times*.

Assuming the *bench* is comfortable, what about the bench*es*? Sitting on the world's most comfortable bench (right back slant, good seat form, perfect height) can still be very uncomfortable if it is isolated or placed back to back with another bench.

People like to watch the action. They enjoy talking across easy distances. Those placing benches can provide another important level of comfort by embracing this need — by grouping, facing, and clustering benches to create spaces off the routes where people walk (but not necessarily out of sight of them). (See Figure 4-16.)

How do people walk? In the outdoors, long strides are normal. To maintain a fluid pace, risers for outdoor steps must be comparatively short and treads relatively long. In the interests of walking comfort, landscape architect Thomas Church suggests the following ratio: twice the riser plus the tread equals 26 (Figure 4-17). Thus, if a riser is 5½ inches, the tread should be 15 inches; where the riser is planned at 6 inches, the tread would be 14 inches. Where more than one foot must be placed on a tread, as in pedestrian ramps, tread length should be such that alternate legs can be used in the stepping-up process (Figure 4-18). To have to step up on the same foot all the time is quite tiring.

Height considerations apply as much to a street curb as to a step riser. Our constant experience and consequent expectation is of a 6-inch change of grade at a curb. (See Figure 4-19.) Much higher or lower spells disaster. Sighted or blind, we expect the 6 inches and will trip over a curb of a different height. Curbs are understood to define traffic separations and are frequently used in protective patterns to enclose planter beds, sculptures, or other special areas. The type of edge definer which is higher than a curb but too low for a seat verges on useless. If the design sense of an area calls for more than a conven-

Figure 4-15　Bench design must consider the physical limitations of the person.

tional curb-size edge, the plan should at minimum call for a sittable 14 to 15 inches, so that the added material also equals added usefulness.

Similar insights should govern fireplace and drinking-fountain heights, as well as point the way to such appreciated conveniences as ramps integrated into stairways for the pushing of baby carriages. (See Figure 4-20.) Comfort should be a hallmark of every design.

The impact of federal legislation mandating accessibility has been so great that at the mention of ramps, most persons think of wheelchairs. We should give a bit more attention to the nature of this legislation while considering human operating needs. The law was developed around the eminently sensible concept of ensuring access for all people to all public places. Although persons in wheelchairs happen to have highly visible access limitations, the law also benefits those with artificial limbs, degenerative diseases, braces, or arthritic ailments, pregnant women, the person with a broken leg, or people suffering from *any* condition which limits mobility. At some point, that's *all of* us.

Under the legislation, the standard *maximum* slope for ramps is 8.33 percent, equal to a ratio of 1 inch rise (vertically) to 12 inches run (horizontally). The ramps must include a handrail. This is a maximum. The ratio can be less — a point frequently misunderstood by designers. In fact, if the slope is 5 percent or less (a proportion of 1 to 20), no rail is required. Given the choice, what slope better satisfies the operating need for accessibility? The 5 percent solution comfortably accommodates all persons, meets accessibility requirements, is good in all weather (including icy conditions in northern climates) and, advancing our next principle, is cheaper since no handrail is required. "Take it to the limit" is only a song lyric; it isn't a design directive.

PRINCIPLE 7: MEET NEEDS FOR LOWEST POSSIBLE COST

Although technical needs are rather easy to identify, their satisfaction and that of more elusive requirements is often balked due to lack of funds. Here is the most classic conflict faced by the designer, one for which he or she must establish a balanced set of priorities: the conflict between needs and budget restrictions.

It is incumbent on designers to avoid unnecessary costs. They must suggest only what can be supported by sound purpose. Yet, in another sense, they are obliged not to skimp, for professionalism dictates that their design must satisfy the true needs of the development. The only way out of this dilemma is through a partnership agreement between the client who is footing the bill and the designer who is assuaging a professional conscience. They must *both* determine what the needs are. And they must *together* ensure that their list of needs is compatible with the monies available to construct the project.

Also, as mentioned in the introduction, the present decrease in resources (both land and money) forces the designer to consider all proposed work in terms of increased productivity from the resources committed. Seasonal use of facilities, use only by restricted populations, use for exotic purposes exclusively — all of these suggest a lack of consideration of this increasingly important aspect of design.

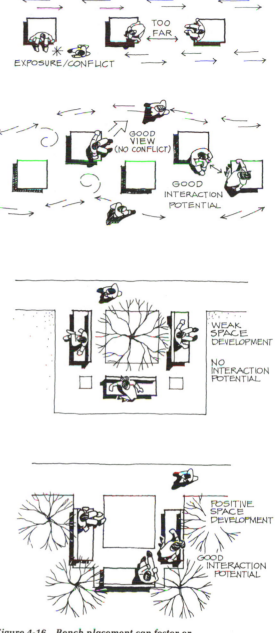

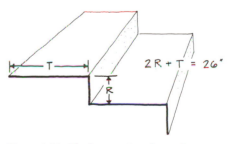

Figure 4-16   Bench placement can foster or frustrate interaction.

Figure 4-17   Ideal proportions for outdoor steps.

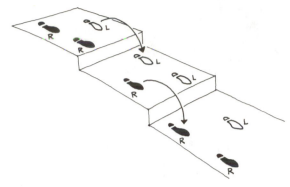

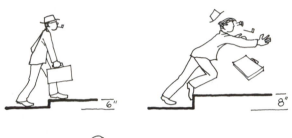

Figure 4-18 Ramps should be designed to allow the user to negotiate the risers with alternate legs.

Figure 4-19 Curbs can be confusing or comfortable depending on height.

Figure 4-20 Consider the comfort of the user in the design of outdoor facilities.

Matters of Concern

7A. *Balance of Needs and Budget* A meeting of the minds between client and designer begins at the onset of design thinking when an initial program of directives is developed in a brainstorming session attended by the landscape architect and the owners or administrators of the project. It continues through preliminary stages when the designer comes back to the client with early ideas which might include objectives not apparent at the time of program development, but revealed during periods of design research. And it follows throughout the final stages, when the work is let for bid among contractors and when changes are being contemplated during construction. A proper balance among needs and budget can be most readily struck if budget is discussed at all such gatherings. How much money is available? What are the alternative ways of meeting goals under financial stringencies? What are the high- and low-priority items? What can be constructed in stages to spread out construction costs over a number of years?

In addition to construction funding, the type, extent, and finances of maintenance will dictate a great many design decisions and therefore deserve an important place in the discussion. It is as foolish to consider exotic plantings if there are no expert horticulturists on the agency's staff as it is to plan for a public swimming pool if there are no funds available for staffing and upkeep.

During consultations dealing with program, it is usually the responsibility of the designer to draw a full expression of needs out of the client and add to them as experience suggests. But initiative for identifying needs can come from either party. Regardless of who is the prime contributor in this regard, the key to success of the partnership in the long run is agreement before final design commitments are made. If this trick is turned, each party is forewarned of minimum needs, their relationship to the requirements of budget, and what must be done in the realm of compromise in order to turn on-paper design into reality.

While designer and client agonize over the restrictions of the budget, the goals it won't reach, and the stretching exercises painfully in process, it is worth putting a last item on the agenda prompted by the pervasive key word *why*. Are these proper goals? Is this Sisyphian trip necessary? Sometimes it may not be.

One park-school complex fought with a boggy area created by outflow drainage of tile lines from several surrounding sites. The ongoing effort was to try to establish turf consistent with the rest of the property while trying annually — and vainly — to set aside bucks enough to permanently drain the area. Neither fight was being won. At the conclusion of a fortunately quiet meeting, the problem was brought into focus. What was the prize being sought? If drained and conventionalized, what was this area to become? It was on the periphery of the property, not within the area programmed for high activity. It was not needed to supplement other space-restricted facilities. By being "unused," it was being used: casual strolling, play, idle curiosity comprised its program. What would it do if nothing further was done to *it*? It did what it had been trying to do: grow into an interesting little nature preserve which, as its species of plants and birds approached a state of stable self-care, became a useful resource for school and park nature programs as well as a point of pleasant contrast to the suburban surround. Best of all the benefits was the price: nothing.

The designer and client must both keep an open mind on an apparently closed issue. Good planning has to be flexible planning, with constant effort being given to turning problems into opportunities. Remember the key word *why* and the key question "What else could *it be?*"

Jerrold Soesbe, chief landscape architect for the Lake County Forest Preserve, in Illinois, provides an example of the problem-opportunity sequence resulting from a budget squeeze.

Acre upon acre of rolling turf at the preserve was a mowing headache in terms of schedule hassles, personnel commitment, and fuel cost for equipment operation. Yet the burden was carried because the clientele, thousands of suburban Chicagoans, cared a lot about the area, used it intensively, and were definitely not bashful in their response to changes. But something had to give. The giving, which proved to be a real gift, took the form of a decision to recognize the value of the original prairie of the area as a historic and ecologically appropriate condition. The next decisions made were to move the turf back in the direction of that prairie by ceasing the mowing and identifying the area as a special place. Subsequently named the Old School Preserve, its special prairie status was further reinforced by a long-term planting program incorporating additional prairie grasses and plants.

The total success of the solution seemed obvious, but also obvious was the need for some very effective public information work. Someone had to explain to the thousands of constituents who had expressed their admiration for the grand sweeps of trimmed grass that the love affair was over. Appreciating the sincerity and depth of public emotion, the staff developed a careful, creative, well researched program to provide education about the concept in practice, its long-term benefits and beauty, the budget considerations — and never needed to exercise any of the effort. Even before the campaign was launched, the visual evidence of softness in the unmowed tracts began to get highly favorable reactions from visitors. The right time and right target resulted in a painless and very successful transition.

The basis for success in this situation was the straightforward recognition of a problem presumably requiring a more-money solution followed by a detour around that solution into opportunity. Although it might seem sheer luck that they were favored by a totally in-tune public, the staff's knowledge of that public and consequent preparation was solid, and they were ready to win their clientele over by the clear demonstration that a limitation had been converted to an asset. The award-winning project has become a major attraction for the region. Before the development, nobody *needed* a prairie restoration, at least not in the sense that someone had identified that need based on some knowledge from or of the client. The need was for a solution of a budget problem. The product was the result of the landscape architect's creative view of the whole situation.

To reprise a familiar refrain, the computer offers potential for great improvement in balancing needs and budget particularly when the issue is maintenance. The prairie conversion mentioned didn't start in that direction; the problem was the cost of current maintenance practices. As a major budget highlight, this one was easy to spot even though the solution required some major imaginative effort.

In a more metropolitan system, however, with a broad variety of park types and even greater variety of maintenance activities, the sheer number of separate services performed makes conventional analysis very difficult. How can a comparison be made of grass cut here to grass cut there? What about paving repairs or upkeep costs in different areas? Replacement costs for various types of equipment used in a number of different locations?

Broad-scale analysis of maintenance has been done with commendable success in some situations — mostly with the help of insight based on experience or a happy combination of observation and raw good luck. Generally, however, because maintenance operations of a large district are so complex, broad-scale analysis has been a failure, although specific procedural details may have been improved.

With use of computer systems, however, a file of records can be stored and overlay comparisons made of data such as (using grass mowing as an example) complexity of the mowing operation in an area (few obstacles, simple; many obstacles, complex), type of equipment used, slope of ground, type of use, public prominence (high or low exposure), and costs of labor associated with each area (dollars per square unit). Using the computer's capability of lightning-speed data review, areas with strong apparent similarities can be compared to determine whether maintenance is cost effective. If Area A has conditions seemingly identical to those in Area B yet costs 20 percent more to maintain, a closer look is appropriate. The importance to both the designer and the user is that each can intensify this search until either a flaw in operations is isolated or a design problem is spotlighted, allowing a better design solution to be developed. The most happy result is the improvement of an environment physically and fiscally.

Beyond the conventional procedures for project development, as "creative" financing has become a standard term in economic parlance, so *creative development* should now mean more than imaginative design. The creative alternatives that deserve consideration are those that offer increased financial capacity and expanded activity opportunities. The possibility of joint public-private financing is one such opportunity. The sharing of resources expands what each party has to offer and benefits both. The park agency, for example, has the property and definitely the audience; the private developer of, for example, a waterslide facility has the expertise and experience to create an exciting and profitable project. Yet neither has the means to succeed without a partner.

Results of this kind of cooperative venture have been successful in varying degrees across the country. The only drawback has been the initial shock experienced by neighbors of the new development. A conscientious park district can eliminate many problems simply by open-eyed preparation of the residents affected and a very thorough, protection-minded investigation of the private developer (accompanied by a carefully prepared contract) before a pact is sealed.

Some developers in areas of the southwest have watched their older, low-density residential properties, incorporating spaciously elegant golf courses, competing feebly with higher-density developments featuring more intense activity centers — tennis, racquetball, basketball, volleyball, exercise and fitness complexes. More activity for more time in less space — increased productivity. One response has been to redevelop these older golf course subdivisions, adding higher-density housing, fitness centers, and 24-hour activity facilities (see Figure 1-7). Along with these facilities have come some creative partnerships with park districts through which staff and program planning are provided in exchange for public access to these private developments.

Partnerships between public and private sectors don't need to be limited to those in which the private partner is the developer. One extraordinary example of financial partnership features the private parties as the funding source and the park district as the developer. The little town of West Lafayette, Indiana, needed a new roof on the city pool's bathhouse. Estimate: $60,000 to $70,000. The city simply didn't have the bucks. They didn't even really have the money to pay the heating bill to keep the pool water warm.

After some amazing brainstorming sessions, topped finally by some revisions to state legislation to permit the action, the city actually arranged with a group of private investors to let them reroof the bathhouse incorporating a complete solar water heating system. The investors lease the roof space from the district for $1 a year, then sell the collected energy back to the district at a set rate. (The rate can be renegotiated at the end of the 9-year contract.) The investors even include maintenance of the system in their offering. Their gain is in the very healthy return from the energy sale and the considerable tax benefits from their investment. The district got a new roof in addition to a new heating system at an excellent price. The system is so productive that during seasons when the pool is not in use, the heat is rerouted to a nearby junior high school where it heats the showers and lavatories.

Apart from the possibility of enlisting private developers as partners, a park district has the built-in potential of joint ventures with its own citizens: programs in which citizen groups take responsibility for elements of the parks system in which they have a special interest. Neighborhood parks are examples of properties that residents may recognize as of significant value to them and be concerned enough about to participate in development programs. In one district, in what was called the "Adopt-A-Park" program, neighborhood people took on in a contract sort of relationship the responsibility for nearly all of the maintenance of their park, thereby saving the district a considerable amount of money and time, as well as increasing the local pride and interest in the park and its programs.

Other examples more commonly encountered but equally important in terms of economic benefits realized include special-project efforts by civic groups — a totlot constructed by a local business club, a picnic area cleaned up by a scout troop, or a fundraising sale by a parents' group to provide money for the park district to make some improvement that would otherwise be unaffordable. In every case, one of the major benefits in addition to the project itself is the pride and even in some cases improved security of the area resulting from the increased attention generated.

7B. *Use of Existing Site Resources*   It is naïve to suggest that extensive projects can be funded for peanuts. You get what you pay for. But the alert designer takes pains to satisfy needs at the lowest possible cost. Paramount is the incorporation of existing site resources into the plan. The designer tries to make best use of what is already there.

The main point here has already been presented in the section on relation of use areas to site; that is, facilities should be assigned only to portions of the site which are compatible with that use. We reemphasize this because it is so often the key factor underlying the success or failure of land-use projects. Implications range from the most obvious — camping can be disappointing if engaged in upon a poorly drained soil and expensive to accommodate if the land must be underdrained — to the less apparent — conifers (especially pines) die quickly where there is concentrated foot traffic, whereas such hardwoods as hickories and sycamores withstand such concentrations relatively well. Hence, certain species must be ruled out for high-impact uses, while others are reasonable candidates, well suited to that purpose. (See related tables in the Appendixes.)

We have also said that use areas should be placed upon portions of the site which, in their unimproved states, approximate the desired finish grade: football fields in the existing flats, toboggan runs on the available north-facing slopes, for example. Doing this satisfies two concerns. It minimizes the cost of earthmoving and simplifies the blending of the new with the old. Not only does such attention to function and aesthetics in the same move support the contention that neither can be separated in design thinking, but it also suggests that the inclusion of aesthetic considerations does not necessarily mean greater expense. Indeed, in this instance, money can be saved.

We noted previously that site modification to provide access for persons with mobility limitations were unaesthetic if developed as a tacked-on afterthought. This is abuse of existing site resources. Let's look at an example of a good use of an existing site resource for access. Tim Nugent, director of the University of Illinois's renowned Rehabilitation Center, has described with pride the planning change made by a large church. In the process of designing a new building, they had planned a generous parking lot in front, a spacious entry porch elevated a few steps above the grade of the lot, and to accommodate their mobility-limited members, a ramp had been proposed winding back and forth from the parking lot to the porch, thereby providing the common point of entry for everyone. Tim's questions about the plan led to the removal of the ramp and the revision of the planned grade of the entire parking lot (still close to prevailing grades on the site) so that the lot itself slopes up to the original porch grade eliminating the need for any steps up to the entry. Access for everybody was simplified. The building gained rather than lost in overall appearance. And the cost? Cheaper. (Same amount of paving for the lot, but less grade modification, less material, and less labor since there was no porch or steps to form.)

Savings can also result from identifying suitable development areas based not on their "natural" conditions (slopes, vegetation, soils) but on their present declined use "transitioned" into a more productive new use. A train station sitting by an abandoned rail line has excellent potential as a picnic shelter especially if the vestigial adjacent paving can be reclaimed for parking and access. The railroad right-of-way itself is an asset convertible to a hiking trail or bikeway with excellent, easy grades for circulation and frequently with interesting, even historical, plant communities associated with it.

When landforms are flattened to provide field-game areas, slopes between use areas may be a necessary byproduct. Even though they are too steep to serve a conventional function, the designer, in the search for additional uses, might identify these slopes as appropriate, safe places to locate children's slides or sled runs. More about these later.

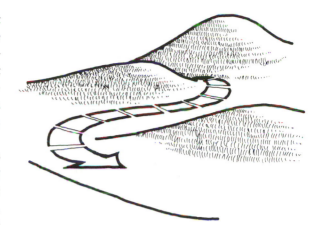

Figure 4-21 *Valley floors are natural drainageways.*

Creative looking may even lead to discovery of *new* natural conditions and recreation resources. Todd Lewis, landscape architect with the AMAX coal company, has noted that some of the old mined properties acquired by his company are examples of almost lunar landscapes resulting from overintensive mining work far in the past. The stripping of surfaces down to seemingly sterile core layers of the earth almost resembles the glacier's depredations of eons before! AMAX scientists looked again at these scarred areas and realized what a significant sequence was occurring. The areas were recovering by creating prehistoric prairie and plains communities just as the same kinds of surfaces did thousands of years before under similar conditions. The areas are living laboratories for observation and education—some of the best recreation money can't buy.

A designer who recognizes the natural forms of the land as a resource is listening to a site's advice. Based on good listening, a case can be made, as an example, for locating roadways in the available linear spaces created by earth forms (Figure 4-21). Since such spaces are usually part of the site's natural drainage pattern, both the aesthetic advantages of enclosure and the functional benefits of eliminating expensive drainage channeling are gained. As shown in Figure 4-22, this is decidedly true where buildings and major use areas have been located on high ground. Following the drainage network of the site, rainwater is thereby encouraged to continue its natural course, running away from the buildings, down the slopes into the roadways, and thence off the site. The site, not the (expensive) bulldozer, has done most of the work for you.

Figure 4-22 *Roadways placed in the valleys readily take away water draining from use areas located at higher elevations.*

Consider other possibilities for checking construction costs. How about using existing buildings to complement the new structures? Renovate the barn into a maintenance facility or put it to use as an arts and crafts center. Slap some paint on the tool shed and it will serve as a control center for the tennis court battery.

The Indianapolis park district recognized potential in an existing site resource. One park contained a huge old swimming pool developed for municipal programs of the post-World War II period. It was vast, it was deep, it was dangerous, it was hard to maintain—and it was practically never used. Kathleen Bodell, the district's director of research and development, noted that the pool might have some value as structural support for a smaller and shallower intensive-use pool, which has been developed and has been very successful. Peripheral deck paving and other supporting facilities have been built using other remnants of the original pool as a base.

What can be done to eliminate the expense of special footings? See that structures are kept off unstable soil and are placed upon naturally solid bases. Why not eliminate the cost of tree removal and the expense of new plantings? Wrap new structures and plantings around existing trees. Place facilities where desired grade already exists so as to minimize the possibility of bulldozer damage. Put facilities enhanced by plantings where plants already exist; place open-expanse facilities in spaces uninhabited by tree groves. Remember that it will take at least 15 years for a newly planted sapling to produce substantial shade and effect, whereas the existing tree might already be of adequate size. How can you ease the financial burden imposed by the construction of lengthy gas, water, electrical, and sewage lines? Locate heavy utility users near existing trunk lines or, in the cases of sewage and water, adjacent to soil suitable for disposal or drilling, thus cutting down the length of feeder pipes and cables.

These and similar measures for taking advantage of what already exists are decided upon in the design stage of development. After design, the advantages are lost. There is usually little excuse for such loss except downright nearsightedness. And that's only a short step from incompetence.

7C. *Increased Productivity* The plan one arrives at by putting all the existing resources of a park site to their most appropriate use is in a sense a two-dimensional solution. It becomes three-dimensional when one takes advantage of overlap potentials to create layers of use occupying essentially the same space. For example, the outfields of baseball diamonds can serve as football and soccer fields, or the roof of a parking structure can serve as a tennis court. The ultimate increase in the productive value of a site has to reach into the fourth dimension — time. Analyzing how often as well as how a site is used is as important as knowing its soil type.

Defining a paved area as a service court, for example, may be a solid choice in respect to its location (adjacent to the recreation center it supports, good connection to the primary circulation, but out of sight of most traffic) and the details of its design (proper dimensions for turning movements of trucks, proper slope for drainage, appropriate thickness and base strength for vehicle loads). But the designer in this case has not factored in the fourth dimension. The area's use times turn out to be fairly specific: intensive early morning start-of-duty action, slight activity at noon, then heavy again at the end-of-duty late afternoon period. The rest of the time — mornings, afternoons, evenings — practically no action. What else could occur on that surface in that location and complete the four-dimensional plan for the space? A natural would seem to be an activity like basketball, which could be added for the minor cost of a backboard and possibly some minor line additions. It may not be an official Olympic layout, but most of the play and most of the fun is found in the most casual circumstances. That's what a pickup game is all about.

Other use innovations may be serendipitous responses to recurring problems. At a Chicago university campus, utility repairs and changes were a constant grief, resulting in what was frequently referred to as the "Trees on Wheels" program. To clear areas for utility or other construction work, trees had to be yanked out of the way, sometimes on uncomfortably short notice. In the best of situations, the trees would be relocated to the last work area. In the worst situations, with no place to put them, they had to be chopped. Recognizing that an adjacent playfield area (about a block square) represented a reasonably flexible site location, planners decided to adjust the south side of the combined baseball and football field to permit a line of trees to be set inside the utility right-of-way line bordering the property. In this strip, the refugee trees were placed as in a nursery (Figure 4-23). The playfield, with no loss of function, gained a spectator shade band, a definite benefit even though none of the trees would necessarily be permanent and the density of the band would frequently change as some of the trees were relocated onto the main campus. The biggest gain was a reduction—in construction-sacrificed trees.

Figure 4-23   Nursery for the "Trees on Wheels" refugees.

A park district in Texas realized that dikes forming a detention basin could be designed to become the amphitheater seating areas for ball games and musical performances staged on the open grass floor of the basin (in dry times, of course). In the midwest, another park district and a local university shared use of a huge fill mound on university property. Fairly remote from active urban areas, the mound changed form constantly as construction for both agencies added or subtracted material. The park district's security personnel struggled in vain to keep dirt bikers off the mound. Finally, the park district turned a problem into an opportunity by programming successful events on the hills. Conflicts between construction traffic and trespassers substantially disappeared as biker groups recognized scheduled events and supported the effort through their own membership.

Accommodating new recreation in the form of specialized vehicles like dune buggies, dirt bikes, snowmobiles, all-terrain juggernauts, or even nonterrain hang gliders means that more users are served, and this means increased productivity. Many of these specialized vehicles can utilize property previously considered fallow ground (too steep, too wet, too inaccessible). However, the designer must carefully appraise the impact of the new use on existing conditions so that the new activity doesn't destroy precious plant or animal life prized by other users for other reasons.

Suppose you discover an area suitable for two or more different uses but realize that the extra functions can't be accommodated because of time conflicts. This need not be a dead end for a good idea. By investigating each activity and its apparent time requirements you may identify some possible changes in scheduling that will allow for increased use. Recognizing the need for additional parking for certain use areas might suggest the building of a parking lot. But a better solution would be to negotiate with the adjacent church for use of their lot at times when the church is unoccupied. The cost is only the rescheduling of events and possibly providing improved circulaton between the park and church.

Faced with some unpleasant bullet biting after Proposition 13 made history, the state park system of California recognized areas of potential productivity gain and made maximum use of its resources. Roadside parking areas with regulations preventing use from sundown to sunrise became overnight camping areas. Campers could park recreational vehicles from 7 P.M. to 7 A.M. The result was a new service for campers on the move during the day, provided without infringing on the daytime visitors who need the parking for their destination-oriented use. The number of satisfied customers was doubled.

Other bonus discoveries require simply a closer look at how space is used. The edges of playfields and the spaces between them may be correctly plotted on the master plan and accordingly constructed on the site, but as many planners have discovered, there is still good space available for threading a jogging trail through these tracts. Even better, exercise facilities can be appended to the trail; little pockets of extra space can be used for the small but high-intensity equipment for chin-ups, sit-ups, stretching, and other specialties for muscular development.

Low-intensity use of field facilities is generally the result of protective concern rather than poor scheduling. Turf doesn't wear well. If it gets bruised in a rugged game, it ordinarily has to be given compensating R and R time for reseeding and recuperation. In a dream scenario, a field heavily used on a given day is taken out of service for a while so new grass can spread back into the damaged areas; play continues on the alternate fields. Sure. Everybody has extra fields lying around—they are kept in the same place where the spare tractors are stored. The reality is that, most of the time, fields get overused when they are needed, and a constant outflow of cash follows in an attempt to bring back the worn areas.

Given the need for higher-intensity use and the impossibility of obtaining more area to absorb that use, the solution to increased productivity in this case may be a short-term cost increase with a long-term payoff: improving the fields themselves to take greater wear. One obvious though prohibitively expensive answer is artificial turf. A more likely alternative is the retention of the natural turf, improved by methods such as the *sand slit process,* originated in Scotland. With this system, major tile lines are cut through the field for increased drainage (lack of drainage seems to be the most prevalent cause of field decline), and subordinate drainage feeders are cut as dense patterns of narrow, sand-filled trenches. Grass grows over these, covering them completely. The addition of irrigation completes a moderate-cost solution. Fields refurbished with this technique have been quickly restored to service. Their use capacity has also been increased dramatically.

Assuming fields themselves are improved to bear increased traffic, the installation of lighting can extend play hours further. Particularly in climates where heat in the summer severely reduces use potential, lighting should be a first priority. The use of utility-grade wooden poles can provide a significant saving over more elaborate metal structures as long as design and placement are carefully considered.

The designer's ability to wrest increased productivity from resources available for recreation has to stem from complete knowledge of the resources—which is only good planning practice anyway. The greater the pressure on the resources, the more important the inventory of data becomes. Information on numbers and kinds of users and on type, character, and quantity of programmed activities, as well as the data about the ecosystems supporting the activities, deserves constant attention and improvement. It is the mine out of which the recreational ore comes. Every effort to make the inventory more complete and constantly accessible *will pay off.* The use of computer files to compile and keep data, and to compare data to reach new conclusions, is not an option but a requirement for owners and designers. It is neither difficult nor expensive. The real expense results from not using every possible means to discover and make use of every possible resource.

7D. *Use of Appropriate Structural Materials* Often, seemingly high initial construction costs can amortize themselves many times over through savings in later maintenance. Conversely, skimping on the construction budget can increase eventual costs by creating maintenance problems. Considering that the money for both construction and maintenance comes out of the same pocket, such long-run viewing justifies many design suggestions which might appear somewhat extravagant at first glance.

This is quite often true in the selection of building materials. For the base plane, an appropriate selection evolves from an analysis of the type and extent of proposed usage. For instance, the designer should be able to determine what the traffic patterns will be. If the pathways people are going to use are not surfaced, they will turn to mud after every rainstorm; they will look messy and be unusable. There are two alternatives. Occasionally disguise the pig wallow with gravel pitched from a wheelbarrow, charting the expense on the maintenance ledger, and watching it exceed the initial costs of a permanent pavement. Or, put down the permanent pavement to begin with and busy your maintenance personnel elsewhere.

Putting the paving where the path is seems a perfectly straightforward solution. It is. However, caution is offered at this point against complacency after the pavement is poured. User groups change in age, social composition, interests, and all the other characteristics reviewed in previous chapters. Cursing the customers as inconsiderate blockheads doesn't help maintain a newly worn path (someplace other than the first pour). What we are all frequently guilty of not considering is the meaning of the change. The old path may no longer serve a need. The choices are still pave or suffer, but before picking one, the overall design of an area should always be considered. A path may disappear by attrition if an improperly sited use is moved.

Assuming the overall plan has been reviewed and the nature of use has been predicted for the foreseeable future, the next step is to select a material which can withstand the rigors of the expected activity. A material is happily matched to its use if it passes the following tests:

Durability. Will it stand up under the anticipated pounding?
Appearance. Is it visually compatible with nearby elements?
Availability. It is economically foolish to haul material from distant sources if comparable material is locally handy.

Figure 4-24 *Surface treatments related to use: soft and drainable under the play piece; durable where constant foot traffic is expected.*

Tactile Qualities. Its feel is especially important where the material will come in contact with the skin as in the case of sitting and playground surfaces.

Climatic Adaptability. Will the material remain stable under such rigors as freezing, thawing, and intense sunlight?

Drainability. Does it allow rainwater to percolate through or run off rapidly and render the area usable after storms?

There are a host of materials to choose from: concrete, brick, cobbles, asphalt, wood blocks, gravel, sand, grass, Astroturf, and others, with many varieties of each. When matching a material with a use, the above criteria should be applied along with whatever priorities are suggested by the activity; for example, in a playground, you might consider concrete for a peripheral walkway since durability is the most essential criterion and place sand under the swings where softness and quick drainage are of paramount concern. (See Figure 4-24.) Or, in a neighborhood picnic ground, you might decide on grass for the unpatterned playfield, gravel on the paths connecting each picnic unit, and a concrete pad under each picnic table and fireplace station.

Suppose a hard surface has been the choice and the options of locally available materials (a *very* important criterion) have been narrowed down to brick and blacktop (the dilemma mentioned in Chapter 2). The designer selecting the best-looking material need not take lumps from a critical client for being extravagant. Paraphrasing an old joke, the benefits of purchasing material today because it's cheap, even though it's ugly, have to be weighed against the vanished cost differential after 10 years' maintenance—when it's *still* ugly.

In fact, faced with cost concerns but having an equal concern for aesthetic standards, a midwestern university found that brick paving for pedestrian circulation could be laid fairly inexpensively dry (no mortar joints) on a modest 4-inch-thick concrete slab. Compared only a few years later to asphalt paving installed for a pedestrian walkway at the same time, the brick not only looked great but weathered well (asphalt didn't), wore well (asphalt didn't), didn't ravel at the edges (asphalt did), and didn't show patch marks after utility lines had to be sliced through it (asphalt *really* did). The bottom line showed the dry-laid brick the winner in both the aesthetic and cost columns.

The challenge in making decisions about materials is the same as in making decisions affecting people. Keep learning more about them and beware of facile assumptions. Critical observation is critically important. Look at nature's treatment of materials. The reason native materials are native is that they live well in their locale. Unlike concrete, which is a composite of not necessarily local materials, stone in its native setting may be an extremely good choice aesthetically and economically because it belongs there—it doesn't self-destruct in a winter that long since gave up doing stress tests on it. Granite curbs, though initially expensive, continue to grace the edges of many east coast roads because they pay off as they outlast most of their concrete competitors.

Grass poses particular problems as a base-plane material. It does well only where it is left untrampled or can be given a chance to recover from the beating it takes from traffic. Thus, if movement is anticipated in a constant line from A to B or is concentrated in a particular area, the immediate vicinity of a picnic table for example, grass quickly gives way to mud and weeds. One solution to this problem is to move the tables periodically. If this is impractical, base-plane materials other than grass are mandatory. These might range from pavement to wood chips or other organic mulch. The mulch requires periodic replacement, but, unlike grass, it does not demand spraying, fertilizing, and mowing. On the other hand, grass might be quite appropriate where use is intermittent or movement from A to B follows several courses with no single pattern predominating.

If mulch begins to become a major material need, some creative effort may unearth some inexpensive sources. Many utility companies clear brush and trees from their rights-of-way and chip the material to ease disposal. It may be free for the hauling. Some wood-processing companies may do the same. Other types of mulch should be considered, such as shell mulches from nut-processing companies or ground-up cob mulches from corn-products companies. What else is going to waste locally? If bush and tree removal is a significant item on a park district's work list, the purchase of a chipper-mulcher may be an excellent investment.

The base plane offers many other possibilities for creative use of structural materials. (See Figure 4-25.) Imagination and willingness to seize an opportunity can help change a truckload of jettisoned brick from junk to be dumped to paving material for a craft court. A street of granite blockstone removed for building construction becomes a mine of surface material for paving around trees in an urban park. Broken concrete sidewalks become rip-rap for stabilizing erosion-prone slopes while vines get established in the interstices. (The teeth-clenching aspect of this creativity is the unfortunately prevalent surprise factor. Nothing becomes available quite in the form or at the time that might be just right.)

The base plane is also dirt (if you don't need it) or earth (if you need more). The sight of trucks full of topsoil driving by on their way to a spoil site further away should inspire you to invent some use for that soil right at home. If a place can be found for it, the soil might be free since the hauler has to pay more to take it a greater distance. Consider a "dune" concept: The mound might screen parking or service areas or provide a wind buffer adjacent to a senior citizens' area. As in the trees on wheels scheme, some useful purpose could be served in the right holding location even though the soil changes shape for a time until it is permanently used (Figure 4-26). Temporary seeding can stabilize the surface. The increased cost of the material later (if you can find it at all) offers a strong inducement to this kind of flexibility.

We will look next at the choice of vertical-plane materials. Here, weathering is the primary culprit creating maintenance problems for fences, walls, and building facades. To minimize long-term expense, it is therefore wise to select materials which need little attention in order to withstand the bombardment of wind, rain, and sunlight. This might mean choosing rust-resistant metals for fittings and fastenings, and stone, brick, and concrete in lieu of wood.

It is also important to cautiously assess the aftereffects of material selections and to make corrective changes if necessary. One agency

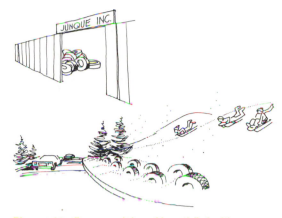

Figure 4-25   Can a special need be satisfied with an apparently "unspecial" material?

Figure 4-26   A "dune" for topsoil storage?

Figure 4-27   Plants can form spaces.

Figure 4-28   Plants can direct circulation.

Figure 4-29   Plants can provide detail interest.

Figure 4-30   Plants can deter wind.

adopted a system of elegant and rugged metal signs made of cast aluminum letters fastened to painted steel faceplates set in aluminum bar frames. The painted panels almost immediately bloomed with rust around the edges. After removing, repainting, and replacing the signs (several times), the agency realized that the fabrication and painting were not at fault. The contact of the steel panels and aluminum frames produced an electrolysis of the two metals which no paint could correct. After aluminum sheets were substituted for the steel faceplates, no more problems occurred.

Where wood is used, tinted stains provide a finish which needs only an occasional refreshing, whereas paint demands recoating at more frequent intervals. In addition, the knocking about that occurs in any public place guarantees that painted surfaces will be chipped and flaking long before they are recoated. However, under the same punishment, stained planes will slowly fade, thereby preserving a reasonable appearance until they can be restained.

Although expensive, redwood is a nearly ideal material, for it not only requires no finishing, but is actually enhanced by weathering; wind, rain, and sun turn its unfinished surface to a soft grey after a few years of exposure.

7E. *Use of Appropriate Plant Materials*   Long-term maintenance expenses can also be minimized by the selection of proper plant materials at the time of design decision. Good judgment here results from a recognition of both similarities and differences between plants and other materials. Like lumber, stone, concrete, and other inanimate materials, plants can define static and directional spaces, provide human-scale detail, screen wind, sun, and views, abate noise, control erosion, and channel circulation. Accordingly, plants, like other materials, must be of such size, shape, and staying power as will suit the job they are given. (See Figures 4-27 through 4-34.)

But plants have unique credentials which set them apart from inanimate materials. Their seasonal changes lend year-round variety which cannot be imitated by nonliving objects which remain first and always as they were set in place. The same plant can be green of leaf in the summer, gold in the fall, laden with berries, branching intricacies, and twig color in the winter, and a kaleidoscope of bloom in the spring.

Further distinguishing plants from other materials is the fact that, as living things, they must be maintained similarly to the way we treat our bodies, which is quite different from the manner in which we keep up our houses. Each species requires specific environmental conditions for survival. Species can be categorized according to *soil needs* (heavy, light, acid, alkaline), *moisture needs* (constant drinker, seldom thirsty), *exposure* (tolerance to sun, shade, wind), and *hardiness* (ability to withstand extreme temperatures). If a plant requires one condition, it will suffer under the opposite. Species which thrive in a swamp will perish if placed in the desert.

In addition, plant species can be cataloged as to *life span, susceptibility to certain diseases and pests,* and *ability to survive surface compaction and fill.* Such information can deter the selection of elm where the Dutch elm disease is rampant, Lombardy poplar where more than a 15-year life expectancy is desired, or beech where soil must be heaped about the base. If these clues about the plant's lifestyle are disregarded, countless hours must be spent assisting the plant in its fight against its environmental enemies. And, even with such help, the species may not make it.

Therefore, why not try to avoid all but the minimum amount of fertilizing, watering, cultivating, spraying, and wrapping with burlap to ward off the winter winds by planting only those species which appreciate the conditions found on the site. Let nature do most of the work for you. You can't beat the prices.

To take advantage of nature's maintenance service, a useful rule of thumb might be: If the site has a great deal of plant life on it, select for the new inclusions only those species which normally fit into the *community* of plants in evidence. Under natural conditions, plants survive by complementing each other; for example, the sun-loving reach above the rest, shadowing the shade-loving. Those who do not contribute to this cooperative arrangement are soon eliminated. To thrust a foreigner among an existing community is to maximize the risk that it will not survive. This rule has its aesthetic benefits as well, for putting like among like helps maintain the prevailing effect.

In the city, where development interferes with the growth of natural communities, plants should still be selected to match the existing (albeit artificial) conditions. In addition to criteria already stated, such considerations as *tolerance to air pollution, salt spray* from icy streets, and *pavement reflection* must direct the selection of city plants. Pavement presents a double problem. Besides throwing sun glare, it prohibits rainwater from reaching roots. It is therefore unwise to pave right up to major trees, and, if this is unavoidable, the pavement nearest the tree should be perforated or bricked with wide sand joints. The installation expense is well justified by future savings in maintenance or replacement costs.

The cost of a free gift deserves a caution in this regard. A tree donated by an owner, even though a dandy and desirable specimen, has to be looked at in terms of the cost and formidable hazards of a move. First considerations should be the "from-to" factors. Can you get *to* it with the necessary equipment? Can you move it *from* its existing location *to* its new home without collapsing the owner's basement wall, dropping utility lines, moving parking meters (easy to overlook), or, worse, having to cut another tree back to a hatrack to make space for this one? If *you* can accomplish the necessary physical changes, can the tree? It is being moved from an unrestricted soil surface at its source location, to a new environment which may challenge it with a hostile soil, a severe exposure, a skimpy water table, and an affectionate audience waiting to love its root surface to death as they play under its branches. Once in place, the care necessary to nurse it along may be the greatest expense of all.

To minimize maintenance chores, the most obvious criteria should also order the selection of plant material. That is, first of all, *plants grow.* Plants should be chosen which have growth habits which naturally fit the circumstances into which they will be placed. (See Figure 4-35.) This will eliminate the extensive pruning required to hold a plant to atypical form. In days gone by, horticultural fanciers got an immeasurable charge out of plants shaped into globes, triangles, and

Figure 4-31   Plants can supply shade.

Figure 4-32   Plants can buffer odors.

Figure 4-33   Plants can suffocate noise.

Figure 4-34   Plants can retard erosion.

Figure 4-35   Plants have predictable forms.

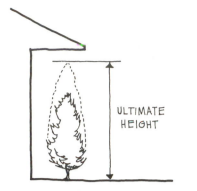

Figure 4-36   Plants have predictable growth rates and sizes.

Figure 4-37   Without undergrowth to take over when the older generation of trees dies, the life of this picnic site is limited.

Figure 4-38   Linear nurseries for beauty with easy service access.

various forms of animal life. Taste aside, perhaps they could afford the grooming effort. With today's burgeoning costs, however, it should be recommended that if one wants to spot a chicken effigy in the park, one should consult a taxidermist rather than a horticulturist.

Along with habit, rate of growth and ultimate size should also be considered. The thinking here cuts two ways. If the selection is slow growing, do you have enough patience to wait for it to fill its appointed place? Yet, if it grows too rapidly, how long before it devours the utility lines or lifts the roof overhang from its joists? To avoid having to wait years for appreciable effect as in the former case, or butcher major limbs as will be required in the latter, it is wise to select a species which will grow at a pace suited to the circumstances—slow if the spot where it is planted is a cramped corner, fast if it must throw up quick screening—and fit its alloted space upon maturity. (See Figure 4-36.)

Plants have limited life spans. Replacement growth must be continually encouraged. An administrative and maintenance policy can be implemented whereby picnic and other areas of intensive traffic are retired periodically to enable underbrush to establish itself. As illustrated in Figure 4-37, a defeating policy would be to wipe out the scrub because "it looks neater." The young material, however disheveled in its infant state, is the best replacement stock and is already in place. Reaching maturity while the taller members decline through old age, the young stock will be ready to make a substantial contribution when the oldsters expire.

A park district can use this kind of natural nursery approach to great advantage if new growth can be integrated with older materials in casual settings. Other opportunities for developing plant material resources on district land should be considered also. Since plant replacements and additions are constantly needed, areas suitable for holding, growing, and transplanting trees should be identified for use but not necessarily developed as typical row by row nurseries. Recalling the multiple-use concept urged earlier, consider nurseries also serving as windbreaks, view screens, use separators, educational arboreta, and sound buffers. Comparatively narrow right-of-way strips can be planted in softly linear, changing patterns, making the parks' drives and trails delightfully scenic while offering easy access for placing and replacing the trees (Figure 4-38). Once suitable locations with flexible boundaries have been identified, a nursery sellout, a tax auction, a donation, or a discovery can be seized as an opportunity and the trees obtained stored with immediate *and* long-term advantages.

Recognize also the opportunities inherent in relationships with research agencies like timber corporations, major nursery companies, and state or federal as well as university departments, all of which may be doing growth studies of large-scale plant materials. Trees developed in these agencies' programs may be intensively used for 5- to 10-year study cycles, then, having passed their test target limits, be disposable. Rather than letting them be cleared away, another agency with an opportune place and purpose may be able to have them purely for the taking. Being aware of available resources is again a key to capitalizing on this kind of opportunity. In fact, an offer of one resource (land) in exchange for another (the plantings) could conceivably lead to the research project being developed on the target site where the trees are ultimately needed. Everybody wins; research results are obtained and the district gets plant materials without needing even to transplant them.

7F. _Energy Conservation_   As mentioned in the discussion of orientation to natural forces, plants offer unique possibilities for energy conservation through control of weather and natural forces. Combining some of the plant abilities previously mentioned, a structure can be buffered from severe winds by mass plantings of dense evergreens, particularly if these are selected by size and species to offer a wedge to the wind (Figure 4-39). Shade is also a vital commodity in an airconditioned world. Trees selected to provide energy-penurious shade must have the growth potential to reach up and out over the structure. Second they have to be accommodated in a location which allows them to take advantage of that potential. A shade tree intended to serve a structure in this capacity may seem to violate conventional design patterns by hugging the building and by being limbed high (by nature or by maintenance) as in Figure 4-40. This confrontation of good design with preconception brings us back to the oft-repeated key word _why_. Preconceptions can be dangerous obstructions to a good answer.

7G. _Attention to Details_   If base-plane materials appropriate to use, vertical-plane materials that will weather well, and plant materials appropriate to the location are specified at the time of design and if materials are placed so as to take every advantage of energy conservation potential, the maintenance budget should breathe a sigh of relief. These are basic matters of concern to which can be added many minor considerations for further savings.

For instance, slopes must be given special attention because they are the surfaces most likely to erode. Intensive traffic should be kept away from steep banks because constant tromping will obliterate the cover which holds the soil in place. Grassed slopes should be rounded at the tops and bottoms, as if stroked with a butter knife, rather than shaped with abrupt edges, as if hacked out with an axe. As indicated in Figure 4-41, such rounding provides for both mowing ease and a smooth visual transition.

One more note on the subject of mowing: Figure 4-42 shows the advantages of paved edging at the base of vertical planes. The mower can cut clean. There is no need to go back with hand clippers to get at the tufts which would have been left by the mower at the base of the wall had the edging not been in place. Granted, a string trimmer would be an easier alternative than handclippers, but the target is to _eliminate the entire step_.

Raising planting surfaces (or depressing walks) can deter people from short-cutting through and stomping on the plants. Similarly, depressing sand areas in playgrounds helps to keep the grit in its proper place. Since sand is a fluid material, it will eventually assume a plane parallel to that of the horizon no matter how it is heaped originally. Therefore, to avoid a slumping overflow, the edges of the container in which the sand is placed should be level.

In the category of many unhappy returns, trees planted by a park

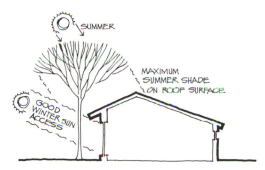

Figure 4-39   *Plants can provide a wind wedge for energy conservation.*

Figure 4-40   *Shade trees, if properly selected and placed, are solar thermostats through the seasons.*

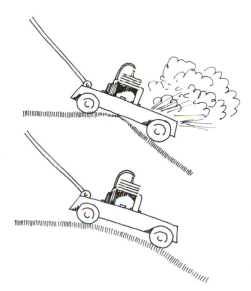

Figure 4-41   *Smooth slope edges (below) are both practical and visually appealing.*

Figure 4-42   *Paving at the base of a wall accommodates one wheel of the mower, thereby leaving a cleanly cut edge.*

district in sidewalk openings adjacent to a street curb were being carefully protected by an epoxy-bound aggregate surface installed over the entire opening (about 4 feet square). The project was well conceived: The aggregate, about the size of pea gravel, makes an easy and attractive walking surface for pedestrians; its porosity is excellent, allowing good air and water circulation to the tree's roots; and the epoxy binder itself has been found to have a good survival capacity in severe weather conditions. The craftmanship was good; installation involved making a neat ring around each tree, about an inch away from the trunk, with a reusable form. However, if the trees have any success at all, they will grow smack into the edges of their holes in 2 years maximum. Obviously the holes will have to be enlarged. But to what extent? The careful craftsmanship is wasted. Since no expansion cuts or lines were provided to allow enlargement in precise steps, a jagged mess will have to be made of a good job. Growth anticipation should obviously be a factor in design of any covers for tree openings, including steel grates or cast materials of any kind. Ask yourself: How can they be made to grow with the tree?

In response to the continuing popularity of bike usage, a number of new types of bike racks have appeared, although many varieties are still based on the traditional bar frames — that is, they have some kind of separator placed vertically at about 6-inch intervals (wood slats, steel bars, concrete slots, or aluminum tubes). The theory of the design is that the small module allows flexibility; any number of bikes can be placed anywhere on the rack. At one university campus, however, comparisons of the 6-inch, all-purpose racks to more apparently inflexible structures with openings 2 feet on center showed that given the choice, people spread their bikes *farther* apart in the 6-inch interval racks. Intervals of 30 inches, 3 feet, or more meant that actual capacity dropped by as much as 50 percent. The racks with 2-foot spaces, however, were used at full capacity.

Garden hoses typically come in 50-foot lengths. Two can be fastened together but when a hose is longer than 100 feet, the friction in the hose itself reduces the outflowing water to a feeble trickle. On a property without a built-in sprinkler system, if the only available water spigots are 200 or more feet apart, there are places that only nature can water.

These are but a few examples of the kinds of details that should be investigated in any design solution. Small in execution, they loom large in significance, for attention to them can prevent major maintenance problems.

PRINCIPLE 8: PROVIDE FOR SUPERVISION EASE

Freedom. It has been suggested that to be unencumbered by overbearing authority is a need common to all. This immediately appears to conflict with an administrative requirement, the need to have people use an area as intended. Obviously, use must be supervised to some extent. And every public place has its share of legitimate *don'ts.* Don't tramp on the flower bed because you will make mud. Don't enter the complex at arbitrary points because this will make it impossible to collect fees. Don't run through the archery range since you may end up with an arrow in you.

But *don't* is a culprit word. It nags. It looms as a challenge. In many cases, it promotes the misconduct it seeks to put down. What is your impulse on spying a *Keep Off the Grass* sign?

To gain the necessary control, yet retain for the user a sense of freedom, landscape architects attempt to replace *don'ts* with *dos* by organizing use areas and circulation routes in a manner that will make it appear reasonable to use the facility as the designer intends and the administrator desires. This is the easiest way to facilitate supervision — let design layout guide visitors into a use pattern that they will find agreeable.

Matters of Concern

8A. *Balance of Use Freedom and Control*   To what degree *can* control be exercised is a question asked early in the design process. It will be found that there are circumstances in which any attempt to control movement or use is a waste of effort, for the directive will be ignored. The simplest example is the situation in which movement patterns cannot be predicted. Where will the user penetrate the large field in order to reach the other side? Unless an obvious purpose such as safety is served by stepping off at a set point, it will be wherever whim suggests. In this situation, it is folly to demand a single entry point, for the regulation will seem unreasonable. Design should allow whim to take its course. Because it will anyway.

There are also instances where use not only cannot, but *should not*, be regulated. Consider a free play area. To the users, it appears to be an arena for doing their own thing. What becomes their attitude, however, when they come across the signboard which spells out what their thing shall be — and also dictates what it shall not be? Shouldn't there be places not only in every system but also in every park where one can express individuality, act freely, exercise discovery mechanisms?

Actually, all we propose is that parks provide the opportunities formerly available on the late, lamented corner lot. Here was gained a release not possible on sites where there is only one way of doing things. Here was freedom of prescribed choice. Truly free space. The lot is no longer with us. But is that reason to do without its rewards? Cannot sites or portions of sites be let to simply sit there beckoning the user to wander, dig a hole, build a shack, fly a kite, or bake a potato? It's the user's choice. It's the user's recreational appetite that needs to be satisfied. It's the user's need which the system proposes to serve.

Who can predict every urge? The recreationist conducting demand studies and the behaviorist spinning theories admit to not even being close. As useful as the information provided by these specialists might be, it will never be absolute. How then do you give the unpredictable its due, if not by simply providing a place and letting it happen? Where freedom of movement and intent is deemed desirable, little design elaboration is necessary except in some cases to ensure maximum use flexibility in the structures and in the organization of the park units.

This is not to suggest that use discipline should never be required, but to stress that restrictions (or lack of them) be for a purpose. Where

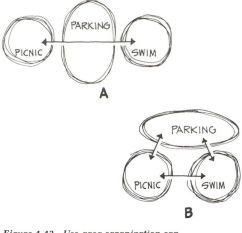

Figure 4-43 *Use-area organization can encourage either an undesirable (A) or an agreeable (B) traffic flow.*

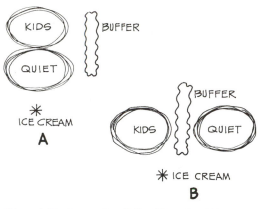

Figure 4-44 *A poor site relationship system (A) can be revamped by taking advantage of an existing site characteristic (B).*

it is apparent to all, especially users, that reasonable purposes are being served, conflict between the controlled and the controller is less likely to arise, and the chances of the directive's being followed are maximized.

8B. *Circulation* In any public facility which serves great numbers of people, movement is an issue of primary concern. If people can get where they want to go readily and without interfering with other activities, a feeling of peace permeates the site. The charge is therefore before the landscape architect: Anticipate flows. Eliminate obstacles and confusion. Provide unobstructed, well-defined, and logical routes.

Obstacles may be natural barriers such as boulders or steep slopes, but they are more likely to be use areas. It is by setting up good relationships among use areas that the designer takes the first step in establishing an efficient circulation system. For instance, as diagrammed in Figure 4-43A, if the parking lot cuts off the picnic area from the swimming beach, it is a cinch that the picnickers will stream through the lot on their way to the water, holding up traffic and endangering themselves, no matter how many signs, railings, and other *don't*s suggest otherwise. But if, as shown in Figure 4-43B, the parking lot is located peripherally, so that the picnic grounds abut the beach, the most direct route will still be followed, but it will be a safe one.

Similarly, how can you expect kids to keep the noise down in the play space shown in Figure 4-44A just because it happens to be next to a quiet zone? And it is just as unreasonable to expect that they will tiptoe through the passive area on their way to the ice cream wagon. Let's say that a natural barrier of earth and trees is nearby as indicated in Figure 4-44B. Use it as a buffer. Assign the play space to one side, place the quiet zone on the other, and locate the refreshment stand where access to it from both sides will be unobstructed.

In both examples, the successful relationship patterns suggest *do*s. The logic of the organization itself tends to supervise the movement, thereby easing the way for the actual linkage of the use areas by roads and walkways. It becomes easy to understand how these routes link the use areas if we divide them into three types: *collector* arteries which connect all major use areas; *secondary* arteries which lead from collectors to connect related spots within a use area; and *minor* arteries which proceed from secondaries to the least-visited facilities.

A designer who understands the collector-secondary-minor premise well can devise access routes to a host of activity units in a manner which simplifies a traveler's decisions and minimizes confusion along the way. First, the designer can eliminate intersections and the accompanying slowdowns from a heavily used collector, by clustering many activity units about a single secondary rather than stringing them out along the main road, where each needs its own separate driveway. While all visitors will be using the collector to enter, leave, and search for objectives, only those interested in a particular group of activities need be on a secondary. Accordingly, travelers do not have to plow through activity group X in search of group Y, for each has been

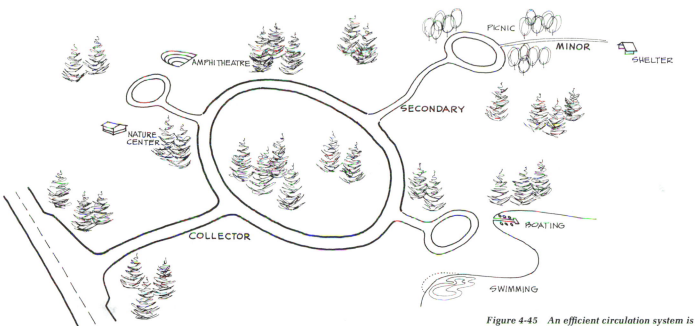

Figure 4-45 An efficient circulation system is distinguished by well-defined routes and consistent alignments.

segregated from the main flow. (Compare Figure 4-45 with Figure 4-46.)

Confusion is further lessened if each road unit flows smoothly, for people have a tendency to follow consistency in alignment. This minimizes inadvertent movements from collectors to secondaries or minors and the subsequent need to move back in search of the artery

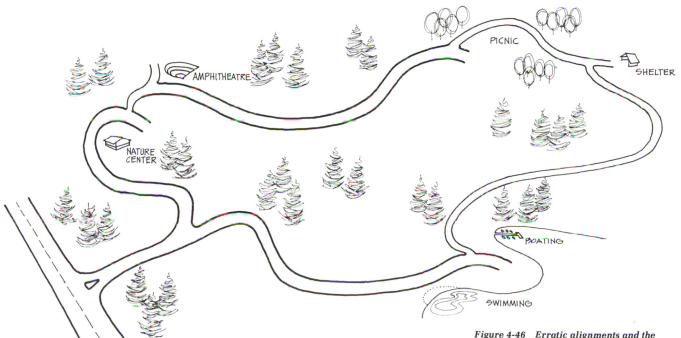

Figure 4-46 Erratic alignments and the separation of related use areas by major arteries are hallmarks of a poor circulation system.

Figure 4-47 A significant physical feature may serve as a point of reference where circulation directions are confusing.

Figure 4-48 Concrete "rumble strips" warn of an approaching intersection.

upon which the journey can be continued. The principle can be applied just as successfully in reverse. The temptation to move down fire and service roads from which the public is excluded is eliminated when such arteries are made to connect with the public way at right angles or otherwise break the main road's continuity.

The way in which turns are treated can often mean the difference between free sailing and eternal congestion. Turns should never be more acute than 90 degrees because at each intersection a decision is being made and the accompanying hesitation, if coupled with a turn that is difficult to negotiate, could cause a traffic tie-up. In addition, each intersection should be cleared of visual obstacles to give a good view of oncoming travelers.

Classic tie-ups are also usual where left-hand turns across traffic are required. Hence, turnoffs should be to the right wherever possible. This is of particular significance for the *entering sequence,* for it is on entering that the traveler, unaccustomed to the layout and searching for objectives, is most confused. A series of left-hand turns, going against the normal right-hand grain that most of us possess and forcing drivers to turn across vehicles speeding from the opposite direction, only adds to that confusion. However, left-hand turns are comparatively inconsequential in the exiting procedure, for by then the traveler has a better feel of the layout, and has a single objective, the exit.

To help the visitor adapt to an unavoidably confusing layout, points of orientation might be inserted. These could be outstanding pieces of architecture (Figure 4-47) or natural features which the scheme would cause to continually pop into view. Points of orientation are handy references that let the visitor know where he or she is at all times: north, south, east, or west; close to, distant from, in front of, or in back of something frequently in view. These references are especially useful in such places as a zoo or fair where there are so many facilities to visit that the possibilities of becoming spun around and lost are high.

What many of these devices and patterns are actually doing is giving information, suggesting to the traveler: Go this way. Go that way. You can find your parked car over there. An abrupt change can also provide information, giving travelers notice that their attention will soon be required. Such changes as dramatic movement from linear to static space, light to dark, human to superhuman scale, smooth pavement to rough, jar the mind, thereby ensuring alertness at the approach to a potential danger such as an automobile crossing. (See Figure 4-48.)

Another kind of change which subconsciously informs is a change in elevation. A slight change such as a curb suggests *keep off.* Unlike the *don't* of a sign, this type of suggestion should breed cooperation. Because it is an effort to mount the curb, the traveler will most likely agree to remain in the depression. Where the requirement is mandatory, the vertical can be increased in height in order to say *keep out* in a stronger voice. The ultimate directive is a vertical elevated above eye level, the barrier in front of the eyes leaving no doubt as to the intended circulation pattern.

Out of intelligent use relationships, a simplified collector-secondary-minor artery system, and such good design details as negotiable turns, right-hand movements upon entering and at other points of vehicular conflict, adequate visibility at corners, minimal intersections, points of orientation, and change comes positive information rather than admonishment, guiding the user without creating an overbearing feeling of regimentation. These and related design moves are meant to minimize the need for signs and supervisory personnel (the traffic cop on every corner). Design does the bulk of the work in their stead.

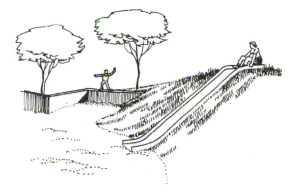

Figure 4-49 Slides, walls, and other play features can be designed for safety without minimizing their challenge potential.

8C. *Safety*   Design can also minimize the number of supervisors needed to ensure the safe pursuit of activities. And where such personnel are required, design can ease their chores.

The need for supervision can be lessened by reducing the potential dangers. Again, many physical hazards can be eliminated by attention to use-area relationships. For example, consider tot or casual areas where users, absorbed in benign pursuits, are oblivious to potential harm. Since their guard is down, they need extra protection from possible collisions caused by spillovers from adjacent areas. It follows that informal spots should be located away from or be well buffered from active areas. In addition, sport fields and the like should be oriented so that errant missiles, such as baseballs and frisbees, will not fly into the midst of those whose guard is down. The most obvious measures for doing away with hazards should also be taken; such blind obstacles as drainage grates in the middle of ballfields should never be allowed.

We have said that the challenge of danger may at times be a part of the experience and should not be eliminated altogether. In such cases, design attention to both challenge and security should be balanced as demonstrated in Figure 4-49. In the playground, walls to traverse might be raised high enough to provide a thrill, yet remain low enough to avoid falls of bone-jarring proportions, and cushioning surfaces can be placed in the potential fall zone. Slides can be incorporated into natural slopes so that falls become tumbles rather than the straight-down variety you buy along with the standard iron-rung slide.

In high-risk areas where supervision is unquestionably called for, whether it be by parents or those on the payroll, the location of oversight stations and related sight angles should be carefully considered. Use relationships again play an important role. Similar facilities, for example a series of spaces used by tots, may need but a single station. If they are organized into a cluster, 360-degree vision is highly possible. If, however, such areas are scattered about the site, stations are needed for each space since there will be no one spot from which all play areas can be seen.

In addition to unobstructed visibility, physical proximity of oversight stations to play areas is desirable. Where physical proximity to all areas is not possible, certain priorities will suggest where the station should go. For instance, if a child who has slipped in the wading pool is plucked out quickly, no damage is done. But there is little one can do to avoid injury to the same child once it begins to fall from the top of a climbing device. If it can't be next to both, the station in this case, while within view of the climber, should be adjacent to the pool.

Since design is for people, the supervisors' comfort as well as their ability to perform should be taken into account. The station should be

Figure 4-50 *A parental station should be located outside of the play zone yet remain within view of the children.*

within view of but away from the actual lines of play to keep supervisors from being trampled. Details count a lot: shade, wind screening, and the like. And as illustrated in Figure 4-50, a low barrier between parents and sand pile is always appreciated, for it keeps the grit from their shoes and out of their reading material.

8D. *Discouraging Undesirables* The problems of hard-core vandalism and perversion are extraordinarily complex matters for which there have yet to appear universal answers. In the search for root causes and solutions, parks sometimes serve as places for testing sociological and psychological theories and for the release of pent-up maladjustments and injustices. Significant along these lines are the works of a few social-action-oriented designers who have coordinated self-help projects in ghettos where residents and gangs have devised and constructed their own recreation areas on vacant land with locally available materials. One purpose is to spark pride through achievement, thereby combating deep-seated frustrations.

A related and very real concern of park administrators is the need to curb disruption caused by vandals and by sexual exhibitionists and potential molestors. Layout and design detailing can either assist or hinder in this.

For discussion purposes, vandalism has two sides, although in actual cases, the lines are most likely to be blurred, so that control measures must be addressed to both categories. Relatively benign is the nuisance or "push over the outhouse for kicks" type of property destruction. Face it, folks. You did this, too. It is reasonable to assume that much of this damage is caused by people whose basic respect for property is momentarily pushed aside by a devilish impulse. A development which is neat and in good repair at all times inspires that respect. It appears worth cherishing and is therefore less likely to be violated than something which is beat up and broken apart to begin with. The latter invites further destruction.

By way of analogy, consider your new automobile. You take pains to keep from getting the first scratch on it. But once the first dent appears, the second does not seem to matter as much. And after the third or fourth, the car becomes in your mind just another beat up old "bomb" not worth worrying about. A park inviting this disdain becomes equally fair game.

But the park which does not have the first scratch upon it is likely to be cared for, the respect it engenders in many cases squelching the

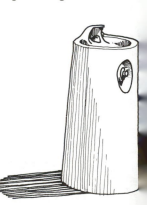

Figure 4-51 *Sturdy yet attractive park furniture.*

momentary urge to cause damage. Accordingly, a park should be designed for easy maintenance so that with a minimum of effort, especially when that first scratch appears, it can quickly be put back into shape. The use of stains in lieu of paints, of appropriate surfacing where circulation will logically occur, and attention to such details as mowing strips are measures already mentioned in this regard.

The seemingly insoluble problems are in hard-core, habitually vandalized areas where the public's entrenched attitudes outweigh a basic respect for property. Where these cases are rampant, developments should first of all be designed for sweeping police inspection: potentially vandalized structures should be clustered rather than spaced about the site; views should be cleared from the street into the park; if the area is fenced, a minimum number of entry points should be located within view of well-traveled arteries.

To fence or not to fence is a subject of argument among law enforcement authorities. Some feel that fences with controlled gateways sufficiently discourage entrants bent upon destruction. Others maintain that fences impede capture; in the inevitable chase, the younger vandal vaulting fences with élan too often eludes the out-of-shape pursuer still struggling hand over hand up the barrier. They reason that the lack of a barrier equalizes the conditions of the chase, perhaps giving an edge to the police officer, who can drive into the park at any peripheral point and move at will over hill and dale without leaving the cruiser.

The structures themselves, whether they be buildings, signs, picnic tables, fireplaces, or drinking fountains should be sturdy. And remember that the fewer the moving parts, the less chance of their being moved into the creek or someone's garage. A problem remains, however, which must be recognized by the designer. How do you provide sturdy structures that appear reasonably attractive, or at least humane? (See Figure 4-51.)

Plants chosen should be those that have a built-in chance to ward off the predations of vandals. Some say: Specify species with thorns; they can at least fight back. However, they also provoke lawsuits and can gouge the innocent. A more reasonable, although not always successful, approach is to box young transplants with fencing until they are large enough to recover from a beating. It has also been noticed that individual specimens are always the first to go, whereas trees grown in clumps remain surprisingly free from destruction.

Many of the measures suggested to thwart vandals, such as opening

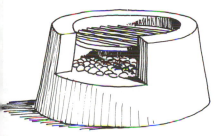

the park to create sweeping views, are equally useful in discouraging deviants who would lurk to frighten or attack the unwary. Opening the park to view not only assists police inspection, it bares the act to the passing public as well, possibly making the psychopath think twice before harassing park users. Within the park, elimination of hidden corners near walls, building alcoves, and understory plantings are also useful, as is good night lighting.

The greatest attraction to marauders is the empty park and the lone person; the greatest discouragement is the park full of people. The designer can help fill the park with people; an experience-laden, efficiently functioning development should attract more people than a run-down, poorly organized facility. But the primary move comes from the park system planner and the recreation programmer. If a park is going to be alive with people, it should be located where a real need exists and activities of high public appeal should be slated. To further protect users, introspective pursuits can be allotted to areas which undesirables are less likely to frequent.

UNDERSTANDING AND HABITS

Generation of awareness is the aim of this chapter as well as of the previous chapter on aesthetics. As with aesthetics, you are urged to establish an excellence scale for workability. Consider whatever aspects of size and quantity, orientation to natural forces, operation of machines, human comfort, administrative procedures, budget, materials, design details, freedom and control of use, circulation, safety, vandal-deviant proofing, and other aspects of park management come to your attention.

From this habit will spring knowledge which will help you rate your own parks and identify their needs, and give you some idea of how these needs might be satisfied. This is not to say that the clever schemes which you find work in one park will necessarily solve the problems of another. What knowledge gained through awareness will certainly do, however, is provide you with enough understanding of how design can satisfy demands per se so that you can judge the relative worth of any design solution proposed to meet your unique needs.

It should be obvious by now that there are many factors to consider in binding requirements into a workable design whole. Up to now, these have been presented in a somewhat scattershot fashion which may have left you lost amid a jungle of considerations, some of which appear to be at odds with others. Certainly, if our discussions are to help you develop an ability to analyze an intricate solution, a more organized framework for considering these issues must be developed.

In addition, while the principles and matters of concern have been held out as design substance or the critical issues which count toward the success or failure of most proposals, they are but categories and quite general at that. To be useful in evaluating a particular project, they must be made specific or be translated into issues which are relevant to the project at hand. To bring the critical issue of increased productivity further into focus, Figure 4-52 offers a catalog of suggestions.

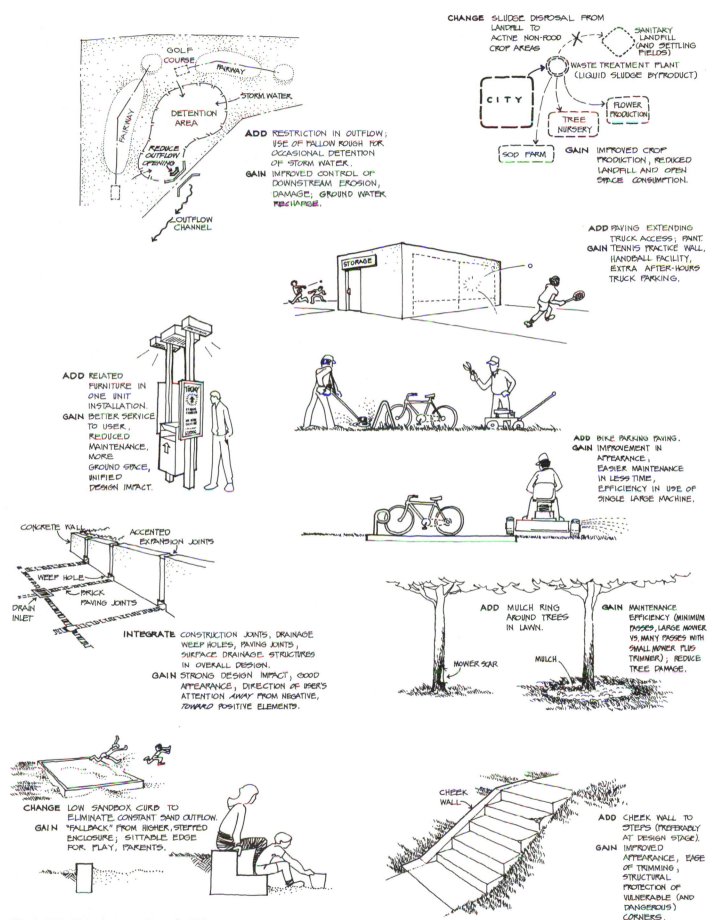

ADD RESTRICTION IN OUTFLOW; USE OF FALLOW ROUGH FOR OCCASIONAL DETENTION OF STORM WATER.
GAIN IMPROVED CONTROL OF DOWNSTREAM EROSION, DAMAGE; GROUND WATER RECHARGE.

CHANGE SLUDGE DISPOSAL FROM LANDFILL TO ACTIVE NON-FOOD CROP AREAS
GAIN IMPROVED CROP PRODUCTION, REDUCED LANDFILL AND OPEN SPACE CONSUMPTION.

ADD PAVING EXTENDING TRUCK ACCESS; PAINT.
GAIN TENNIS PRACTICE WALL, HANDBALL FACILITY, EXTRA AFTER-HOURS TRUCK PARKING.

ADD RELATED FURNITURE IN ONE UNIT INSTALLATION.
GAIN BETTER SERVICE TO USER, REDUCED MAINTENANCE, MORE GROUND SPACE, UNIFIED DESIGN IMPACT.

ADD BIKE PARKING PAVING.
GAIN IMPROVEMENT IN APPEARANCE, EASIER MAINTENANCE IN LESS TIME, EFFICIENCY IN USE OF SINGLE LARGE MACHINE.

INTEGRATE CONSTRUCTION JOINTS, DRAINAGE WEEP HOLES, PAVING JOINTS, SURFACE DRAINAGE STRUCTURES IN OVERALL DESIGN.
GAIN STRONG DESIGN IMPACT, GOOD APPEARANCE, DIRECTION OF USER'S ATTENTION *AWAY* FROM NEGATIVE, *TOWARD* POSITIVE ELEMENTS.

ADD MULCH RING AROUND TREES IN LAWN.
GAIN MAINTENANCE EFFICIENCY (MINIMUM PASSES, LARGE MOWER VS. MANY PASSES WITH SMALL MOWER PLUS TRIMMER); REDUCE TREE DAMAGE.

CHANGE LOW SANDBOX CURB TO ELIMINATE CONSTANT SAND OUTFLOW.
GAIN "FALLBACK" FROM HIGHER, STEPPED ENCLOSURE; SITTABLE EDGE FOR PLAY, PARENTS.

ADD CHEEK WALL TO STEPS (PREFERABLY AT DESIGN STAGE).
GAIN IMPROVED APPEARANCE, EASE OF TRIMMING, STRUCTURAL PROTECTION OF VULNERABLE (AND DANGEROUS) CORNERS.

Figure 4-52 Major increases in productivity can result from minor design changes.

After a slight pause to discuss the mechanics of plan presentation, we will try to do this. First will be offered a process which designers use to organize their own minds, for they too need some systematic method for ferreting significance out of a jumble of possible determinants. The design process will then be used as a model which, with a few twists, will be converted into a critical procedure: a method which should turn generalities into specifics and allow you to strike at the heart of a design question while keeping the loose ends tidy as you proceed.

chapter five
Plan Interpretation

*B*efore we proceed to the planning process, we should discuss the plan itself and the symbols which have to be interpreted in order to grasp its meaning. Actually, there are several types of plans with which you should become familiar.

PLAN TYPES

There is first of all the *master plan* (Figure 5-1), which shows the essential organization of the park including commitments regarding circulation and major relationships: park to surroundings, use areas to site, use areas to use areas, and major structures to use areas. You will find that most documents specifically labeled *master plan* are for extensive developments devouring hundreds of acres or more and are drawn at a scale of 1 inch = 100 feet or 1 inch = 200 feet, the large scales enabling the entire layout to be seen on one sheet but limiting what can be shown to the most general. Even though design decisions are broad stroke at these scales, they still reflect much of the landscape architect's thinking about the blending of the new with the old, area sizes and quantities, orientation to natural forces, and use of existing site resources. What a large-scale master plan lacks is a full representation of proposed lines, forms, textures, and colors, all but the most major contour adjustments, the location of minor structures like light fixtures and drinking fountains, and the handling of other details too small to be drawn in.

These are left to be indicated on the *site plan* (Figure 5-2), drawn at a scale of, say, 1 inch = 20 feet or 1 inch = 40 feet. In addition to rendering more exactly the larger-scale commitments, the designer can also show aesthetic character, spatial framework, and the location of

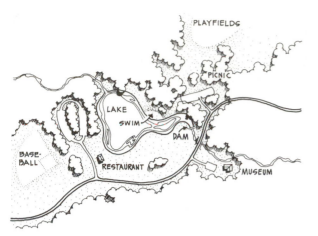

Figure 5-1 *A portion of a master plan.*

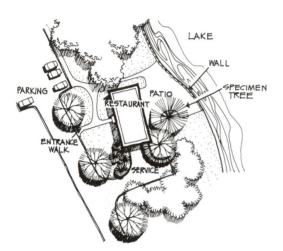

Figure 5-2 *A portion of a site plan enlarged from Figure 5-1.*

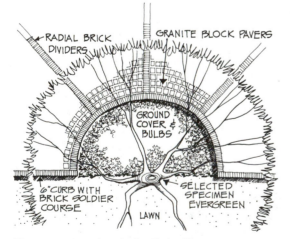

Figure 5-3 *A portion of a detail plan blown up from Figure 5-2.*

many minor structures on this drawing. The site plan can be a blowup of a portion of the master plan, or it can itself serve as the master plan when no drawing precedes it. The latter is usual if the area under study comprises about 50 acres or less, its moderate size being suited to a rather detailed solution presentation on one sheet of paper.

Where it is required that every fly speck, including such details as curb widths, sign locations, and pavement textures be shown, a *detail plan* (Figure 5-3) drawn to a scale of 1 inch = 10 feet or less is in order. This can be an enlargement of a portion of the site plan or, if the area is quite small (a totlot or bus waiting space, for example), can serve alone as a mini-master plan.

Accompanying each of the above might be *schematic plans* (Figure 5-4), illustrating circulation patterns, major relationships, or whatever else the designer believes are the keystones of the solution. Schematics are abstracted from the morass of plan detail as a courtesy to the reviewer. They are often used as backup material for verbal presentations or to accompany written reports which provide an explanation both of the plan and of the supporting data.

There are other terms by which master, site, and detail plans are known. *Development plan, master development plan,* and, in some loquacious circles, *master site development plan* are a few which come immediately to mind. It is useless to suggest which label goes officially with which plan type inasmuch as there is no general agreement among designers, many using *master plan* to refer to what we have called a *site plan, development plan* for either site or *master plan,* and an infinite number of other combinations.

What is more important than haggling about titles is understanding what kinds of information each plan type provides, regardless of what the designer you are working with has chosen to call it. This will help you in two ways: If you know the degree of design commitment possible at each scale, you are most likely to concentrate your critical focus on relevant issues rather than waste energy searching for the location of benches on a 1 inch = 200 feet layout scheme; secondly, knowing what each plan can show will allow you to participate in decisions regarding what kinds of drawings are necessary.

What we have called a master plan is the first statement of development intent and suggests how all the pieces will fit. With a master plan available, each piece can be built separately with full confidence that, when development is finished, all pieces will knit and work well together. The master drawing is often accompanied by a *staging plan* which indicates how construction might be phased in instances where budget does not permit construction in one stroke. The master plan can also be considered a record document showing both the existing and proposed at any given moment. On it can be charted changes brought about by new demands that arise between plan creation and implementation. And because the plan provides an overview of the project, it is easy to spot the side effects of the changes, and to see what measures need to be taken to retain the original "fit" of the interrelated parts.

What we have termed the site plan gets us closer to construction, for the scale at which it is drawn allows the designer to pinpoint locations and draw rather precise forms. The site plan, often accompanied by detail plans of some of its parts, provides the basis for *construction plans,* (Figure 5-5) which show measurements, material specifications, structural diagrams, and all the computations needed by contractors. It is also a guide for the *planting plan* (Figure 5-6), which is a type of construction drawing indicating to landscapers where plant material is to be installed.

All of these plans are interrelated, one laying the groundwork for the next. As you can see, there are two phases involved in seeing a job through to construction. The first is the stage of *ideas,* expressed in the master, site, and detail plans. These are the primary talking documents, discussed and modified a number of times before agreement is reached between client and designer. It is only after the ideas are agreed on that the designer can turn to the next, or *working drawing,* phase, the construction and planting plans. Most nonprofessionals lack the technical background necessary for an in-depth review of the working drawings which will be turned over to contractors. Thus, it is during the earlier phase that your chief opportunity to participate as a critic occurs. Fortunately, this is a crucial period, for decisions reached at the idea level dictate most of what will be done in the working drawing phase.

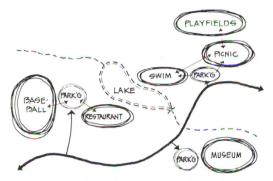

Figure 5-4   A schematic plan simplified from Figure 5-1.

AIDS TO EXPLAINING PLANS

A plan drawing is the usual form in which a site design solution is presented because it is the least time-consuming to prepare of the devices available to illustrate solution essentials. Unfortunately, it is a difficult document for the unschooled reader to comprehend, for while it is two-dimensional, its reality is three-dimensional. A scale model is a useful alternative. But unlike a plan, a model cannot be photocopied. It is also expensive to construct. Therefore, clients usually resign themselves to accepting a plan along with the mental gymnastics required to understand it.

To help a reviewer visualize the plan, the landscape architect often provides various types of sketches illustrating portions of the solution. These may be *elevations,* flat representations of objects seen on selected vertical planes (Figure 5-7); *sections,* slices through horizontal planes showing the goings-on above and below ground level (Figure 5-8); *eye-level perspectives,* three-dimensional sketches drawn as people might experience the development from chosen vantage points (Figure 5-9); or *bird's-eye perspectives,* overall three-dimensional views of the development as it might be seen from the upper story of an adjacent building (Figure 5-10).

While all these aid in putting the plan's message across, they can only show selected aspects of the solution. Even a comprehensive bird's-eye sketch has its shortcomings, for you cannot see behind and underneath many of its elements. Accordingly, you must examine the plan itself to decide most questions.

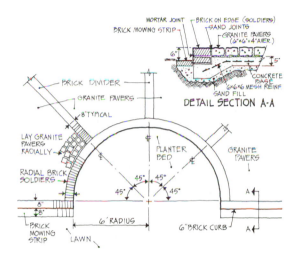

Figure 5-5   A construction plan for Figure 5-3.

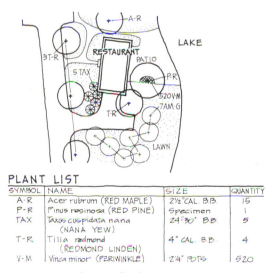

PLANT LIST

SYMBOL	NAME	SIZE	QUANTITY
A-R	Acer rubrum (RED MAPLE)	2½"CAL. B.B.	15
P-R	Pinus resinosa (RED PINE)	Specimen	1
TAX	Taxus cuspidata nana (NANA YEW)	24"-30" B.B.	5
T-R	Tilia redmond (REDMOND LINDEN)	4" CAL. B.B.	4
V-M	Vinca minor (PERIWINKLE)	2¼" POTS	520

Figure 5-6   A planting plan for Figure 5-2.

HOW A PLAN IS DRAWN

Using a variety of line weights and colors, the designer attempts to create several illusions that will ease the reviewer's interpretive chore.

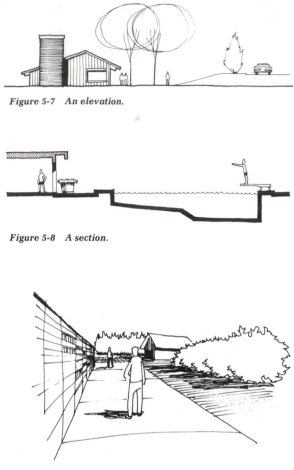

Figure 5-7   An elevation.

Figure 5-8   A section.

Figure 5-9   An eye-level perspective.

Figure 5-10   A bird's-eye perspective.

(Refer to plan drawings in Chapters 6 and 7.) In this regard, a successful drawing is one that appears uncomplicated no matter how much information it includes. The designer accomplishes this by setting down visually important objects with heavy strokes and lesser elements with progressively lighter marks. Hence, those objects which define space or form the skeleton of the plan (canopy trees, buildings) pop out, while the other elements (pavement patterns, curblines) recede into the background. When there are several levels of visual strength each level can be read cleanly, whereas a monotone drawing would serve up the same amount of information as a sheet of unintelligible spaghetti.

The plan should also have a three-dimensional feeling about it to help readers make the transition from two to three dimensions in their minds. Edging plan features with shadow marks is a typical technique, but most of the job can be accomplished by the aforementioned line variations. Where this is well done, the plan's parts read in order of diminishing strength as if you were hovering over the site in a helicopter — which in a sense you are doing when going about your inspection of the drawing. The illusion thus created would also be analogous to the impact were you experiencing the actual development at eye-level. That is, buildings, trees, and other spatial definers would both read strongest on the plan and catch your eye first on the ground. Those elements just under the canopy or second to the buildings in height, such as fences and small flowering trees, which are drawn with the next heaviest line, would also follow the spatial definers in actual visual impact. Details such as grassy patches, cobblestone areas, curblines, would be drawn with the lightest lines, for in reality these would be the last elements to impose their presence upon you.

The symbols on the plan, standing for items which the designer proposes to have installed, can be labeled, but to facilitate interpretation they should also express something of the character of the items. Thus, designers might delineate trees as roundish bubbles with ragged edges so that they may be quickly distinguished from buildings drawn with unyielding lines and hard corners. They may symbolize brick with waffle-iron marks so you can immediately judge its extent in relation to the concrete shown on the same plan as a scored sweep and the grass depicted by texture stipples. They may also color the trees purple and cross-hatch the water. Good luck to these dilettantes. They will have to spend most of their allotted time with you explaining what all those funny looking things on the plan stand for.

CONTOURS

However, there are some odd-looking things on the plan which cannot be avoided. These are the *contour lines* wiggled over the paper to represent peaks, valleys, slopes — the three-dimensional form of the land surface. (Note following letter references in Figure 5-11.) Contours, imaginary strokes connecting equal points of elevation, are usually the lightest lines. The term *elevation* stands for a height above or below an assumed plane of reference or datum, the usual datum being sea level which is expressed as elevation 0. Thus, if a contour is

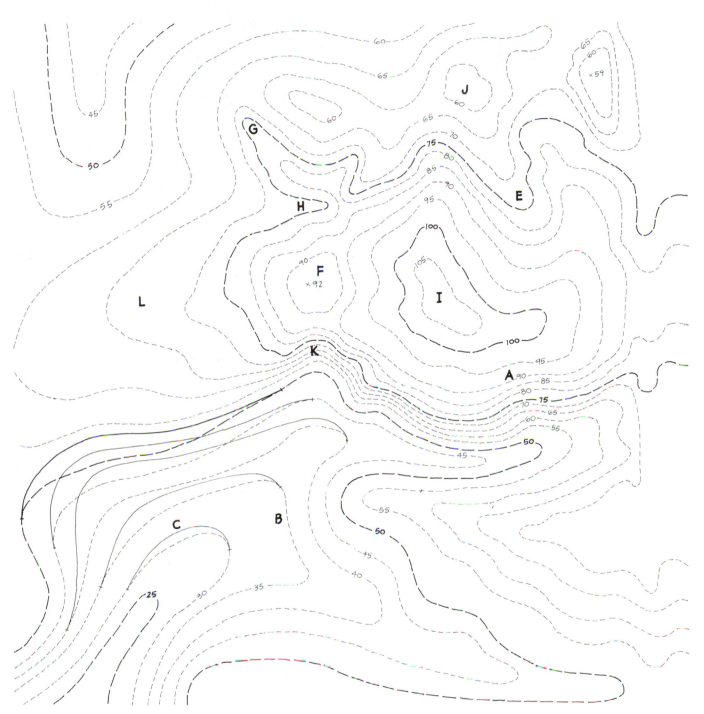

Figure 5-11   A topographic map.

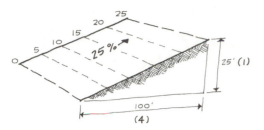

Figure 5-12 *The slope of the land can be referred to in terms of a ratio or a percentage.*

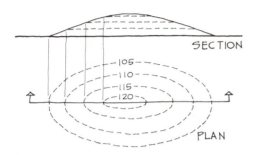

Figure 5-13 *Visualized in cross section, these contours indicate a peak.*

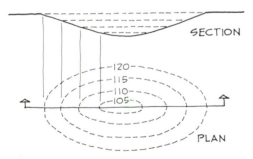

Figure 5-14 *A cross section shows that these contours depict a depression.*

labeled 90, the points which it connects are 90 feet above the surface of the sea (A).

On most plans, dashed lines (B) represent the existing contours, while unbroken lines (C) indicate those proposed. However, if only existing contours are shown, they may be entire lines, the usual rule being violated by those labor-conscious designers who feel that unbroken lines can be put down faster than dashes.

Visualization of the land configuration as expressed by contour drawings is a hard-to-come-by facility, but if the knack is acquired, the greatest obstacle to seeing the plan in three-dimensions virtually disappears. Thus, a real effort to grasp the picture portrayed by these funny lines pays off manyfold. Here are a few technicalities you must consider in reading contour lines:

1. Every plan has a *contour interval.* The interval is designated in the plan legend (D) and stands for the vertical distance between adjacent lines. For readability's sake, every fifth contour is heavied (E). Therefore, if the contour interval is 5 feet, light lines connect, for example, elevations 80, 85, 90, and 95. The 75 and 100 foot contours are darker.
2. *Spot elevations* ($\times$ 92 on the diagram) are occasionally inserted to indicate critical points lying between the contour lines (F).
3. Bends (sometimes called *noses*) in a contour line point either down a ridge (G) or up a valley (H).
4. A closed contour indicates either a summit (I) or a depression (J) in the ground.
5. The closer the contours, the steeper the slope (K); the farther apart the lines, the more gentle the pitch (L).
6. The steepest part of the slope is that which runs perpendicular to the direction of the contour lines.
7. *Gradient* (slope pitch) is usually expressed either as a ratio of horizontal run to vertical rise (for example, 4 : 1), or a percentage. (A vertical rise of 25 feet per 100 feet of run would be a 25 percent gradient.) (See Figure 5-12.)

The gradient can be easily computed from a plan where contours are shown. If you wish to express the grade as a ratio, first determine horizontal run by measuring the ground surface distance between several contour lines. This measurement can be taken with either an engineer's scale (marked off in decimals) or an architect's rule (scored in fractions) flipped to the side which represents the scale at which the plan has been drawn. Then multiply the number of contours found in the area of horizontal measurement by the contour interval. This gives you the vertical rise which is divided into the run measurement to arrive at the ratio. To express the grade as a percentage, simply count from the contour lines the number of feet the ground rises in 100 horizontal feet and place a percent symbol after the result.

Certain visualization exercises will help you get a feel for the relative steepness of the slopes represented by these figures and should otherwise give you a feel of the land. Develop the habit of doing cross sections or slices through the areas you wish to visualize. Do dozens on paper initially as demonstrated in Figures 5-13 and 5-14 and soon you will find yourself drawing them automatically in your head every time you spy a contour map or want to answer such questions as: Is that a peak or a valley? How rugged are those undulations? How flat is the surface proposed for the ball diamond?

Concurrently, you might run 100-foot measuring tapes out in the hall. Have one end held on the floor, raise the other the number of feet required for the grade percentage you wish to picture. The "slope" of the tape will be the actual pitch of the ground whose contours compute to the figure you are using.

Begin to check out plans on the site. As you move through the development, picture yourself walking inside the plan. Eventually, you should be able to reverse this process so that every time you pick up a plan drawing, you will immediately climb in, walk around, and come away with not only a feeling for the landforms, but a three-dimensional impression of all the other design essentials as well.

chapter six

Site Design Process

*T*he ability to design recreation areas is similar to that required to solve any kind of land-use problem, the primary difference between a park design and, say, a subdivision design being the inputs which are analyzed. Accordingly, you will find that most designers have worked their way into a park design specialty from a general education in landscape architecture, just as doctors receive a basic medical background before turning to brain surgery.

Development of design expertise does not occur overnight; it requires an inordinate amount of time and patience spent in simply doing: testing, discovering, and prodding latent talents to the surface. Much of the trial, error, and frustration that this entails is due to the fact that no one has yet invented a design cookbook containing procedures which guarantee results. However, many designers do use with some success a process which helps them sort out the facts, premises, and possibilities, and arrive at a solution.

The process aids the landscape architect by systematically focusing attention on all factors which could affect the design's outcome and otherwise lends a semblance of organization to the attack. By illuminating relevant factors, it can also trigger flashes of inspiration. The process therefore bolsters both the rational and intuitive powers that the designer must call upon. While the process provides a framework, its ultimate value as a design tool is contingent upon the designer's ability to exercise those powers interchangeably within it.

A systematic approach to site design includes three phases. The first is a *survey,* or an assembling of facts and data. The second is *analysis,* or the making of value judgments about the effects of one fact upon another. The third step may be called *synthesis,* or the weaving of the results of analysis into a comprehensive solution to the problem. The steps may not be done strictly according to this chronology, for there is much feedback and interplay among them. In addition, the process must remain flexible in order to allow each designer to use his or her mental powers in the way he or she finds most comfortable.

SURVEY

Program Development

Each design phase has several parts. The first step in the survey phase is the preparation of a program expressing the early requirements of the project. Either handed to the landscape architect by the client or its development delegated to the designer if the client does not have the means to shape it up, the program establishes goals to be accomplished. These might be set down as: *tangible items* (ten tennis courts), *capacities* (picnic facilities for 200 people), *physical benefits* (nonabrasive play surfaces), or *intangible gains* (being an educational institution, the school should have grounds which show respect for the natural environment). Agency *policies* whose implementation would depend upon how well the site was developed might also be included (a desire to collect entrance fees), as well as information regarding available *construction and maintenance funds.*

The program gives direction to the designer's thinking, yet it is always a flexible document, subject to modification as that thinking progresses. This is because not only the answers but many of the questions remain unclear until the end.

In the book *Problem Seeking,* William Pena's small masterpiece on Caudill Rowlett Scott's programming techniques, Pena emphasizes the importance of controlling the "data clog" that results when the client provides too much information without any organization or priorities. The client needs the control offered by the designer's objective view of inflowing information: Is it important? Interesting? Irrelevant? Some data may seem very important to users because of current political or financial pressures yet have little long-term impact on the design. Other data may have to be obtained by, in effect, prying open apparently closed issues so that clients can recognize elements which they take for granted and think of as unimportant but which have a direct bearing on the success of a project. For example, means of *increasing productivity* by intensifying or coordinating uses may not surface unless someone makes the effort to analyze the status quo of all facilities and then investigate both *"Why?"* and *"What else?"* In an urban park in an ethnic neighborhood where the prevailing pattern is one of gregarious camaraderie along the street perimeters, conversation pits in the interior created by the original designer for adult users sit unused (and unmentioned by the users in the designer's information-gathering phase because, though they aren't a solution, they at least aren't a problem). Ask *"Why?"* and *"What else?"* Conversion to a safe play area could be a major program feature but only if the opportunity is not overlooked.

Additional items might be suggested to take advantage of site potential discovered midway through the analysis phase: a skiing complex proposed to exploit the many steep slopes. Capacities may have to be adjusted due to site restrictions: fewer cabins planned to ensure that sewage distribution fields are not overloaded. In some cases, items may have to be eliminated entirely from consideration as unfeasible: swimming taken off the list because the water is found to be polluted.

As the designer begins to uncover solution possibilities, the program may also be augmented with criteria unique to the job at hand. Many will be spun from those principles and matters of concern found to be most relevant to the project. For instance, in the study of use-area relationships, the designer might realize that day users will be drawn to different attractions than overnight guests and conclude that facilities for the former should be separate from those for the latter. Additional directives might come from research into the technical requirements of the program items.

On counts other than the debated territorial imperative, in large measure the program should reflect the voiced desires of the people whom the park will eventually serve. However, on some sad occasions, this is not the case, the list of facilities being drawn up in a vacuum by either the designer or administrator. As a result, the park may include only those things its developers like to do.

The citizenry becomes involved when many of the program items come from demand-study interpretations, the questionnaire route being quite satisfactory for most developments serving the diverse population that would be attracted to either a citywide complex or one located away from population centers. When development is proposed for a neighborhood, however, more direct public involvement in program preparation, including continuing face to face consultations with the designer, is highly desirable. One district has created a full-time position for a public coordinator. The coordinator's responsibility is to know each neighborhood and the citizens living there, and to be their liaison with the park district on all issues — design, maintenance, security, program, anything affecting their use of and regard for the parks. If not able to answer a particular question or resolve a specific concern, the coordinator brings the district's designer or maintenance superintendent or other appropriate person directly to the place or person concerned to provide a hands-on response and, if possible, a proper solution.

This kind of involvement is especially significant for developments serving the urban poor, to whom the neighborhood is essentially the entire world and a major source of identity. To deny the residents direct participation, while outsiders ram through ideas they alone imagine to be cute, is both arrogant and patronizing. This is the way public alienation is created.

Inventory of On-Site Factors

After the program has been thrashed out, the designer begins gathering facts about the site, securing information from maps and personal inspections of the area. Such data could include the location of and other information about existing:

1. Constructed elements
    a. Legal and physical boundaries, private holdings, and public easements

TOPOGRAPHY

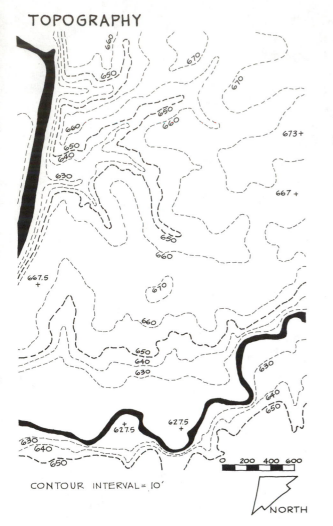

CONTOUR INTERVAL = 10'

NORTH

200 400 600

Figure 6-1   Site data—topography.

b. Buildings, bridges, and other structures including those of historical and archeological significance

c. Roads, walks, and other transportation ways

d. Electric lines, gas mains, and other utilities

e. Land uses: agriculture, industry, recreation, and others

f. Applicable ordinances such as zoning regulations and health codes

2. Natural resources

a. Topography, including high and low points (Figure 6-1), gradients (Figure 6-2), and drainage patterns (Figure 6-3)

b. Soil types, by name if available, for clues regarding ground surface permeability, stability, and fertility (Figure 6-4)

c. Water bodies, including permanence, fluctuations, and other habits

d. Subsurface matter: geology of the underlying rock including existence of commercially or functionally valuable material such as sand and gravel, coal, or water

e. Vegetation types (mixed hardwoods, pine forest, prairie grassland, others) and individual specimens of consequence (Figure 6-5)

f. Wildlife, including existence of desirable habitats such as low cover for pheasants, caves for bears, or berries for birds

3. Natural forces (including both macroclimate as generally found over the entire site and microclimate characteristics or changes from the norm experienced in isolated patches)

a. Temperature (air and water) especially day, night, and seasonal norms, extremes, and their durations

b. Sun angles at various seasons and times of the day

c. Sun pockets such as might be found in forest clearings; frost pockets which may be found in low places where the wind that sweeps away the morning dew is blocked

d. Wind directions and intensities, both daily and seasonal

e. Precipitation: rain, snow, and sleet seasons and accumulations; storm frequencies and intensities

4. Perceptual characteristics

a. Views into and from the site; significant features

b. Smells and sounds and their sources

c. Spatial patterns

d. Lines, forms, textures, colors, and size relationships which give the site its peculiar character

e. General impressions regarding experience potential of the site and its parts

Inventory of Off-Site Factors

The designer must also accumulate information about the constructed, natural, and perceptual elements on the properties which surround or otherwise affect the site. These might include both existing and anticipated:

1. Land-use patterns
2. Stream and drainage sources
3. Visuals, smells, and sounds

SLOPE GRADIENTS

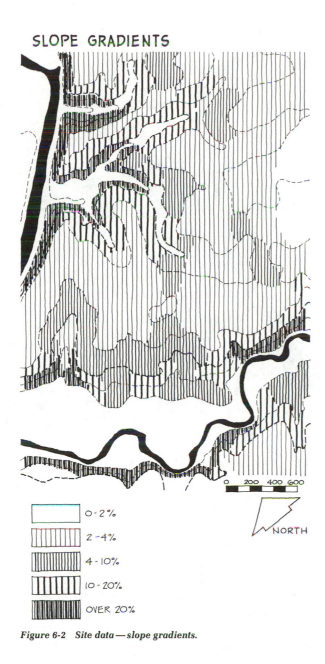

☐	0 - 2 %
▦	2 - 4 %
▥	4 - 10 %
▦	10 - 20%
■	OVER 20%

NORTH

Figure 6-2   Site data—slope gradients.

DRAINAGE PATTERNS

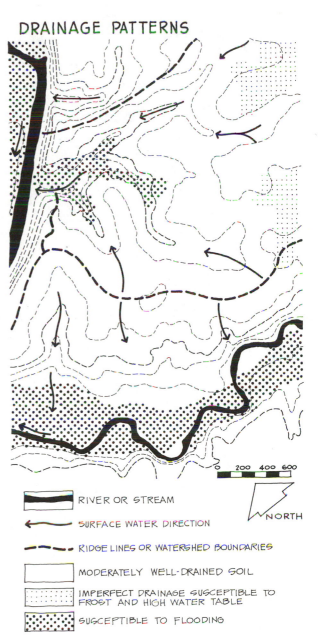

▬	RIVER OR STREAM
←	SURFACE WATER DIRECTION
– – –	RIDGE LINES OR WATERSHED BOUNDARIES
☐	MODERATELY WELL-DRAINED SOIL
⋮⋮	IMPERFECT DRAINAGE SUSCEPTIBLE TO FROST AND HIGH WATER TABLE
⦂⦂	SUSCEPTIBLE TO FLOODING

NORTH

Figure 6-3   Site data—drainage patterns.

4. Aesthetic character
5. Public utility locations and capacities
6. Transportation ways and systems

Each step in the survey phase begins in isolation, the first facts collected simply being those which are immediately handy. Soon all steps become intertwined, each giving direction to the others in order to turn general notions of what might be needed into specific requirements and ensure that everything which could affect the project's outcome has been considered. The designer must shift back and forth between program and inventory. Program items suggest to the designer not only what information must be collected, but also what is inconsequential. The fact that a playground is being planned sends the landscape architect after data about sun angles and the peripheral traffic situation. It suggests little urgency to seek out a map showing

SOIL TYPES

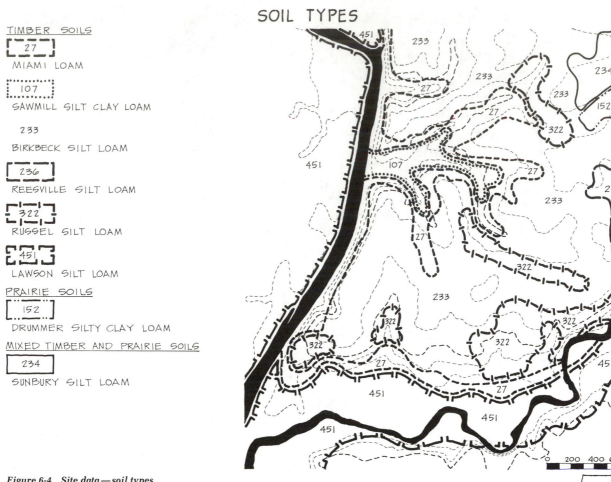

TIMBER SOILS

27
MIAMI LOAM

107
SAWMILL SILT CLAY LOAM

233
BIRKBECK SILT LOAM

236
REESVILLE SILT LOAM

322
RUSSEL SILT LOAM

451
LAWSON SILT LOAM

PRAIRIE SOILS

152
DRUMMER SILTY CLAY LOAM

MIXED TIMBER AND PRAIRIE SOILS

234
SUNBURY SILT LOAM

Figure 6-4   Site data—soil types.

the location of bear dens and pheasant cover. In a complementary fashion, as we have discussed, data garnered might make it clear that modifications are necessary in the program. The information gathered must be assigned some value in relation to program elements. The value may be a simple plus or minus, or data may be assigned to a numerical scale (for example, 5 or 10 = good or desirable, 1 or 0 = poor or undesirable). Unless the designer assigns specific values to the data, he or she may be misled by the data, or find it hard to draw conclusions.

The recurrent question is: ''Why?'' What is the purpose of gathering this data? The target in site analysis is to use the information either to *find a place for a particular use* or *find a use for a particular place.* Generally with a program developed and uses identified, the focus of the analysis becomes the search for the right place.

To see how the survey phase and subsequent phases work, look at the accompanying case study, which has been simplified to eliminate confusing details. First, note in Figure 6-6 the program comprised of items which we will assume have been agreed upon as meeting the needs of the park users. Relate the items to the drawing labeled *site analysis* (Figure 6-9) in order to see what categories of survey informa-

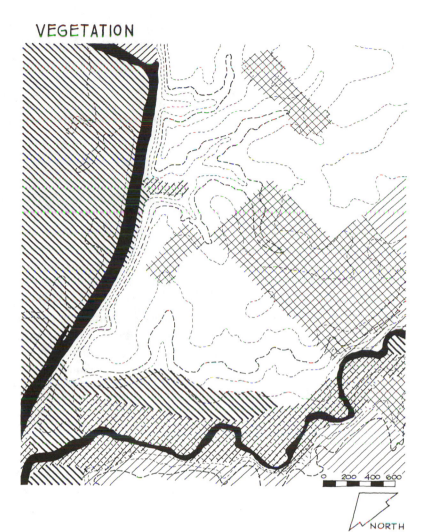

VEGETATION

OAK-HICKORY ASSOCIATION

MIXED UPLAND

MIXED UPLAND REGENERATION

BOTTOMLAND MAPLE ASSOCIATION

MIXED BOTTOMLAND

0 200 400 600

NORTH

Figure 6-5   Site data—vegatation.

tion the program has suggested. Then reflect on the diagrams and drawings in turn as each is explained in the following.

ANALYSIS

Program Relationships (Figure 6-7)

While data are being collected, design ideas are germinating, but they are held in the back of the designer's mind until a more comprehensive look at development possibilities has been taken. This begins by grouping program items in order to understand something about their interrelationships.

Relationship Diagrams (Figure 6-8)

These interrelationships are then translated into diagrammatic form, the designer investigating how the major units might work well together and how circulation might be facilitated between them. Neither scale nor site information enters the landscape architect's mind at this point; the concentration is solely on functional relationships and lines of travel. Many combinations will be tried as the landscape architect

PROGRAM

ENTRY CONTROL BUILDING
NATURE CENTER
SERVICE YARD
BOAT REPAIR AREA
NATURE TRAILS
PICNICKING
PLAYFIELD
COMFORT STATION
SWIMMING
MARINA
ROWBOAT & EQUIPMENT
   RENTAL BUILDING
PARKING
CONCESSION
BATHHOUSE

Figure 6-6   Design process case study—program.

PROGRAM RELATIONSHIPS

<u>1. NATURE CENTER</u>
   A. TRAILS
   B. PARKING

<u>2. PICNICKING</u>
   A. PLAYFIELDS
   B. COMFORT STATION
   C. CONCESSION
   D. PARKING

<u>3. SWIMMING</u>
   A. BATHHOUSE
   B. CONCESSION
   C. PARKING

<u>4. MARINA</u>
   A. RENTAL BUILDING
   B. BOAT REPAIR
   C. CONCESSION
   D. PARKING

<u>5. SERVICE YARD</u>
   A. ENTRY CONTROL

Figure 6-7 Design process case study — program relationships.

attempts to work out the bugs of prior diagrams in subsequent ones. Finally, a scheme is developed which, in the designer's estimation, represents an ideal functional pattern for the program's major use areas.

Site Analysis (Figure 6-9)

Now the designer turns an analytical eye on the site, first compiling the inventory items on a topographic map. Those which lend themselves to graphic representation, such as vegetative cover, water, and soil, are expressed in sweeping patterns and color coded according to variety or condition. This is done so that the character of the site can be read at a glance, allowing the designer to quickly spy areas suited for certain of the program items. For instance, landforms might be marked off in four colors: one designating slopes of less than 1 percent where drainage is always a problem; another standing for surfaces of 1 to 3 percent that may be suitable for all types of construction with little or no earthmoving; the third indicating areas of 4 to 9 percent grade, the land suited to building and roadway installation with moderate grading; and the fourth showing slopes of 10 percent or greater which will require major site adjustments if built upon. Breakdown increments will vary with each project, depending upon the slope requirements of the program units.

In addition, natural and perceptual influences like wind directions and noise sources are illustrated with bold symbols, and other considerations are set down in note form on the map. The latter might be directives the designer has established internally according to the ideas which have been germinating in the back of the mind: "Save rock outcropping." Or, because by now there is a feel for the program requirements: "Good place for entrance."

In the analysis phase of the design process, the designer strives to gain a full understanding of program requirements and an intimate knowledge of the limitations and potentials of the site before beginning to make concrete decisions. This phase also serves to flash possibilities for solution in the designer's mind, alternatives founded in the logic of the analyses being made.

As in the survey phase, analytical steps are first taken singly, but soon swing into a back and forth effort, with a growing knowledge of program needs directing the search for particular site qualities, and a rising feeling for the site illuminating what can be done to satisfy the program's demands. Concurrently, both research and criteria reevaluations are proceeding so that, when the time comes to put the pieces together, the designer knows full well what tests a successful synthesis must pass.

SYNTHESIS

Design Concept (Figure 6-10)

Up to now, one issue at a time has been placed in front of the landscape architect in a progression of interrelated complexity. Proceeding in such a fashion, the designer is less likely to be panic-stricken by the

RELATIONSHIP DIAGRAMS

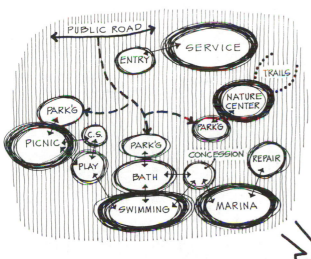

+ ENTRY CONTROL NEAR PUBLIC ROAD.
+ PARKING — SPLIT, DOESN'T PENETRATE ACTIVITIES.
+ ONE CONCESSION FOR SWIMMING & MARINA WHICH SHOULD BOTH BE NEAR WATER.
+ PICNIC & SWIMMING SHARE PLAYFIELD.
− MARINA NOISE & DEBRIS CONFLICT WITH SWIMMING.
− PICNIC DIVORCED FROM NATURE CENTER.
− NATURE CENTER WEDGED BETWEEN NOISY SERVICE AND REPAIR.

+ BATH–CONCESSION COMBINED TO SEPARATE SWIMMING & MARINA.
+ PICNIC & NATURE CENTER PARKING COMBINED.
+ SWIMMING & MARINA PARKING COMBINED.
+ REPAIR & SERVICE (NOISE & MESS) COMBINED.
− PICNICKERS GO THRU N.C. AND TRAILS TO SWIM & BOAT.
− ROADS CUT PICNIC FROM BOATING.

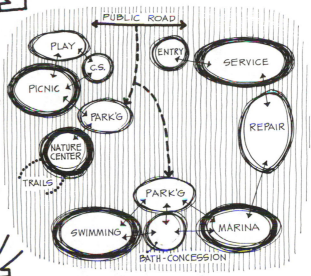

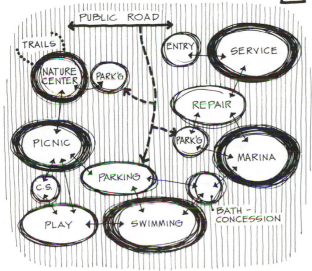

+ PARKING — SPLIT, DOESN'T PENETRATE ACTIVITIES (PEOPLE DON'T CROSS ROADS TO GET TO ANYTHING).
+ N.C. ISOLATED BUT CONVENIENT TO PICNIC AREA WHICH WILL PROVIDE MAJORITY OF VISITORS.
+ BATH–CONCESSION SEPARATE MARINA & SWIMMING.
+ PLAY SEPARATE BUT USABLE BY BOTH SWIMMING AND PICNIC.
+ MARINA, REPAIR & SERVICE TOGETHER — NOISE ISOLATED FROM REST OF PARK.
+ ENTRY CONTROL NEAR PUBLIC ROAD, FIRST CONTACT.

THIS IS IT !

Figure 6-8   Design process case study — relationship diagrams.

SITE ANALYSIS

NORTH

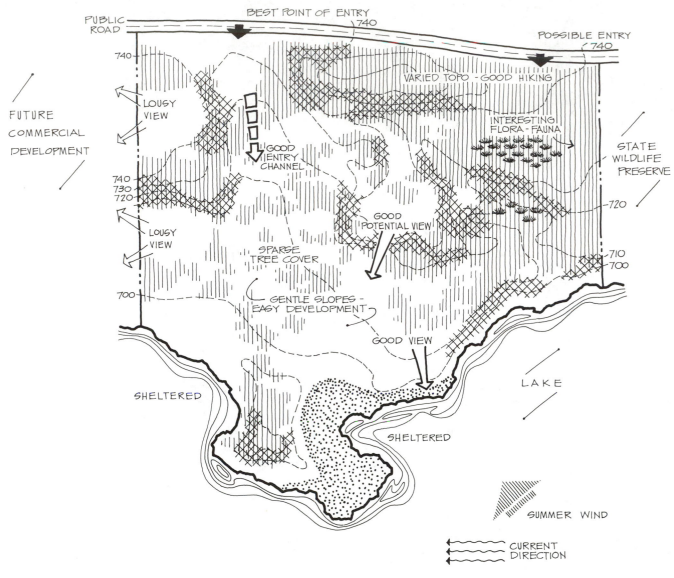

PUBLIC ROAD

BEST POINT OF ENTRY

740

POSSIBLE ENTRY
740

740

VARIED TOPO - GOOD HIKING

FUTURE COMMERCIAL DEVELOPMENT

LOUSY VIEW

GOOD ENTRY CHANNEL

INTERESTING FLORA - FAUNA

STATE WILDLIFE PRESERVE

740
730
720

720

LOUSY VIEW

GOOD POTENTIAL VIEW

710
700

SPARSE TREE COVER

700

GENTLE SLOPES - EASY DEVELOPMENT

GOOD VIEW

SHELTERED

LAKE

SHELTERED

SUMMER WIND

CURRENT DIRECTION

LEGEND

▦	WOODED AREA
▨	SLOPES EXCEEDING 5%
▦	MARSHY AREA
▦	SANDY AREA
— · — · —	CONTOUR LINE

Figure 6-9   Design process case study—site analysis.

DESIGN CONCEPT

NORTH

RELATION OF USE AREAS TO SITE

1. NATURE CENTER
- GOOD VIEW
- APPROXIMATE TO DIVERSE NATURAL INTEREST AREA
- ISOLATED BY TOPO FROM OFFENSIVE TRAFFIC & NOISE

2. PICNICKING
- FLAT SITE
- STABLE SOIL
- CANOPY TREES
- VIEW OF WATER, YET AS SAFETY MEASURE, SEPARATED FROM LAKE BY TOPO
- IN PATH OF SUMMER BREEZES FROM LAKE
- RELATED PLAY AREA IN FLAT, TREELESS SPACE

3. SWIMMING
- SANDY SOIL
- SHELTERED COVE
- MAXIMUM SOLAR EXPOSURE

4. MARINA
- SHELTERED
- APPROXIMATE TO COMPATIBLE COMMERCIAL DEVELOPMENT
- FLAT SITE
- STABLE SOIL
- RELATED REPAIR AREA FLAT AND TREELESS, UNAFFECTED BY POOR VIEW

5. SERVICE YARD
- FLAT, CLEARED SITE, UNAFFECTED BY POOR VIEW
- STABLE SOIL
- SEPARATED FROM PUBLIC AREAS BY TOPO

6. ROADS & PARKING LOTS
- FLAT TOPO AVOIDING EXCESSIVE CUT & FILL
- STABLE SOIL
- SPARSE TREES PROVIDE COVER YET ALIGNMENT AVOIDS REMOVAL OF VEGETATION
- EXISTING SPATIAL CHANNELS

Figure 6-10   *Design process case study — design concept.*

magnitude of the problem than if attempting to address the entirety of the project at the onset.

Once the designer has a good handle on required relationships and site influences, the synthesis phase is opened with an attempt to fit the ideal functional diagram to the site. What the designer reads from the diagram and tries to visualize on the ground is a functional essence rather than a literal image; that is, a diagrammatic sketch which shows one use unit next to another does not demand that one must appear to the right of the other on the final plan. Rather, it offers the more general suggestion that they must be adjacent on the site. The designer is therefore free to reverse, shift, rotate, warp, or otherwise manipulate the diagram elements so that all use units end up on desirable portions of the site in a pattern which retains the essential relationships of the abstract diagram.

What takes place in the designer's mind during synthesis is impossible to describe except to say that it entails a series of impulsive reactions to the conditions of the problem as they unfold. In no particular order, save one he or she feels at ease with, the designer may start by selecting a perfect location for one use area, work circulation to it, then roll the other units from it. The designer may relocate areas whose initial positioning violates the sense of the relationship diagram or revise the whole to ameliorate the negative effects of the relocation, and then turn to refinements that satisfy a single criterion. Gathering steam, the designer begins reacting to all factors at once, working simultaneously among all the solution aspects until at last the whole is visualized.

The product is a skeleton concept, much like an outline for a book, only presented in graphic form. Use units are illustrated in approximate size and form where they belong on the site. Traffic channels are indicated. The spatial structure is set. Additional work remains, for the skeleton must be fleshed out with a myriad of details, but these will supplement rather than materially change the major commitments made at this point.

Refined Plan (Figure 6-11)

Within the concept framework, the designer proceeds to make precision adjustments, add minor use areas and structures, and do whatever else is necessary to give the solution its finished form.

Final Plan

The work is now drawn up as a *preliminary plan* ready to be reviewed by the client. A single refined concept may be presented if the landscape architect feels that the problem can be solved in only one manner. A number of alternatives may be trotted out if the designer has either evolved several equally desirable relationship diagrams or discovered that a single diagram can be fitted to the site in a variety of ways.

During the review session, the designer explains the reasons behind the moves while the client darts a question here and there, mulling over the ideas generated by the drawings. A successful review ends with agreement about the proposal usually contingent upon the incor-

REFINED PLAN

NORTH

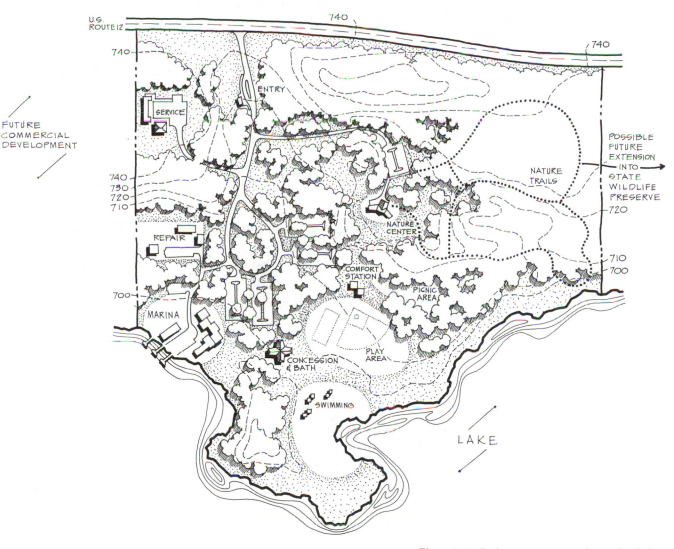

Figure 6-11   Design process case study — refined plan.

poration of modifications requested by the client. Back on the drawing board, the revisions are made and the plan is finalized.

Computer Support

As we have seen, the site analysis generates criteria that guide the siting of the program uses. These criteria are established by relating the program items to the inventory information collected on the site. Organization of the inventoried information can at first seem like an overwhelming task, both in terms of raw volume of data and number of possible interrelationships. In the case we just looked at, for example, fourteen different uses are considered in relation to more than a dozen different criteria, including steepness of slope, vegetation cover density, and highway access.

SPREADSHEET FOR SITE ANALYSIS — Project 6/85
Suitability Criteria

FACILITY TYPE		I	IIA	IIB	III	IV
SLOPES	0–2%	x	x	x	x	x
	2–4%	x	x	x	x	x
	4–10%	x		x	x	x
	10–20%	x				
	20%+	x				
DRAINAGE	Good	x	x	x	x	x
	Fair	x		x	x	
	Poor	x				
SOIL	Good	x	x	x	x	x
	Fair	x	x	x	x	
	Poor	x				
VEGETATION	Good	x		x		
	Fair	x		x		x
	Poor	x	x		x	x

FACILITY TYPES INCLUDE:
I.   Nonconstruction: nature trails
IIA. Minimal construction: playfields
IIB. Minimal construction: picnicking
III. Moderate construction: roads, parking, service yard
IV. Intensive construction: all structures

Figure 6-12 Typical spreadsheet format for preliminary computer-based site analysis.

SPREADSHEET FOR SITE SELECTION—
PLAYFIELDS

SITES		A	B	C	D
CRITERIA					
SLOPES	0–4%	x	x	x	x
DRAINAGE	Good				x
SOIL	Fair to Good	x		x	x
VEGETATION	Poor to Absent	x			x
SCORE		3	1	2	4

Figure 6-13 Typical spreadsheet for site selection of playfields.

The application of computer technology offers some powerful means of dealing with Pena's data clog difficulty — and some shortcuts in the mind-boggling process of collating the information. Using software created for management and display of data (usually referred to as data base management systems), a matrix can be generated showing interrelationships of all the uses being considered and all the criteria assembled so that uses with similar requirements can be identified and grouped easily (Figure 6-12). This consolidation can make the selection of suitable sites easier. The criterion most limiting to all uses is apparently steep slopes. Plotting these data on the base map would immediately eliminate consideration of many areas for an entire block of uses. Dense vegetation is another major criterion that can be plotted, further narrowing the array of site choices.

Reversing the telescope, the data management matrix can be used to display isolated criteria for single uses. Instead of analyzing a single site for many uses, this kind of application compares several sites for a single use. In such a situation, the question addressed could be: "Of these four sites for potential acquisition, which would be best for field-games development?" The output would include the focused criteria list as shown down the left of the matrix in Figure 6-13. However, the facility type column heads would be replaced by the roster of sites showing their respective *scores* for each of the criteria. The selection process would then at least start with a ranking of known data, to be confirmed by more detailed physical observation of the properties. In this situation the highest score (site D) would be most suitable.

If the computer's only function in the site analysis process was to provide these matrix displays, it would have to be considered simply an expensive assistant. The dramatic importance of this technology is in the step beyond the first presentation of collected data. The game of "What if?" can next be played simply by changing any of the criteria. What if each slope could be increased by 2 percent? For the individual park site, all affected uses immediately are displayed with revised relationships. Some uses might be possible in areas previously indicated as off limits. For the specific use, the several sites being evaluated might suddenly have a new rank order with a consequent change in purchase priority. Interesting. What about a 3 percent increase? What about *decreasing* by 2 percent? The instant display of results is a vitally important adjunct to the effort to make the best decision about resource utilization; it guarantees that the maximum possible number of alternatives has been considered and the minimum number of surprises will be encountered.

Assuming that a computer system will be a necessity for any agency, a conscientious effort toward its care and feeding will include stuffing its data files with statistics and facts about sites, uses, and local population, and with management data and economic information, regardless of whether the specific data are needed at the moment. The stored resource, created at relative leisure, will prove invaluable when needed under pressure.

In the capacity of a user, be wary when evaluating an analysis presented in support of a proposed plan, no matter whether the source is in-house staff or a remote consultant, whether the plan is computer-generated or laboriously hand drawn. Sheer volume of paper does not necessarily equal impact. A successful analysis is not measured in pounds, only in quality. A large amount of inventoried data is useful only if actually relevant to the analysis performed. How are the *conclusions presented* related to the *data collected*? Why were the data needed? The analysis should be a record of an orderly thought process leading to a logical plan.

chapter seven

Plan
Evaluation

lthough their chores are different throughout, designers and critics
A are confronted with many similar situations. Beginning with
little understanding of solution direction, both are vulnerable to panic
in the face of the project's magnitude and both need a clear view of
where to begin. While both might have early feelings about what is
needed, such general feelings must be turned into specific requirements in order to direct attention to the significant determinants of the
case. The success of the end product — the architect's drawing or the
critic's evaluation — hinges on the ability to make correct value judgments about the synthesis.

The best aid that can be suggested for the critic — as well as for the
designer — is a systematic approach to sorting out determinants, although this cannot guarantee results since a favorable outcome depends upon how well the critic operates within the framework provided by the system. While any evaluation procedure is therefore but a
tool, the one suggested here should arm the critics with enough understanding to give them some confidence in their conclusions.

SELECTING THE DESIGNER

The process of ensuring an appropriate solution to your land-use
problem begins long before the plan is developed. It starts with the
selection of the landscape architect. If you find a good one, your
critique becomes but a cordial review, lasting just long enough to
satisfy your curiosity, leaving ample time in the evening to toast both
your fine judgment and the landscape architect's at a parlor of good
cheer.

When designers are employees of your agency, you already know something about their work and abilities. However, many park departments do not budget a full-time design staff, preferring to contract the preparation of each development plan to a private consultant. Selecting a qualified consultant is an art which should be mastered by the financing party to the contract. It involves a searching analysis of the designer's references and past performances. Several candidates should be asked to present their credentials; while one might appear adequate to the task, comparison with the qualifications of others will confirm a decision that the best has been chosen.

There is frequently a tendency to keep the money at home by selecting a designer from the immediate area, but this should be tempered by a desire to choose a consultant who is detached from the pressures of local politics and vested interests. Whether from around the area or from out of town, the landscape architect must be able to provide an objective solution to the problem.

Those landscape architecture firms that devote all or portions of their practices to the design of recreation areas should be asked to supply examples of prior works similar to the one you are planning. Inspect the graphics and accompanying texts and draw conclusions about depth of analysis and breadth of thought (these chapters have suggested what should be expected of a competent designer). During the formal interview, quiz the designer regarding the handling of issues which have been discussed here.

While specialty experience deserves consideration, don't overlook landscape architects who have not done park projects, remembering that their education proposes to equip them to treat all types of land-use problems. Even the office with the highest number of recreation areas under its belt started somewhere. In reviewing samples of their work, look for the handling of design aspects similar to those associated with parks such as circulation, use-area relationships, resource utilization, and aesthetic experience. Excellence in these categories and professional presence under examination may very well indicate a capacity to meet your specific challenge and provide the quality you seek.

Landscape architects compete for commissions on the basis of ability rather than price, for their code of ethics prohibits fee bidding. This is not to suggest that you should avoid negotiating with the designer over both the extent and cost of the work. Determining whether or not you can afford the service is your right as well as a most practical consideration. However, such discussions should be delayed until after you have measured the consultant's competence, for it is on this that the solution to your problem depends.

PREPARATION

A landscape architect—the type from whom you would not want to buy a used car—once said that he could convince a client to accept anything because, when he presented a proposal, he was the only one prepared. Fortunately, such cavalier attitudes are rare, but the lesson remains: All parties to an issue should be familiar with its details if they wish to guard their interests when the issue comes up for discussion. To those who have a stake in the quality of a park design proposal, preparation for discussion means getting at least a feeling for the problem and some understanding of the factors which could affect its solution.

This can be yours through knowledge of program requirements and site characteristics, the former gleaned from cursory research or by virtue of personal acquaintance with program activities; for example, you may be an expert equestrian and thus quite knowledgeable about stable development and bridle path layout. Site information can come from a topographic map or an on-the-ground reconnaissance. From these thoughts can evolve a list of factors which you consider important in resolving the problem.

If more thorough preparation fits your mood or the circumstances, you can expand your list of important considerations by setting each of the principles and matters of concern against what you understand about the program and site. When played against the particulars of the problem, the principles and matters of concern act as triggers, dislodging from the back of your mind a host of specific issues which you feel the designer should ponder on the way to solution.

To see how this might work, let's assume that a baseball diamond is required by the program. Baseball is selected because most of you are probably familiar with the game and need do no research in order to participate in this exercise. Go down the following list, asking yourself what each item brings to mind in terms of design decisions which should be made regarding the diamond's function and aesthetic appeal.

1. Everything must have a purpose.
   a. Relation of park to surroundings
   b. Relation of use areas to site
   c. Relation of use areas to use areas
   d. Relation of major structures to use areas
   e. Relation of minor structures to minor structures
2. Design must be for people.
   a. Balance of impersonal and personal needs
3. Both function and aesthetics must be satisfied.
   a. Balance of dollar and human values
4. Establish a substantial experience.
   a. Effects of lines, forms, textures, and colors
   b. Effects of dominance
   c. Effects of enclosure
5. Establish an appropriate experience.
   a. Suited to personality of place
   b. Suited to personality of user
   c. Suited to personality of function
   d. Suited to scale
6. Satisfy technical requirements.
   a. Sizes
   b. Quantities
   c. Orientation to natural forces
   d. Operating needs
7. Meet needs for lowest possible cost.
   a. Balance of needs and budget

  b. Use of existing site resources
  c. Provision of appropriate structural materials
  d. Provision of appropriate plant materials
  e. Attention to details
8. Provide for supervision ease.
  a. Balance of use freedom and control
  b. Circulation
  c. Safety
  d. Discouraging undesirables

Following are some thoughts which these categories might trigger. But don't look at them until you have first gone through the suggested procedure and set down your own ideas. Your purpose will be to identify areas in which design decisions must be made; the form is inconsequential. They may be stated as directives which should be followed, questions you want answered, or specific concerns whose treatment deserves inspection.

As you proceed, you may draw a blank on some items, but this is to be expected since certain categories will be less applicable than others, with a few totally irrelevant to particular facilities. For example, the category *relation of use area to major structures* is probably irrelevant to the example we are considering: a baseball diamond in a complex of amateur sport fields. But even this negative conclusion has value in preparing for evaluation; having considered the issue, you have some assurance that an exception has not been overlooked.

In addition, do not be frustrated if repetitions emerge as you tick off the categories. Double checks have been built into the principles and matters of concern in accordance with the contention that if one phrasing does not dislodge a significant thought, perhaps a synonymous one will. That is, if the fact that a baseball diamond needs a flat surface does not dawn on you when you dwell upon *relation of use areas to site,* there is a chance that it will be brought to mind by *use of existing site resources.*

When you have completed this exercise, compare your list with the one below to see how close you come, or if indeed you have uncovered other factors.

Some Factors Affecting the Design of a Baseball Field

Buffer noise and flight of errant baseballs.

Flat surface draining to periphery.

Direct access from parking lots or pedestrian entrances to spectator area.

Location of drinking fountains, comfort stations, concession stands.

Maintenance equipment stored near diamond or elsewhere?

Positioning of bleachers or other viewing accommodations.

Static space.

Cleared field.

Dark outfield background.

Layout dimensions according to rules of the game including at least 300 feet down each foul line.

Is fee control necessary?

Sun out of eyes of batter and pitcher.

Soil appropriate for grass growth.

Permeable soil.
Avoid access to other park units across outfield.
No hidden obstacles in playing field.
Lighting system on egress routes for twilight games.

Go through this process for all units in the program. While it may take a bit of time to evolve lists of factors for the first few units, the pace should quicken with subsequent ones as your concentration improves and as you begin to pick up common factors; for example, areas for lawn bowling and tennis need to be laid out according to the official dimensions of the games just as the baseball diamond does. Checking off the principles and matters of concern against all units in the program should also make you conscious of relationships — lawn bowling and tennis courts should be located away from the baseball field — which should be jotted down as they occur to you.

Not much more than an hour of uninterrupted concentration should be all you'll need to effectively run through most programs regardless of their lengths. It is not necessary to work out solutions to the problems you uncover or do more than speculate about how determinants might best be handled. This is what the designer is doing for you. Remember also that, while you may see some directions which you think a solution might take, your ideas are most likely fragments not tied to other considerations. Therefore, you should not carry into critique prejudgments regarding what the final form and organization might be, for your thoughts have not been tested against the full range of priorities. Nor is it required that you come up with an all-inclusive list of concerns. In fact, it would be as impossible to derive an all-inclusive analysis of the problem at this stage as it would be for the designer to predict all aspects of the solution while in the middle of analysis.

With these cautions in mind, any information you gain, no matter how cursory or brief your examination, serves the primary purpose of the procedure: orienting you to the problem so that you will not have to approach the plan drawing cold. By raising awareness of what may be involved, the procedure also sharpens your ability to react to the proposal as presented by the designer.

In addition, you have developed a checklist comprising focus points or items which will demand your attention during critique. They can also be starting points from which an ensuing discussion, allowed to take its course, may direct eyes to other significant matters.

A desire to become oriented and identify specific focus points should also motivate your inspection of the site. Warming up for evaluation, you should work toward discovering as many site limitations and potentials as possible given the time allowed for the study and the information you have available.

Your site review may be assisted by the principles and matters of concern, triggering thoughts in a fashion similar to that suggested to help cull information about the program. Or your attention might be directed to site determinants by points on the program checklist. Consider our baseball example. The fact that the facility requires a flat surface and permeable soil should send you searching after those characteristics on the site. Your findings are additional focus points, in this case, site potentials and limitations whose management in the solution should be observed. These may be compiled as an addendum to the program checklist or, better yet, jotted down in place on a topographic map of the site. Since the designer will be presenting conclusions on a map, this should facilitate comparisons.

You should now be quite able to approach the proposed solution *on its own terms.*

CRITIQUE

The opportunity to evaluate may occur in many ways. It may come in the form of a plan routed across your desk. In this case, the plan is unlikely to be accompanied by its designer. Or you may be given a written report outlining the essentials of the proposal to which the plan is attached. You may also attend a preliminary plan presentation made personally by the landscape architect. While the following approach supposes that the designer is present, most of the steps fit the other instances as well.

I. *Understand what the designer has done.* During the presentation, make notes when questions come to mind. During the discussion period which usually follows the unveiling, pin down the designer for justification. If you cannot follow the reasoning, ask for clarification. If you cannot read topographic relief, character of lines, forms, textures, and colors, and the nature of the spatial sequences from the plan, ask to have them explained. If you feel that something has not been made clear, ask to have it reexplained. If you do not understand the significance of an issue, ask. Ask. Ask. There are no stupid questions. Only questions.

II. *Consider the designer's goals.* These are the primary objectives or criteria which support the major design decisions and should show up in the designer's opening remarks or appear early in the written report. Are they valid?
   A. If you approve of the purposes, proceed to the next step.
   B. If you are not entirely convinced by the reasoning underlying some goals, go on to the next step, but qualify subsequent judgments accordingly.
   C. If you feel that the designer's criteria are completely unfounded—they are as muddle-headed as "tree cover should be obliterated inasmuch as it adds nothing to the value of the site"—forget about the next step. Critique only the goals and write off the work as a completely misguided effort.

III. *Evaluate goal realization.* The following guidelines should help you concentrate and also help you sum up your thoughts during presentation and discussion. It can also be used as a procedure for treating in detail those plans which are available for lengthy study.
   A. From the plan, abstract its concept. Do this in your mind or on tracing paper and you will have an uncluttered view of the proposal's functional and aesthetic skeleton: its major use areas, circulation patterns, and spatial structure.

B. Either mentally or physically, overlay this skeleton on a site analysis (perhaps the topographic map on which you compiled preparatory impressions). Actually, a concept abstraction and site analysis should be available to you from the designer as part of the presentation package.

1. On these drawings, bring to bear the full force of your knowledge about design in general and the specific thoughts you have regarding the particular project, treating first the *complex at large.* From the schematics, with an occasional allusion to the original drawing, make broad judgments regarding:

   a. Satisfaction of stated goals and additional criteria which you feel are warranted.
   b. Relation of park to surroundings.
   c. Relation of use areas to site.
   d. Relation of use areas to use areas.
   e. Relation of major structures to use areas.
   f. Circulation.
   g. Spatial experiences.
   h. Aesthetic character.
   i. Provisions for order and variety.

2. Now go back to the parent drawing and make more detailed judgments about *each major use area.* Go through the areas in some reasonable order: right to left; north to south; as found along the major arteries; passive areas, then active ones; or from day use units to overnight facilities.

   a. Concentrate on issues a – i, above.
   b. Consider relevant focus points from your checklist.

3. Draw conclusions about *each object in each use area.* Throughout, but especially here, you should consider the degree of design commitment possible at the plan scale and the type of drawing being studied. As we said in the chapter on plan interpretation, the location of light fixtures is not a decision reached at 1 inch = 200 feet; the naming of plant species is not a requisite of the master plan but belongs on the planting plan.

4. At this stage, you should have a comfortable understanding of the solution proposal. Finally, go over all the principles and matters of concern in order to see if any issues remain. Now you are ready to sum up.

CASE STUDIES

Let's try out the procedure. Following are some plans waiting to test your insights. Case 1 (Figure 7-4) is adapted from an actual professional proposal originally drawn at l inch = 50 feet scale. The accompanying program (Figure 7-1), site analysis (Figure 7-2), concept schematic (Figure 7-3), and summary explanation of the proposal's strong and weak points should make the evaluation easy for you. The summary gives reasons for the conclusions and offers further tips on how to approach the drawings. Your critique, addressed only to the substance of the plan, need not be as verbose. With this in mind, you may wish to attempt a review of your own before turning to the evaluation of Case 1 and comparing your findings with it.

Case 2 (Figure 7-5) is another solution for the same problem. This was not the consultant's answer; it was worked up especially for this book to illustrate some errors which could render a proposal useless. No explanation is provided; you will have to find the weaknesses yourself, using the same program and site analysis, but abstracting your own version of the concept.

You are on your own for the four subsequent cases (Cases 3–6); here you will evaluate alternate design proposals for two new parks on undeveloped sites. Following the new-park studies are two redevelopment studies (Cases 7 and 8) for existing parks. We will further discuss the concepts of life cost and obsolescence in connection with these last case studies. Cases 3–8 are all hypothetical, created for this book to illustrate a number of the points we have discussed. They typify many situations you might come up against when dealing with "live" circumstances. In all cases, you must supply the concept abstraction and evaluation.

Both problems and solutions for the new-park studies are presented in simplified form on the assumption that these are among your first attempts to evaluate a design proposal. You should also be aware that a complete examination of program and site requires more knowledge than you can glean from the program and map provided. For instance, little is indicated about surrounding influences and there is no description of applicable ordinances. Unavailable too are the nuances perceived by someone who has walked the site and is familiar with the locality and the affected population. While this knowledge would be handy in actual circumstances, enough information is presented in these hypothetical cases to confront you with a meaningful challenge.

Until you become quite well acquainted with professionally prepared plans and their ingredients, it is suggested that in evaluating these cases, you attempt to follow the procedure outlined in this chapter from preparation to critique. This is not to promote the procedure as the only one possible, nor is it to imply that everyone will feel comfortable using it. Indeed, there are circumstances where it will prove to be unwieldy, but since it is comprehensive and offers a technique for unearthing specific determinants, its use at the onset should encourage the development of similar traits in whatever other system is eventually embraced. While you are still a neophyte, it should give order and fullness to the review; later it can serve as a plane of departure from which a personal method for scrutinizing the anatomy of a park plan may be developed. Such a pattern is sure to emerge as your maneuvers become progressively more automatic.

CASE 1: EVALUATION OF A SCHOOL PARK SITE PLAN
(Figures 7-1 through 7-4)

Note: The solution evaluated here was adapted from a plan for the Thomas Paine School-Park, Urbana, Illinois, prepared for the Urbana School District and the Urbana Park District by landscape architect Phillip E. DeTurk.

A SCHOOL PARK   PROGRAM

SCHOOL UNITS

GRADES K-2
- TOT LOT
- PLAY COURT (PAVED)
- FREE PLAY AREA (TURF)
- STORY CIRCLE

GRADES 3-6
- PLAY COURT (PAVED)
- FREE PLAY AREA (TURF)
- APPARATUS AREA
- SOFTBALL FIELD
- TOUCH FOOTBALL-SOCCER FIELD
- TWO BASKETBALL COURTS

PARK UNITS

- CRAFTS AREA
- SHELTER
- SPRAY POOL
- TOT LOT
- THREE TENNIS COURTS
- ICE SKATING RINK
- LITTLE LEAGUE BASEBALL FIELD
- OFF-STREET PARKING (30-35 CARS)

CRITERIA

1. ISOLATE SCHOOL FACILITIES FROM PARK UNITS TO MINIMIZE OVERLAP INTERFERENCE DURING SCHOOL HOURS. YET, IN ORDER TO TAKE ADVANTAGE OF THE SCHOOL-PARK CONCEPT (AVOIDS FACILITY DUPLICATION; REQUIRES LESS LAND THAN COMPLETELY SEPARATE DEVELOPMENTS), ACCOMMODATE A DUAL USE FLOW FOR THOSE PERIODS WHEN SCHOOL IS NOT IN SESSION.

2. PROVIDE EDUCATIONAL EXPERIENCES.

3. RELOCATE EXISTING SERVICE DRIVE TO MINIMIZE HAZARDS OF MIXING KIDS WITH VEHICLES.

4. PROVIDE RELIEF FROM THE LOCAL ENVIRONMENTAL DULLNESS THAT RESULTS FROM THE COMMUNITY BEING SURROUNDED BY ENDLESS FLAT CORNFIELDS.

Figure 7-1   A school park program.

Goal Validity

1. The decision to separate school units from park areas seems appropriate. To minimize the chaos which could be caused by competition for facilities, an organizational system must be developed which will allow vacationing adults, tots and parents, adults on afternoon breaks, and others who might be in the park during school hours to have free run of the areas most attractive to them. Yet, their noise and physical presence must be kept from disturbing school kids and teachers. This separation should not be difficult to achieve. The trick will be to come up with a plan that will both achieve this goal and satisfy the seemingly contradictory demand: the fusing of school and park facilities so that after-hours and summer programs can be efficiently administered over the entire site.

A qualification is in order. Essential to the success of any school park operation is a prearranged agreement between school and park authorities regarding responsibility for staffing, maintenance, and liability for injury when one authority programs activities on another agency's land. Unless this is spelled out and followed through on, the concept is in trouble no matter how well the facilities are organized.

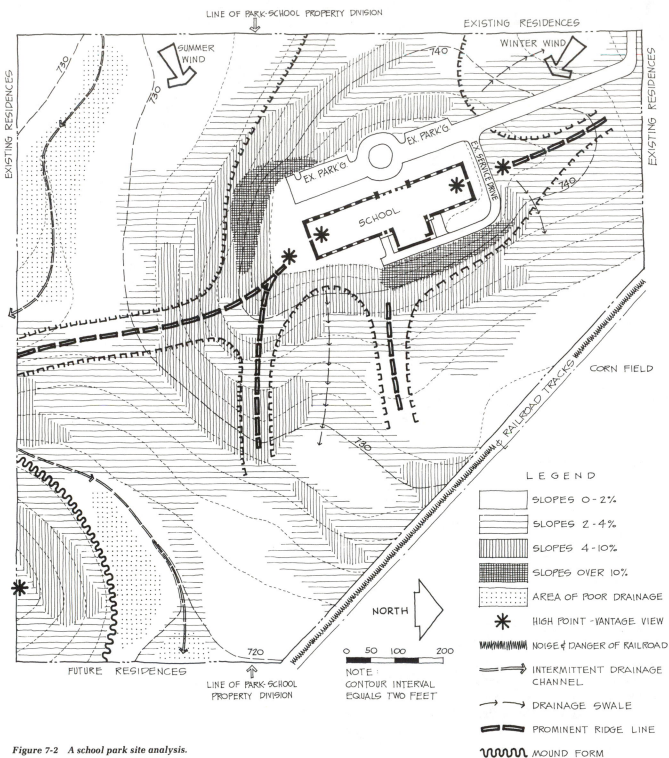

Figure 7-2 *A school park site analysis.*

LEGEND

SLOPES 0-2%

SLOPES 2-4%

SLOPES 4-10%

SLOPES OVER 10%

AREA OF POOR DRAINAGE

HIGH POINT - VANTAGE VIEW

NOISE & DANGER OF RAILROAD

INTERMITTENT DRAINAGE CHANNEL

DRAINAGE SWALE

PROMINENT RIDGE LINE

MOUND FORM

AREA PARTIALLY ENCLOSED BY TOPOGRAPHY

SOIL: SLOW PERCOLATION RATE

NORTH

0 50 100 200

NOTE:
CONTOUR INTERVAL
EQUALS TWO FEET

LINE OF PARK-SCHOOL PROPERTY DIVISION

SUMMER WIND

EXISTING RESIDENCES

WINTER WIND

EXISTING RESIDENCES

EXISTING RESIDENCES

EX. PARK'G.

EX. PARK'G.

EX. SERVICE DRIVE

SCHOOL

CORN FIELD

RAILROAD TRACKS

FUTURE RESIDENCES

LINE OF PARK-SCHOOL PROPERTY DIVISION

730

740

730

720

A SCHOOL PARK   DESIGN CONCEPT · SOLUTION 1

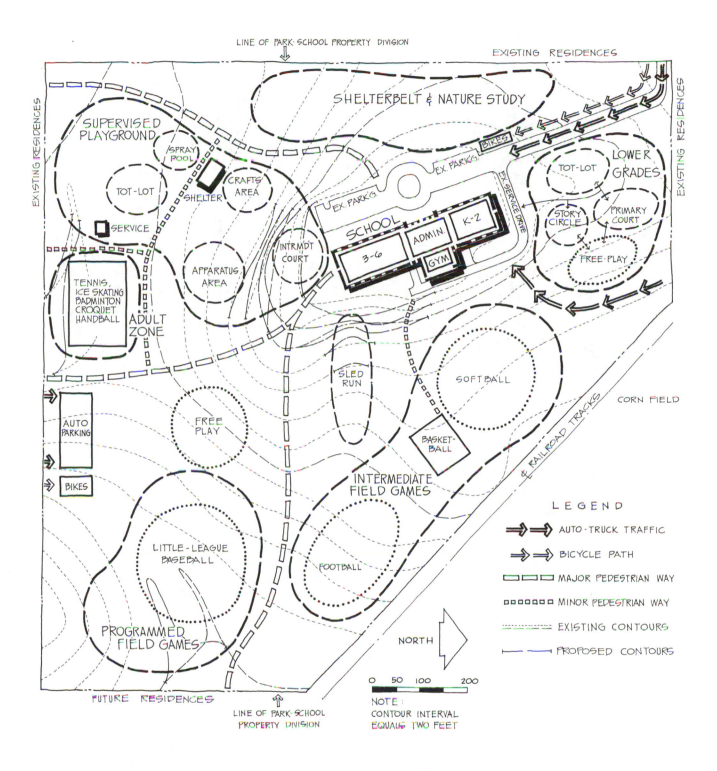

Figure 7-3   A school park design concept—solution 1.

A SCHOOL PARK   SITE PLAN · SOLUTION 1

Figure 7-4   A school park site plan—solution 1.

2. Arguing against the goal of providing educational experiences is like disparaging motherhood and apple pie, especially in a development associated with a school.

3. Foresight would have eliminated the need for the financially wasteful third criterion. For, while traffic on the service road is only sporadic, hence posing but a moderate hazard, the fact that the road was built where it is at all illustrates in microcosm what can happen when building design and site planning are not coordinated.

The school structure was sited and built before the landscape architect was approached to consider the rest of the land. When the landscape architect is not present to consult with the building architect, an overview of the entire development is missing. As a result, the building architect, unable to judge the effects of such decisions on land-use efficiency, may very well divide up land suited for companion use units by access roads or locate buildings on land more appropriate for other purposes, to give only a couple of examples. This also works in reverse. When laboring in isolation, the landscape architect may tie down a building to a place on the site which could pose restrictions on the design of the structure. What should have been called for, as it should be in any project comprising buildings and extensive land usage, was a collaborative study of the entire 33 acres by building architect and landscape architect treating the full acreage as a single problem.

However, hindsight will not rectify this mistake. Since the service road abuts the building at the door out of which the kindergarten kids are expected to flood, and it can be anticipated that this age group will be oblivious to the potential danger, the road should be relocated. Although traffic is sporadic, the prospect of but one accident is too chilling an alternative to leave it alone.

4. Those who have experienced central Illinois know it as a flat sheet of corn and soybean fields that presents itself to the eye in expanses guaranteed to anaesthetize the senses. Too much of a muchness, as one wag has put it. To secure environmental diversity is therefore a worthy criterion. How this is done deserves special attention because, even though the basic charge is to instill variety, the character of the place must also be retained in order to avoid the embarrassment of establishing a 33-acre sore thumb.

The Complex at Large

Goal Realization Separation is achieved simply by placing most of the school units on school property and the majority of park facilities on the park-owned land. No big deal. However, the designer receives a standing ovation for the balancing act he has done with the use areas within each property. Note first of all that the tennis and handball courts and the totlot and park shelter, which are high-attraction units for school-hour park visitors, are placed at some distance from the school building, which also puts them handy to the park entrance. Thereby, the park population is concentrated where conflict is unlikely to occur during school hours. In addition, the park's play apparatus and free-play space, which may have minor use during the school day but be major attractions after classes let out, are separated from the building by sloping topography. Note, though, that they are adjacent to the school's intermediate court and are thus available if school leaders desire. Now, refocus on this quadrant. You can see a complete activity setup suited to an after-hours or summer program for young children, with the shelter serving as a centrally located supervisory station.

By virtue of its proximity to both the school's intermediate court and game fields, the free-play area can be used in conjunction with the former and as overflow for the latter, thus creating use possibilities for the park's open area, an area which might otherwise lie fallow during school hours. Flowing together, yet with delicate separations preserved, the full complement of school park fields offers a range of combinations for evening, weekend, or summer sport programs — big areas, small areas, places for structured events such as playground tournaments, spaces for unprogrammed activities such as kite flying, model airplane soaring, or just plain running around. Between scheduled events, the field half of the site is an ideal arena for satisfying whim — from pickup games to unpredictable role playing, up and down its slopes, under and around its trees, in its small and large spaces — for it is well buffered from the game courts and the youngest children's activity areas where greater use control must be exercised.

A break in this pattern may be noted; the basketball court is located near the softball field rather than proximate to the tennis courts where it would be more available for adult school-hour use. However, since it has been requested as a school-related unit and is likely to be of greatest attraction to the after-school set, a location removed from the other courts seems justified.

Therefore, the layout appears to meet the first goal; it contains enough flexibility to fit a range of use combinations, yet has an appropriate number of relationship safeguards to ward off use conflicts. There is only one major duplication, that being the totlots which show up both north and south. This appears unavoidable since totlots may be demanded by both residents and kindergarteners during the same hours, and, with the building already in place, there is no way a single area can meet these requirements. Given this double demand, it is as reasonable to place the school's lot next to related classrooms as it is to site the other near the park entrance. But even here, the designer is on his creative toes, providing the park's lot with a trike run and thereby lending it a special flavor. Coincidentally, a bonus is gained by providing two tot areas. After school hours and during the weekends and summer, residents to the north have a totlot more convenient to their homes than the one slated for the park proper.

To the possibilities for education which already exist on the site — the nearby railroad, including the original prairie grasses which still grow along its right-of-way, the adjacent cornfields reflecting the region's agricultural heritage — the designer has added a nature study shelterbelt and encouraged human interaction by providing several catalysts for gatherings. Judgments on questions such as the suitability of the crafts facility and the educational horizons of the play apparatus must wait until more detail can be seen; the scale prohibits full disclosure of the designer's intentions for these.

The nature study area suggestion is an illustration of a liability turned into an advantage. Shortly before the preparation of this plan, the roof of the school was lifted from its rafters by storm winds, and the pieces scattered to Munchkin Land. Fortunately, there were no children in the building at the time. Wind screening is therefore advisable, lest this happen again with more dire results. The designer translates the shelterbelt into a nature study place, thereby exploiting the dual-use principle. Happily (since the designer had no choice as to its location), the shelterbelt lies adjacent to the school and reaches conveniently toward the park shelter from which interpretive programs can emanate.

While human interaction can take place wherever there are people, in this plan design ploys have enhanced the possibility. The park shelter, centrally placed for observation of child play, and the spectator slopes, convenient to the softball and little league fields, are two gathering places which are immediately evident. Other potential sitting spaces associated with totlots and game courts remain to be exploited in further detail studies.

The handling of the service-drive relocation is another example of the turning of an obstacle into an asset. Once obstructing the passage from the classrooms to the area best suited for primary play, the road now separates the younger children's activities from the older kids' sport fields, thereby discouraging overlap. The drive still nestles next to the gym, but this seems unavoidable because of the location of the building's service docks. While this expanse of pavement at the foot of the building will still look unattractive, the remaining safety problem is relatively negligible. It can be assumed that traffic movement has subsided at this point, the road becoming primarily a storage and maneuvering surface, and that the older children passing across the pavement will be more alert to the vehicles than the primary graders.

When it comes to the fourth goal, instilling environmental variety, the designer is in luck, for the site sits on one of the glacial moraines which occasionally interrupt the pervasive flatness of the region. As fortunate as he might have been to begin with, the manner in which he has followed through must be logged to his personal credit. Recognizing that the site itself supplies a welcome contrast to its surroundings, the designer has intensified its character, thereby managing order and variety with the same stroke. Use units have been settled into existing pockets formed by the site's rolling topography. The sculptural character of the ridges have been accented with brows of tree masses. And to ensure that users experience the views associated with the changes of grade, collector walkways have been placed on the crests of the topographical rolls.

Relation of Park to Surroundings   The shelterbelt screens the school's parking lot and entry road from residences to the west. Reaches of pavement required by tennis and parking to the south are also adequately buffered from residential view. The totlots are guarded from surrounding traffic by distance and plantings. Areas of highly concentrated use have been kept away from the railroad. The chain-link fence proposed to edge the right-of-way should keep bouncing balls from the tracks, while the high trees should handle errant flies. The fence should also thwart those who would wander onto the roadbed at times when there is no teacher supervision.

Relation of Use Areas to Site   In addition to recognizing the existence of topographic pockets, the designer has perceived that variations in grade are a distinguishing characteristic of the site. In matching uses to the land, he has been faithful to the following realities regarding relative slope severity:

1. Since slopes of 0 to 2 percent are essentially flat and the soil which covers the entire site heavy and resistant to immediate percolation, drainage would be slow if they were planted in lawn, but rapid if they were paved. Hence, slopes of this type are suited for court games such as basketball, tennis, volleyball, and dodgeball.
2. Slopes in the 2 to 4 percent range are fairly flat, yet steep enough to provide adequate surface-water runoff if planted in lawn. These slopes are appropriate for sport fields: softball, baseball, football, soccer, and others.
3. Slopes ranging from 4 to 10 percent have rapid surface runoff, but are too steep for organized field sports or court games. If they are planted in lawn and intensive use imposed, erosion could be a major problem. Slopes of this type can be used for general free play where use is sporadic and does not conform to a set pattern.
4. Slopes over 10 percent are too severe for concentrated use. Erosion is a definite problem requiring such slopes to be stabilized with ground covers, rough-cut lawns, trees, and other soil holders. These grades should receive only intermittent traffic or special use where steep pitches are essential to the play experience (see built-in slides, sled run, roll slope, and other uses on the plan). These areas can also serve to separate incompatible activities.

Only slight earth reshaping is needed to accommodate these appropriate matches. This occurs notably south of the school, extending the existing shelf to a size adequate for intermediate court installation, and near the tennis courts to the southwest and the little league field to the southeast. The latter moves relocate the existing swales in order to improve drainability, while allowing the site's natural drainage pattern to remain intact.

Relation of Use Areas to Use Areas   Most of these have been covered under goal realization. In addition, note that the park's car lot is central to the game courts and little league field, which makes sense inasmuch as these facilities will draw many adults who will arrive by auto. Primary adult attractions like tennis, handball, and badminton are well buffered from nearby play areas slated for youngsters.

Relation of Major Structures to Use Areas   While students deserve a better view from the western windows than a parking lot, the landscape architect had no control over the location of the lot and entry drive; their placement was determined when the building was constructed. Since the kindergarten, first, and second grades occupy the north wing of the school, the proximity of the totlot and primary court is advisable. There is similar wisdom in the proposed location for the intermediate court, adjacent to the door which leads to the third to sixth grades. Commotion associated with these areas is subdued somewhat by plantings. The playfields are handy to the gym entrance, noise being minimized by distance.

Circulation As has been stated, vehicular access and parking lots for the school were set before the site study was begun, and the relocation of the service drive has already been discussed. The parking lot to the south sits on the park periphery, happily minimizing vehicular penetration of the grounds.

Bicycle routes also penetrate the site only slightly, thereby freeing the bulk of the acreage for unimpeded pedestrian travel. It is proposed that bicycles be stored both near the school and in the park in spaces next to the auto parking lots, which seems reasonable, although after alighting bicyclists must cross the entry drive to get to the school entrance, presumably at the same time that school officials are driving up the road to the building. This bug remains to be worked out. Separate bicycle lanes are wisely suggested to avoid the hazards of mixing pedestrians with wheeled vehicles.

Pedestrian access seems sufficient with walking routes across the park providing for a direct flow to the school. This is certainly necessary due to the amount of daily traffic seeking that objective. The fact that walks follow the ridgelines wherever possible not only suggests the availability of views, but ensures quick drainage during inclement weather as well. Paved access from the gym to the basketball courts and ballfields also eases the need for follow-up maintenance when the ground is soggy.

The three-prong circuit from the southern and eastern edges to the school additionally serves as collector routes for the park from which secondary walkways extend to various interior facilities. Walks are adroitly placed between use units so as not to interfere with play, for the most part also acting as psychological barriers between separate facilities.

Paved access to field areas is adequate since entry and exit patterns will be unpredictable, and will not be confined to the paved walks.

Since service circulation for park maintenance will be minimal, the walkway system or lawn areas can be used as necessary.

Spatial Experiences A full assessment of spatial character requires a review of commitments still to be made during subsequent detail studies. However, at this scale, it is essential that the designer set up the overall three-dimensional network which will govern follow-up thinking. Therefore, what deserves attention on this plan is evidence of a spatial structure per se. This landscape architect has met the objective well, compartmentalizing use units with tree masses or in topographic pockets which he has reinforced with plant material, closing off one compartment from another where separation is advisable, and linking them where circulation or viewing suggests a need to do so.

A clue to sensitivity to the need for three-dimensional thinking is found in a designer's massing of major plant material (rather than scattering isolated trees about as if they had been thrown at a dart board by a drunk). Where the plant materials are attractively massed on a large-scale plan, there is an excellent chance that detail studies will establish appropriate spatial qualities. However, if spatial relationships are not considered at the larger scales, as exemplified by an inebriated attitude toward the plantings, it is unlikely that they will be well handled in later stages of the project.

Aesthetic Character A complete evaluation of the proposal's aesthetic qualities must also wait until the design of each use unit can be seen in full detail. However, as with spatial structure, what can be sensed at this scale is aesthetic *potential* as indicated by the general appearance of lines, forms, textures, colors, and spaces. While not final commitments, these show what the designer has in mind and will strive to develop in later studies.

The lines, forms, and spatial network should be given the closest attention. At the scale of this plan, textures and colors are used primarily to separate out the various ground surfaces to enhance the drawing's appeal and readability. However, at the same time, they might also reflect something about the project's liveliness or sterility.

Are experiences provided? Will they be substantial? This plan seems to say yes, for it contains not only a strong spatial structure but a consistent form "flavor" as well. *Both* spatial and line configurations are spirited, complementing each other and hinting that the designer has indeed opted for a dominant effect.

Will the effect be appropriate? The answer once more appears to be yes, for the plan's parts have an animated and playful feeling, well in keeping with a recreational enterprise of this type. The organic quality of the spaces and forms also suggests a fidelity to the rolling topography of the site.

Order and Variety Points already discussed, such as fitting use units into topographic hollows, remaining faithful to slope, and intensifying existing site character leave little doubt that the blending of new with old will come off successfully, thereby fostering environmental order.

Variety potential shows up in the tree-accented topographic changes, varying sizes and configurations of spatial openings, and the exploitation of views. Additional enrichment should arise from the detailing of the use areas and selection of plant species. While this remains to be done, the fact that the designer has indicated so much feeling for the problem within the restrictions of the plan scale gives a reasonable assurance that his detail work will be equally successful. A less confident posture would have to be struck had the designer been lax in presenting such clues to his aesthetic sensitivity.

Each Use Area in Turn

Some general comments are in order before we proceed on the tour of the use units. Additional design steps are required after acceptance of this plan, and focus on each area may trigger suggestions to be incorporated into ensuing detail studies. It benefits both client and designer to think ahead in order to initiate further study on a basis of mutual agreement. Comments augmenting the plan are usually volunteered by the designer or brought out by the client's question: "What else do you have in mind for this area?" Therefore, ideas for future study are expressed below, as they might be during the course of a typical design presentation. The reader must clearly distinguish these ideas from objections, which are also raised.

The first thing you should notice as you begin the evaluation of the individual units is that use units not originally required by the program are proposed. The additions all seem compatible with project purposes and fit in well with the other areas. The service building and facilities for handball, badminton, croquet, tricycling, and bike parking are adjuncts to initially specified units. The nature study shelterbelt and sled run are further exploitations of the site. Assuming that the designer has determined that such activities fill a neighborhood need, plaudits are due for appropriately broadening the use of the property.

In addition, note that all areas seem to be sized properly and oriented correctly. An exception in the latter category is the sled run slated for an eastern slope, not an ideal orientation. Such a compromise may be excused, for the run is located on the longest steep surface on the site.

By now, evaluation has been almost completed, for during the complex-at-large investigation much has been said about the functional and aesthetic qualities of each use unit. This round will begin with the school's totlot, then move clockwise, stopping at each area to clean up what might have been missed previously.

Interior circulation works well north of the building, for the route to the primary court bypasses the totlot, thereby minimizing interruptions. The free-play turf is well located for handling overflow from the court. The entire cluster can be readily supervised from one spot. Also easing supervision, the totlot is well contained by plantings as is the free-play space, the latter safely barricaded from the service road. In his detail studies, it is hoped that the designer will retain the flowing forms and provide rich material contrasts in order to stimulate imaginations and sensory faculties. It is also hoped that equipment design will provide for a full range of play experiences: sliding, climbing, running, jumping, rolling, balancing, and digging. In this rather small space, this will probably mean the inclusion of several multipurpose pieces; the square footage does not appear adequate for many separate items.

The basketball court will have to be buffered from the softball diamond's foul line. Visual supervision of the entire field-sports area can take place from the walkway. In the actual placement of trees on the sledding slope, the need to maintain unobstructed sliding channels must be considered. Utilizing the vacant ballfields for the sled landing exemplifies the dual-use principle.

Affording a view of the little league field, the nearby mound should attract spectators, thereby encouraging the experiencing of the highest point in the park. The adjacent free-play space can be used for practice and little league tryouts, establishing another possibility for dual use.

Dual use also shows up in the designer's thinking in the employment of the tennis courts for ice skating. Surfacing material which can withstand the rigors of freezing and thawing will have to be selected to make this idea work. Expansion possibilities for the tennis courts seem to be thwarted by their being hemmed in on all sides by other construction. Tennis demand is frequently underestimated, and if a clamor for more courts should be raised, a real problem exists. To make the courts available for those whose schedule permits only evening play, night lighting should be considered in the detail thinking as should sitting accommodations for those crowded days when players must wait their turns. Since it is centrally located among the tennis, badminton, and croquet areas, the service house can be used to control reservations and equipment loans.

The tricycle circuit suggested for the totlot can provide a host of fun possibilities if eventually laid out with varying curves, grade changes, and tunnels. Some precautions will have to be taken to minimize conflict with whatever more-sedentary pursuits are planned for the same area. As with the north lot, seating accommodations should be slated for the comfort of supervising parents.

The play spaces surrounding the park shelter are clustered well, allowing sweeping visual inspection from the shelter at the hub of the complex. The spray pool (a safety problem) and crafts area (requiring direct student-teacher contact) are wisely made to abut the shelter. However, measures will have to be taken to keep wind-whipped spray in check. Further exploiting dual-use possibilities, the crafts surface and structure may serve for small group picnics held as part of a summer playground program. Consideration of this possibility leads to the thought that the shelter might contain equipment storage facilities and an outdoor fireplace, but raises a question about the inclusion of toilets. While a convenient comfort station is desirable, the flushing sounds sure to be heard through the walls might very well dull appetites. Perhaps public toilets could be incorporated into the service building a few yards south, thereby providing a handy convenience for adults as well.

Situated well on the other side of the shelter from the totlot in order to minimize age-group conflict, the on-grade slides, apparatus, and roll slope present intriguing possibilities for stimulating play. The plan sets this up as an action area, a theme which should be carried through in the detailing. Accordingly, criteria for selecting apparatus should include the pieces' potential for stimulating adventures, fostering role playing, and triggering imaginations. Grass chosen for adjacent slopes should be the toughest strains in anticipation of the activity which will be encouraged upon them.

To fully exploit the potential of the shelterbelt as a nature area, possibilities should be left open not only for plant identification but insect, bird, and small wildlife study as well. The grove should therefore be allowed to mature in its own way, with undergrowth taking over naturally. This rules out grass mowing. Undoubtedly, to get the shelterbelt going, the installation of small trees will be called for, since the cost of covering such an expanse with mature specimens would be prohibitive. Accordingly, if the plan is to be implemented in phases, the belt should be included in the first stage. Then it can be growing to full usefulness while funds for the remaining work are being pursued.

Objects within Each Use Area

Other than the few speculations above, no questions can be directed to this plan regarding such individual items as drinking fountains, curbs, drainage catch basins, or trash receptacles. Critical commentary on objects in the use areas must wait until commitments at detail scale are seen.

Summary

Distinguished by balanced attention to aesthetics and function, order and variety, spatial and ground patterns, use freedom and control, people and mechanical devices — and by an organizational system tailored to the site which separates school from park yet produces an overlap appropriately patterned for maximum use flexibility — this is an excellent plan. Most concerns raised during the critique involve matters easily handled in the detail stage without affecting the major components of the proposal. The only real problem foreseen is the difficulty of expanding the tennis courts. If they have a handle on demand, park authorities can readily judge the degree of risk involved. Hence, the decision to revise the court area or leave it as proposed rests in their hands.

CASE 2: ALTERNATE SOLUTION FOR THE SCHOOL PARK SITE (Figure 7-5)

Critique the alternate solution in Figure 7-5. What aspects of this plan make it inconvenient for users and inappropriate to the site? What favorable comments could you make, if any? Are there any aspects of this proposal that you think could be incorporated into the DeTurk plan? What significant difference between the two plans should immediately clue you in to the inadequacy of the second proposal? Go through the critical procedure as in Case 1, then compare your results with the results for Case 1.

CASES 3 AND 4: ALTERNATE DESIGN PROPOSALS FOR A STATE PARK (Figures 7-6 through 7-10)

Cases 3 and 4 are alternate design solutions for another new park: in this instance, a state park on an undeveloped site. You are provided with a program (Figure 7-6) comprising a list of uses and an initial criterion, or goal statement. There is also a topographical map (Figure 7-7) with some notes on soil types and slope limitations (assume that these have been transferred from other documents that have not been made available to you) and a site analysis (Figure 7-8). Evaluate the two solutions (Figures 7-9 and 7-10), beginning by commenting on the initial goal statement. The scale of the plan drawings is 1 inch = 100 feet.

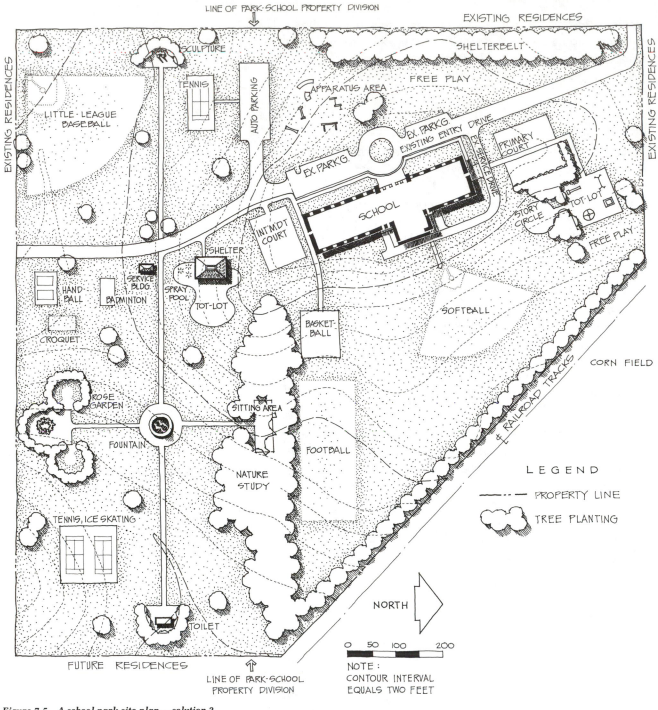

Figure 7-5   A school park site plan—solution 2.

A STATE PARK   PROGRAM

<u>UNITS</u>

LODGE BUILDING -
   GUEST AND MEETING ROOMS, RESTAURANT, RESERVATION DESK
   FOR LODGE AND CABINS.

LODGE PARKING -
   30 SPACES FOR GUESTS, 50 SPACES FOR GENERAL USE,
   10 SPACES FOR EMPLOYEES.

30 HOUSEKEEPING CABINS

CABIN PARKING -
   ONE SPACE EACH CONVENIENT TO EACH CABIN.

CAMPING AREA -
   200 SITES

FAMILY PICNICKING AREA -
   100 SITES

OUTDOOR AMPHITHEATER

BOAT DOCK -
   ROWBOATS, CANOES

WALKING TRAILS

RENTAL STABLE

BRIDLE TRAILS

MAINTENANCE BUILDING AND SERVICE YARD

STAFF HOUSING -
   DETACHED HOUSES FOR MANAGER AND ASSISTANT
   MANAGER AND FAMILIES.

<u>CRITERION</u>

PROVIDE OPPORTUNITIES TO EXPERIENCE THE NATURAL QUALITIES
OF THE SITE.

Figure 7-6   A state park program.

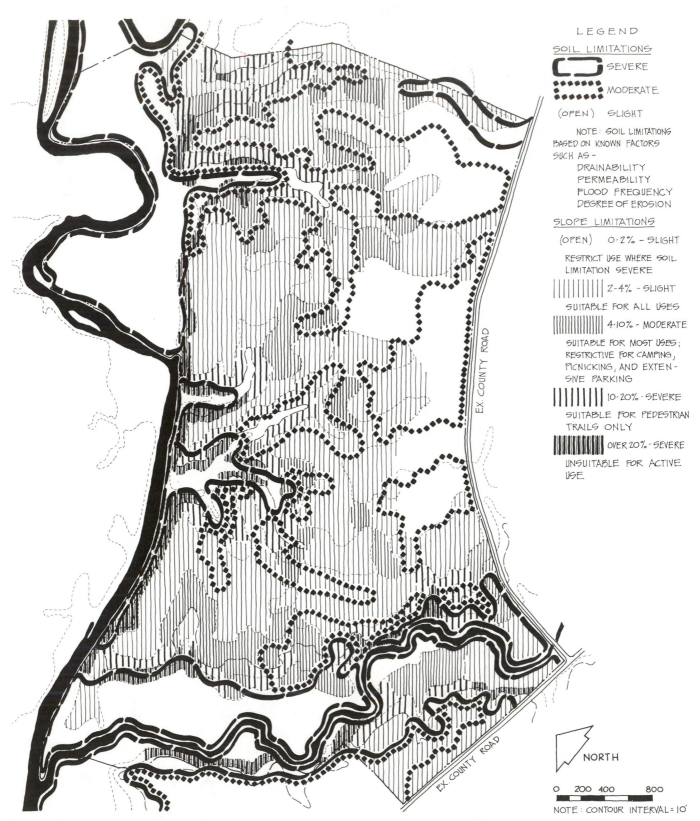

Figure 7-7   A state park site analysis, 1 of 2.

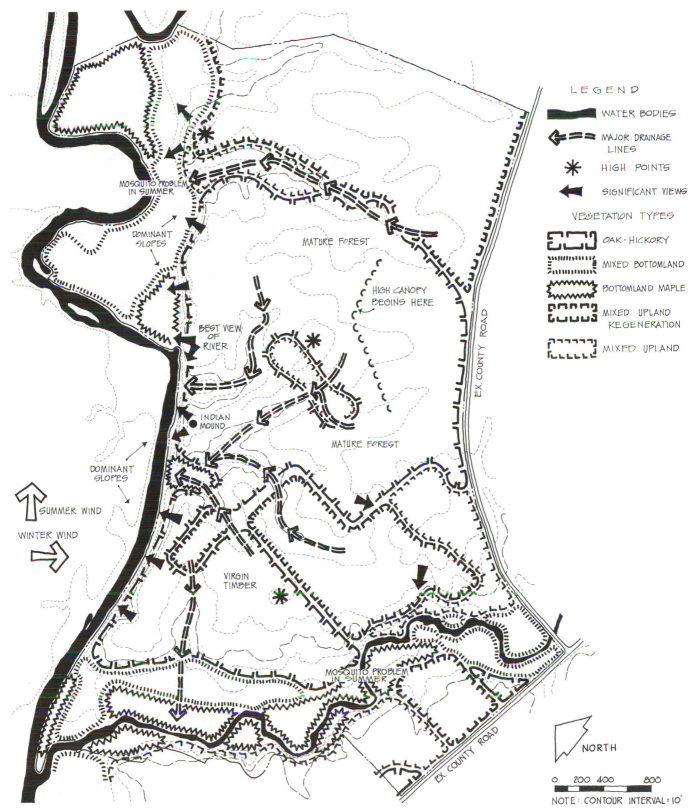

LEGEND

WATER BODIES

MAJOR DRAINAGE
LINES

HIGH POINTS

SIGNIFICANT VIEWS

VEGETATION TYPES

OAK-HICKORY

MIXED BOTTOMLAND

BOTTOMLAND MAPLE

MIXED UPLAND
REGENERATION

MIXED UPLAND

MOSQUITO PROBLEM
IN SUMMER

DOMINANT
SLOPES

MATURE FOREST

HIGH CANOPY
BEGINS HERE

BEST VIEW
OF
RIVER

INDIAN
MOUND

MATURE FOREST

DOMINANT
SLOPES

SUMMER WIND

WINTER WIND

VIRGIN
TIMBER

MOSQUITO PROBLEM
IN SUMMER

EX. COUNTY ROAD

EX. COUNTY ROAD

NORTH

0   200 400   800

NOTE: CONTOUR INTERVAL = 10'

Figure 7-8   A state park site analysis, 2 of 2.

Figure 7-9 A state park master plan—solution 1.

A STATE PARK   MASTER PLAN   SOLUTION 2

LEGEND

━━━━ RIVER
═══ PARK ROADS
─ ─ ─ WALKING TRAILS
═╫═╫═ STEPS
⋯⋯⋯ BRIDLE PATHS
⌒50⌒ CONTOURS
⌒10⌒
─·─·─ PROPERTY LINE
TREE AREAS

NORTH

0   200 400   800

NOTE· CONTOUR INTERVAL· 10′

Figure 7-10   A state park master plan — solution 2.

CASES 5 AND 6: ALTERNATE
DESIGN PROPOSALS FOR
AN URBAN PARKLET
(Figures 7-11 through 7-14)

Cases 5 and 6 again present alternate design solutions for a new park: this time an urban parklet to be developed on a corner lot which is now essentially waste space. Once again you are provided with a program and initial criteria (Figure 7-11) and a site analysis (Figure 7-12). Go through the evaluation procedure for each of the design proposals (Figures 7-13 and 7-14) and compare your conclusions. The plan scale is 1 inch = 10 feet.

PARK REDEVELOPMENT: LIFE COST
AND OBSOLESCENCE

Two old-park case studies (Cases 7 and 8) will be presented to you next. Again, the analysis of the design is your responsibility. However, more background on the park, its location, and the people it serves is introduced than in the new-park studies, to help you evaluate the status of the existing design. The study of an existing park is necessarily a four-dimensional effort because the clock is already running. Since a park is already in place, the necessity of increasing the productivity of its resources motivates many of the procedures in each study. The study must consider the existing park for preservation or change as well as the creation of something new.

Life cost, as introduced in Chapter 2, is arrived at by assessing the initial installed value of an element of a park plus the value of effort necessary to maintain this element throughout its theoretical useful life. In this application *maintenance* is defined as the work of keeping an element in good enough condition to serve its intended purpose. The greater the effort required to perform this service, the higher the ultimate life cost of the element. If the element is useful, the investment is a good one. If the element is not useful, the effort and investment are wasted.

Usefulness is the test of *obsolescence*. The test of usefulness must be applied to all elements of a park; this includes the plan itself. A plan can be obsolete even before construction if the functions it organizes will be obsolete when the work is done.

In order to evaluate the obsolescence of park plans, a "thermometer" test is offered (Figure 7-18), to be applied in Cases 7 and 8. This test is not a design evaluation. It is a subjective review of information about each plan, limited by the data available. From this review, however, conclusions can be drawn as to whether the plan is obsolete or not, and deserves to be pursued further.

It is important to note that data are essential to the proper evaluation of obsolescence (and this is a further strong argument for constant devotion by a park district to developing and using good record-keeping systems for all operations). The thermometer test is only a comparison and offers a basis for further investigation where questions remain. For other sites, more or different factors could be included.

AN URBAN PARKLET   PROGRAM

UNITS _____   CRITERIA

    1) BENCHES
    2) DRINKING FOUNTAIN
    3) WASTE CANS
    4) APPROPRIATE PLANTING
    5) WALKWAYS

    1) ACCOMMODATE PEDESTRIAN
       MOVEMENT PATTERNS.
    2) PROVIDE SITTING AREAS FOR
       SHOPPERS AND BUS PATRONS.

Figure 7-11 An urban parklet program.

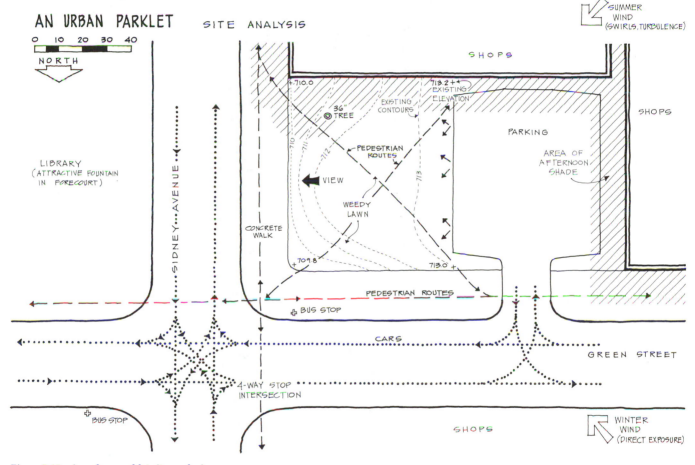

Figure 7-12 An urban parklet site analysis.

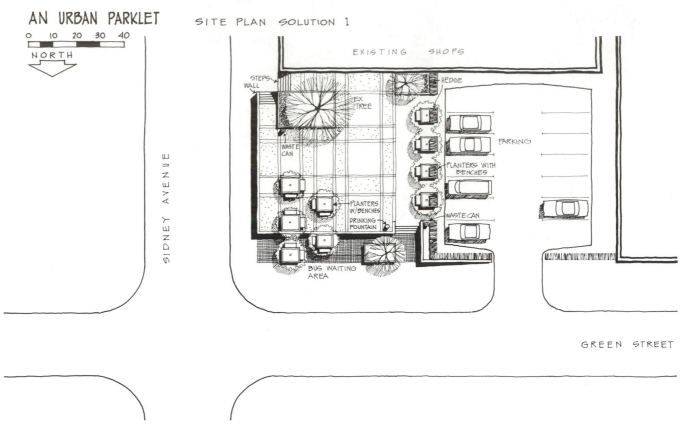

AN URBAN PARKLET

0 10 20 30 40

NORTH

SITE PLAN SOLUTION 1

EXISTING SHOPS

STEPS
WALL

EX. TREE

HEDGE

WASTE CAN

PARKING

PLANTERS WITH BENCHES

PLANTERS W/BENCHES

DRINKING FOUNTAIN

WASTE CAN

BUS WAITING AREA

SIDNEY AVENUE

GREEN STREET

Figure 7-13   An urban parklet site plan — solution 1.

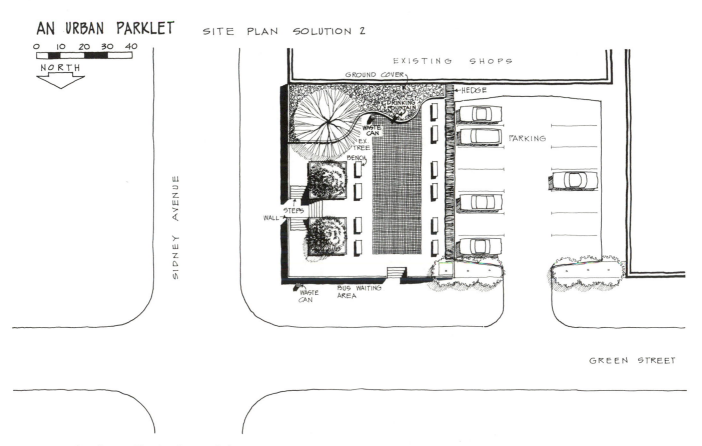

AN URBAN PARKLET

0 10 20 30 40

NORTH

SITE PLAN SOLUTION 2

EXISTING SHOPS

GROUND COVER

HEDGE

DRINKING FOUNTAIN

WASTE CAN

EX. TREE

PARKING

BENCH

WALL

STEPS

WASTE CAN

BUS WAITING AREA

SIDNEY AVENUE

GREEN STREET

Figure 7-14   An urban parklet site plan — solution 2.

CASE 7: REDEVELOPMENT OF
AN EXISTING URBAN PARK
(Figures 7-15 through 7-18)

In this case, modeled after a real and very similar situation, you will evaluate a redevelopment plan for an urban park. The park has an existing plan created for a user family of nearly a century ago. The genteel neighborhood of large and graceful homes occupied by single wealthy families was appropriately served by a large and very low-intensity park to be looked at, strolled through, discussed affectionately, and never touched. The existing plan now has to be reevaluated for a user population occupying those stately homes as apartment tenants — at three or four times the original density. The need for recreation facilities has increased in the same proportion.

First, look at the background information that accompanies the existing plan (Figure 7-16). Based on this information, an obsolescence evaluation (see the Figure 7-18 thermometer chart) has been made. We will now discuss the obsolescence evaluation point by point.

Congruence of needs and facilities involves a judgment on how closely the plans dovetail with the needs of the current users (Figure 7-15). These needs are learned by observing activities in the park, by interviewing users, or by surveying potential users. The park's facilities can then be evaluated in terms of the users' needs. Are the users there in spite of the park or because it "fits" them? The volleyball players are an example of people adapting facility to need.

The quality of the decisions made in this category is proportional to the range of users contacted. The need for data from all ages, social groups, and interest areas cannot be overemphasized.

The existing park is rated very low on congruence because it offers very little that the user doesn't have to adapt to use. The proposal (Figure 7-17) is rated high because it uses the park's framework to advantage in presenting settings for most of the needs identified.

To evaluate *supportive maintenance,* it is necessary to inventory all the work done to maintain the park and identify the activities each operation supports. Supportive maintenance would be regular and reasonable work directed toward continuing a desired condition. In the existing park, the lawnmowing and fertilizing in the area of the intensive volleyball wear is work done to support an obsolete activity (observation of the green as part of a park "picture") and opposes a use that fulfills a very real need (they even supply their own equipment!).

The existing plan is rated moderately low since it does foster the open-space activity occurring east of the pool. The proposed plan shows a better correlation of activities to physical facilities. In addition, required maintenance for the new facilities might be less than for the present ones, for several reasons: less detail effort (elimination of shrub shearing); better material selections (the flowering trees for maximum results with minimum care, the grass pavers for the festival area, reducing the chance of damage and the resulting need for repair); and elimination of recurrent problems (removal of the asphalt paving, the pool with fountain, and the security-problem shrubs at the corners). The new plan also apparently makes feasible the use of larger equipment and simpler maintenance procedures.

Productive maintenance relates to activities plus elements. Produc-

AN EXISTING URBAN PARK   PROGRAM

UNITS   (OBSERVED*, REQUESTED•)

1) VOLLEYBALL*
2) PICNICKING/LUNCH *
3) OPEN SHELTER•
4) TENNIS •
5) MULTI-PURPOSE COURT/EXHIBIT SPACE
6) ENTERTAINMENT/SPECIAL
    PERFORMANCE AREA *
7) SEATING *
8) BUS WAITING *
9) BASKETBALL•
10) FIELD GAMES *
11) PLANTING/COLOR AREAS

CRITERIA

1) RETAIN USABLE SITE FACILITIES.
2) REDUCE COUNTERPRODUCTIVE
    MAINTENANCE.
3) ADAPT TO CURRENT USERS.
4) PROVIDE FLEXIBILITY FOR FUTURE.
5) PROVIDE INTERACTION OPPORTUNITY
    FOR USERS.
6) PROVIDE PEOPLE-WATCHING
    ENVIRONMENT.

Figure 7-15   An existing urban park program.

tive maintenance would be specially scheduled work, a life-extending or renovating procedure—another installment payment on a good investment. It is not productive if the work is inefficient due to the design or materials used or if the activities it supports are obsolete. Restaining the shelter in the new plan for the first time after many years of good service would be productive maintenance. Shearing the memorial evergreens, for the second time in 6 months, to keep the ball shapes symmetrical is not productive maintenance. Amending the soil annually to provide a special acid condition for the flowering plants in the new proposal (assuming other equally effective materials are available) would not be productive maintenance.

The existing plan is a disaster in this category. The most painful example is the pool since, even though it has no function, until a decision to eliminate it is made, it must still be maintained. The proposed plan eliminates the elements that don't offer program support and thus puts maintenance on a positive track. (Primarily, maintenance will consist of mowing with possible annual special service for paved areas, shelter, and some other portions of the site.)

Life potential for plants or construction materials is the average time the material can be expected to survive in reasonably good condition with reasonable maintenance. Life potential of plants or construction materials must be evaluated first in terms of the element's usefulness. If it is obsolete for its original use and there are no other arguments for keeping it, the life potential is zero.

If usefulness is established, can reasonable maintenance work maintain the element's function and appearance? Maintenance requirements for the fountain in the center of the existing park were no longer "reasonable" when the plumbing system aged to the point that overhauls of the mechanism became necessary twice a year, imported parts were needed, and plumber's rates exceeded those of the district's director.

If reasonable maintenance work seems sufficient for the foreseeable future, then is the cost of that maintenance for the element's anticipated life less or greater than the cost of a new equivalent? At any point a new acquisition offers the elimination of all the old problems

AN EXISTING URBAN PARK   SITE AND USE ANALYSIS

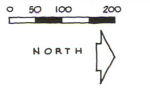

NORTH

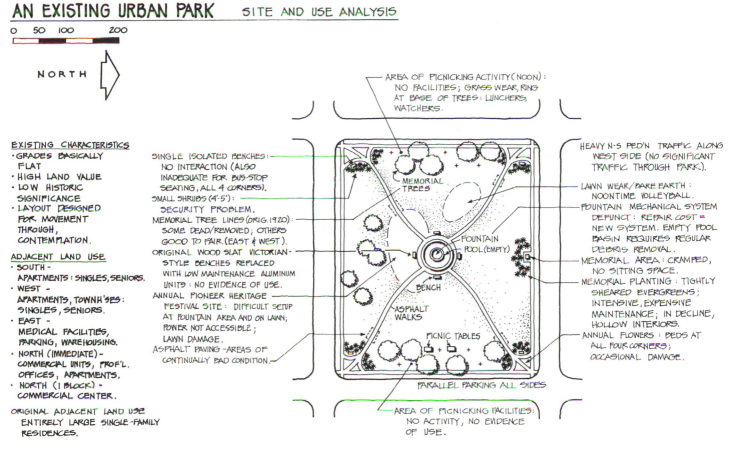

AREA OF PICNICKING ACTIVITY (NOON):
NO FACILITIES; GRASS WEAR, RING
AT BASE OF TREES: LUNCHERS,
WATCHERS.

EXISTING CHARACTERISTICS
- GRADES BASICALLY FLAT
- HIGH LAND VALUE
- LOW HISTORIC SIGNIFICANCE
- LAYOUT DESIGNED FOR MOVEMENT THROUGH, CONTEMPLATION.

ADJACENT LAND USE
- SOUTH – APARTMENTS: SINGLES, SENIORS.
- WEST – APARTMENTS, TOWNH'SES: SINGLES, SENIORS.
- EAST – MEDICAL FACILITIES, PARKING, WAREHOUSING.
- NORTH (IMMEDIATE) – COMMERCIAL UNITS, PROF'L. OFFICES, APARTMENTS.
- NORTH (1 BLOCK) – COMMERCIAL CENTER.

ORIGINAL ADJACENT LAND USE ENTIRELY LARGE SINGLE-FAMILY RESIDENCES.

SINGLE ISOLATED BENCHES: NO INTERACTION (ALSO INADEQUATE FOR BUS-STOP SEATING, ALL 4 CORNERS).

SMALL SHRUBS (4'-5'): SECURITY PROBLEM.

MEMORIAL TREE LINES (ORIG. 1920): SOME DEAD/REMOVED; OTHERS GOOD TO FAIR (EAST & WEST).

ORIGINAL WOOD SLAT VICTORIAN-STYLE BENCHES REPLACED WITH LOW MAINTENANCE ALUMINUM UNITS: NO EVIDENCE OF USE.

ANNUAL PIONEER HERITAGE FESTIVAL SITE: DIFFICULT SETUP AT FOUNTAIN AREA AND ON LAWN; POWER NOT ACCESSIBLE; LAWN DAMAGE.

ASPHALT PAVING – AREAS OF CONTINUALLY BAD CONDITION.

MEMORIAL TREES

FOUNTAIN POOL (EMPTY)

BENCH

ASPHALT WALKS

PICNIC TABLES

HEAVY N-S PED'N TRAFFIC ALONG WEST SIDE (NO SIGNIFICANT TRAFFIC THROUGH PARK).

LAWN WEAR/BARE EARTH: NOONTIME VOLLEYBALL.

FOUNTAIN MECHANICAL SYSTEM DEFUNCT: REPAIR COST = NEW SYSTEM. EMPTY POOL BASIN REQUIRES REGULAR DEBRIS REMOVAL.

MEMORIAL AREA: CRAMPED, NO SITTING SPACE.

MEMORIAL PLANTING: TIGHTLY SHEARED EVERGREENS; INTENSIVE, EXPENSIVE MAINTENANCE; IN DECLINE, HOLLOW INTERIORS.

ANNUAL FLOWERS: BEDS AT ALL FOUR CORNERS; OCCASIONAL DAMAGE.

PARALLEL PARKING ALL SIDES

AREA OF PICNICKING FACILITIES: NO ACTIVITY, NO EVIDENCE OF USE.

Figure 7-16   An existing urban park site and use analysis.

AN EXISTING URBAN PARK   PROPOSED REDEVELOPMENT

NORTH

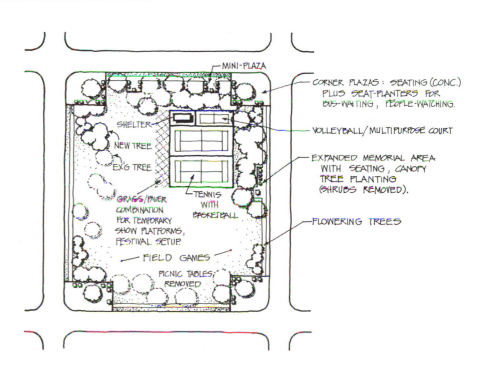

MINI-PLAZA

SHELTER

NEW TREE

EX'G TREE

GRASS/PAVER COMBINATION FOR TEMPORARY SHOW PLATFORMS, FESTIVAL SETUP.

FIELD GAMES

PICNIC TABLES; REMOVED

TENNIS WITH BASKETBALL

CORNER PLAZAS: SEATING (CONC.) PLUS SEAT-PLANTERS FOR BUS-WAITING, PEOPLE-WATCHING.

VOLLEYBALL/MULTIPURPOSE COURT

EXPANDED MEMORIAL AREA WITH SEATING, CANOPY TREE PLANTING (SHRUBS REMOVED).

FLOWERING TREES

Figure 7-17   An existing urban park's proposed redevelopment.

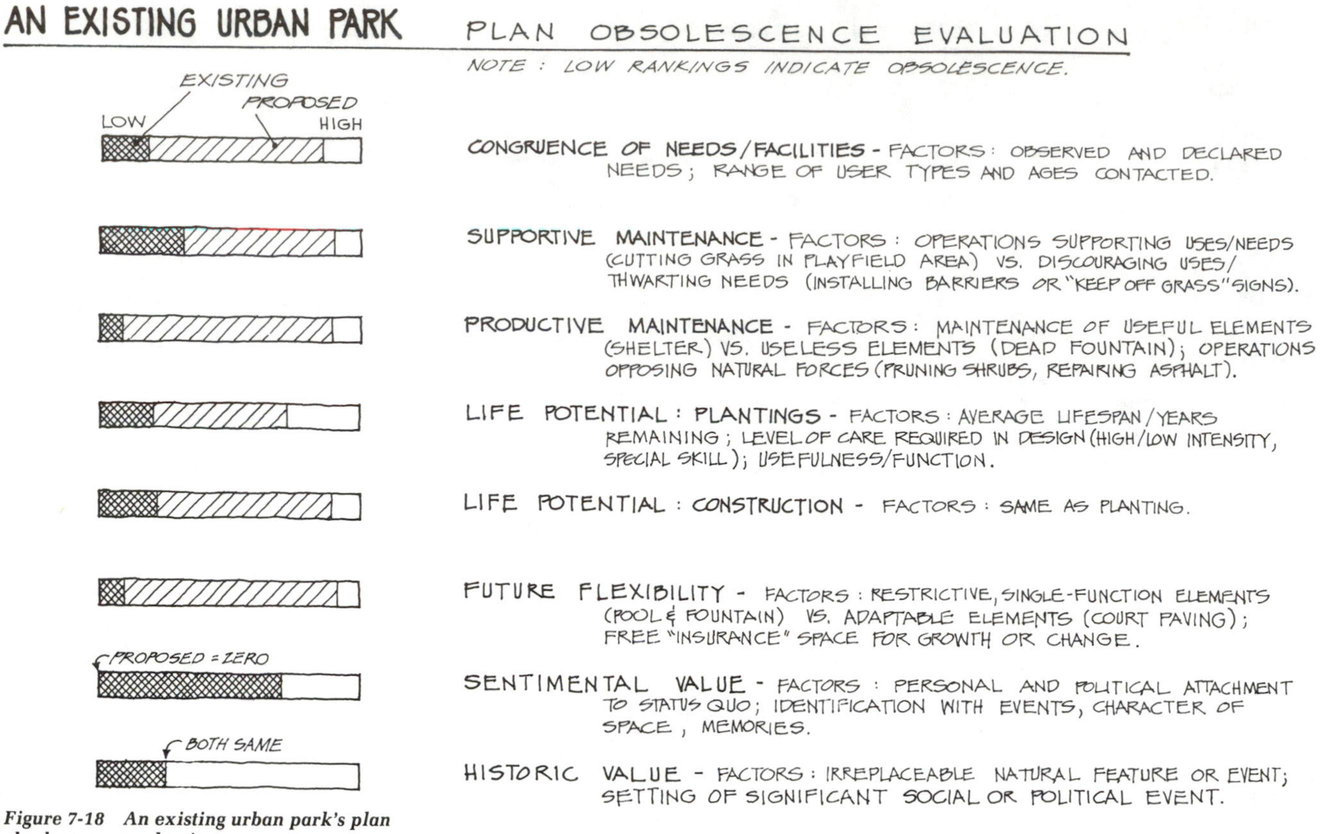

PLAN OBSOLESCENCE EVALUATION

NOTE : LOW RANKINGS INDICATE OBSOLESCENCE.

EXISTING
PROPOSED
LOW   HIGH

CONGRUENCE OF NEEDS/FACILITIES - FACTORS : OBSERVED AND DECLARED NEEDS ; RANGE OF USER TYPES AND AGES CONTACTED.

SUPPORTIVE MAINTENANCE - FACTORS : OPERATIONS SUPPORTING USES/NEEDS (CUTTING GRASS IN PLAYFIELD AREA) VS. DISCOURAGING USES/ THWARTING NEEDS (INSTALLING BARRIERS OR "KEEP OFF GRASS" SIGNS).

PRODUCTIVE MAINTENANCE - FACTORS : MAINTENANCE OF USEFUL ELEMENTS (SHELTER) VS. USELESS ELEMENTS (DEAD FOUNTAIN) ; OPERATIONS OPPOSING NATURAL FORCES (PRUNING SHRUBS, REPAIRING ASPHALT).

LIFE POTENTIAL : PLANTINGS - FACTORS : AVERAGE LIFESPAN/YEARS REMAINING ; LEVEL OF CARE REQUIRED IN DESIGN (HIGH/LOW INTENSITY, SPECIAL SKILL) ; USEFULNESS/FUNCTION.

LIFE POTENTIAL : CONSTRUCTION - FACTORS : SAME AS PLANTING.

FUTURE FLEXIBILITY - FACTORS : RESTRICTIVE, SINGLE-FUNCTION ELEMENTS (POOL & FOUNTAIN) VS. ADAPTABLE ELEMENTS (COURT PAVING) ; FREE "INSURANCE" SPACE FOR GROWTH OR CHANGE.

PROPOSED = ZERO

SENTIMENTAL VALUE - FACTORS : PERSONAL AND POLITICAL ATTACHMENT TO STATUS QUO ; IDENTIFICATION WITH EVENTS, CHARACTER OF SPACE, MEMORIES.

BOTH SAME

HISTORIC VALUE - FACTORS : IRREPLACEABLE NATURAL FEATURE OR EVENT ; SETTING OF SIGNIFICANT SOCIAL OR POLITICAL EVENT.

Figure 7-18   An existing urban park's plan obsolescence evaluation.

and the advantage of some new opportunities. The memorial evergreens in the existing park, assuming they could be tolerated with only one shearing per year, would still in a very short time consume a maintenance allowance that would permit buying new plants selected to grow within the design limits without requiring special pruning.

The existing plan is rated low on both its plantings and its construction elements. The plants are all in stages of advanced age. The high-maintenance materials have the lowest functional value. The medium-height shrubs creating the security concern at the corners are doubly bad since any work on them not only costs money but further exacerbates the problem. The proposed plan scores well in this category because its plant materials are simple, big, and useful. The design groups them in most places, thus providing backup so that the individuals are neither so important nor so vulnerable. The construction materials are basically all simple with none of the complexity of the pool or the vulnerability of the narrow asphalt paths.

Future flexibility is not easily evaluated. What will be needed in the distant or near future is impossible to determine. It can be assumed, however, that a facility with a single, very specific function will not be very useful if that function becomes obsolete. A facility like the pool with central fountain offers no possibilities for change. However, a paved area painted with current game patterns and identified as a multipurpose court can later be repainted and continue its useful life in a new capacity. Likewise, an area designated as playfields can, if "insurance" space has been included in the plan, expand or contract as necessary to accommodate new activities.

Other than the open lawn areas, the existing plan offers little flexibility and is scored low. Its facilities are restrictively designed to do only one thing and are not amenable to change. The proposed plan scores well because it provides facilities which could be easily adapted to new uses without much more effort than a title revision. The design also makes prudent use of the park's space by not committing the center of the site to the paved court complex. The remaining open lawn area permits multiple activities with some buffer between.

Sentimental and historical value are confused with each other in some cases, especially by the user who remembers with teared eye and lumped throat *that* day in the park. Sentimental attachment to a park is expressed in user reaction against *any* change. The more important consideration is that of historic elements, either natural (as an unusual geologic formation, plant community, or event—like Capistrano's swallows) or sociopolitical. If significant enough, these elements don't become obsolete simply because time is frozen for them.

There is evidence of sentimental concern for the existing park on the part of some users (and consequently a high rating). There is no evidence of any historic significance except for the memorial structure and the trees. Both of these elements are maintained (in fact enhanced) in the proposed scheme. The historic rating is consequently equal for both plans. The attraction of a new development could be weighed against the sentimental attachment to the existing one through a further effort at user contact in the surrounding area.

Summary

The judgments recorded in the thermometer chart in Figure 7-18 are subjective assessments of the limited data available. The proposal scores well for many reasons, most of which are summarized as *increased productivity* from the resource. The existing facility would simply be used more effectively for better purposes.

Rather than a high-low range, it would be more descriptive in this sort of evaluation to provide a numerical score (ranging from, say, 5 for a condition that meets the criteria to 1 for an unsuitable or obsolete condition). A low total score would indicate that a plan is obsolete; this method also permits a quantitative comparison of the obsolescence of rival plans. As more data are assembled about a park, the quality of evaluation improves; and the evaluation can be more confidently presented to the clientele knowing the direction suggested can be supported by the facts. For the next case study, you will be required to do your own thermometer evaluation, this time of an existing plan and two alternate redevelopment plans.

CASE 8: REDEVELOPMENT OF AN EXISTING REGIONAL PARK
(Figures 7-19 through 7-23)

This study is also based on a real site with considerable significance to its district because of its central location in the urban area and its large size. The program (Figure 7-19) is a distillation of data obtained through broad public contact. The incorporation of commercial ele-

AN EXISTING REGIONAL PARK PROGRAM

UNITS (SOURCE: SURVEY OR OBSERVATION)

ENTERTAINMENT FACILITIES
1) WATERSLIDE
2) OBSERVATION TOWER OR EQUAL LANDMARK
3) NEW CARNIVAL RIDES
4) CHILDREN'S THEATER
5) SEPARATE, EXPANDED CHILDREN'S PLAY AREA
6) RETAIN/IMPROVE:
   A) ZOO
   B) BAND SHELL
   C) LAGOON
   D) ROSE GARDEN
   E) GAZEBO
7) ZOO SERVICE BUILDING
   A) EXPAND FOR MORE MAINTENANCE/
      STORAGE SPACE (NOW IN CONJUNCTION
      WITH HEADQUARTERS SERVICES).
   B) SEPARATE H.Q. (TO ANOTHER SITE);
      EXPAND FOR ZOO SUPPORT AS
      INTERPRETIVE/EDUC. CENTER.

EDUCATION FACILITIES
8) CONSERVATORY ADDITION FOR ADULT
     AND SPECIAL EDUCATION CLASSES.
9) OUTDOOR TEACHING FACILITY IN CONJUNCTION
     WITH THE CONSERVATORY.
10) IMPROVE HISTORIC CABIN SITE FOR PROGRAMS
11) GARDEN FOR MAJOR EXHIBITS, FESTIVALS;
     SUNKEN FORM REQUESTED FOR
     DEFINITION OF SPACE AND CONTROL.

SUPPORT FACILITIES
12) EXPAND PARKING 20%-30%
13) CONCESSION STRUCTURE(S)

Figure 7-19 An existing regional park program.

CRITERIA

1) UTILIZE EXISTING FACILITIES TO
   SATISFY NEW NEEDS.
2) PROVIDE MAXIMUM SEPARATION OF
   CONFLICTING UNITS (NOISY/QUIET,
   EDUCATION/ENTERTAINMENT, ETC.).
3) PROVIDE MAXIMUM EASE OF CIRCULATION.
4) PROVIDE EFFICIENT CONTROL FOR
   COMMERCIAL ELEMENTS (WATER SLIDE,
   FEE PARKING, ETC.).
5) IMPROVE POTENTIAL FOR EFFICIENCY
   OF SERVICE, MAINTENANCE.
6) RETAIN MAXIMUM VALUE OF NATURAL
   RESOURCES ON SITE (WOODS, WATER,
   ANIMAL HABITAT).
7) REDUCE COUNTERPRODUCTIVE MAINTENANCE.

OTHER FACTORS

1) USE INTENSITY IS LOW ON TENNIS COURTS.
   SINCE MAINTENANCE CONTINUES AT NECESSARY
   LEVEL, OPTIONS TO INCREASE USE OF
   SURFACE SHOULD BE EXPLORED.
2) HEADQUARTERS COULD BE RELOCATED OUT
   OF PARK IF REDUCED CONFLICT AND
   INCREASED USE POTENTIAL WOULD RESULT.

ments like the waterslide has been reviewed at great length and accepted as a positive direction for the district without legal or principle conflicts.

Initially (about 1900) the population of the surrounding neighborhood was low to middle income, of European heritage. Through the 1930s popular activities were car touring, picnicking, and some field sports. Other uses grew by vogue or accumulation of tradition. The park continues to attempt to serve nearly everyone for everything.

The current population in the local area is still predominantly single-family. However, the park now serves a much wider region because of the ease of access to it. Major roads on the edges of the park connect it to the entire urban area. Consequently a broad spectrum of users considers this their park.

In addition to those with a strong desire for the commercial activities programmed, there is a very lively population interested in the existing natural resources of the site. All-season hikers, bird watchers, and naturalists enjoy the park. There is a strong garden club in the community with the financial and organizational ability to actively support development efforts. Equally active are several groups concerned

AN EXISTING REGIONAL PARK

PRESENT DEVELOPMENT

SITE CONDITION NOTES:
1. BAD INTERSECTION.
2. BAD INTERSECTION PLUS SERVICE TRAFFIC.
3. SPRINGS AND SEEPAGE; RECURRENT PAVING DAMAGE; BASE AND BANK EROSION.

OVERALL SITE MAINTENANCE: FAIR TO POOR.

ROSE GARDEN

CONSERVATORY

TENNIS COURTS

ZOO SERVICE

CEMETERY

PROPERTY LINE

ZOO

GAZEBO

FLOWER GARDEN (ABANDONED)

CABIN

BASEBALL

HDQTRS

CARNIVAL RIDES & PLAYGROUND

PICNIC

PARKING

BANDSHELL

BOATHOUSE (ABAN.)

LAGOON

PICNIC

PARKING

SINGLE FAMILY RESIDENCES

HEAVY TRAFFIC VOLUME

STATE ROUTE 147

SINGLE FAMILY RESIDENCES

SINGLE FAMILY RESIDENCES; SOME APARTMENTS

MODERATE TRAFFIC VOLUME

STREAM

INSIGNIFICANT TRAFFIC VOLUME

SINGLE FAMILY RESIDENCES

NORTH

0   100   300   500

Figure 7-20 *An existing regional park's present development.*

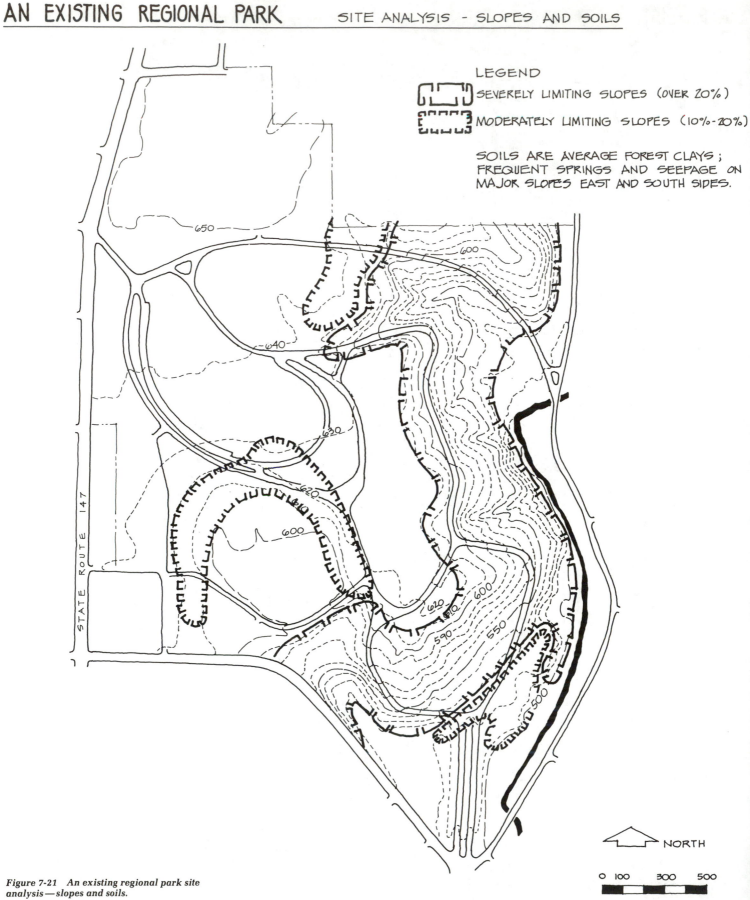

LEGEND

SEVERELY LIMITING SLOPES (OVER 20%)

MODERATELY LIMITING SLOPES (10%-20%)

SOILS ARE AVERAGE FOREST CLAYS; FREQUENT SPRINGS AND SEEPAGE ON MAJOR SLOPES EAST AND SOUTH SIDES.

STATE ROUTE 147

NORTH

0 100 300 500

NOTE: CONTOUR INTERVAL = 10'

Figure 7-21 An existing regional park site analysis — slopes and soils.

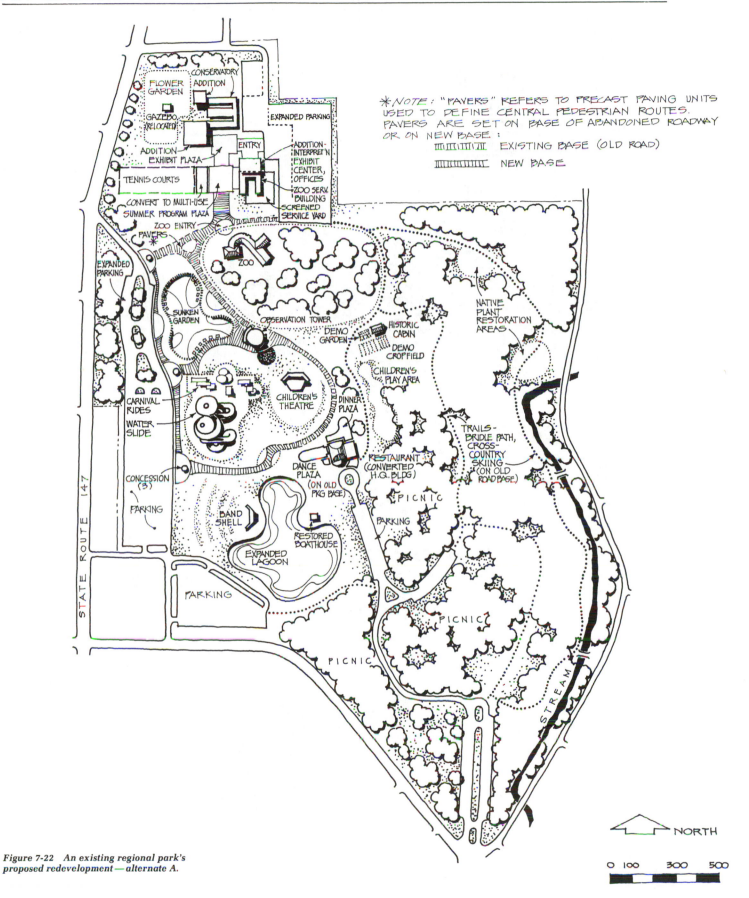

NOTE: "PAVERS" REFERS TO PRECAST PAVING UNITS USED TO DEFINE CENTRAL PEDESTRIAN ROUTES. PAVERS ARE SET ON BASE OF ABANDONED ROADWAY OR ON NEW BASE:

IIIIIIIIIIIIIII EXISTING BASE (OLD ROAD)

IIIIIIIIIIIII NEW BASE

FLOWER GARDEN
CONSERVATORY ADDITION
GAZEBO (RELOCATED)
EXPANDED PARKING
ADDITION - EXHIBIT PLAZA
ENTRY
ADDITION - INTERPRET'N EXHIBIT CENTER, OFFICES
TENNIS COURTS
ZOO SERV. BUILDING
CONVERT TO MULTI-USE SUMMER PROGRAM PLAZA
SCREENED SERVICE YARD
ZOO ENTRY
PAVERS
EXPANDED PARKING
ZOO
SUNKEN GARDEN
OBSERVATION TOWER
DEMO GARDEN
HISTORIC CABIN
NATIVE PLANT RESTORATION AREAS
DEMO CROP FIELD
CHILDREN'S PLAY AREA
CARNIVAL RIDES
CHILDREN'S THEATRE
DINNER PLAZA
WATER SLIDE
TRAILS - BRIDLE PATH, CROSS-COUNTRY SKIING (ON OLD ROAD BASE)
CONCESSION (3)
DANCE PLAZA
RESTAURANT (CONVERTED H.Q. BLDG)
PARKING
(ON OLD PKG BASE)
PICNIC
BAND SHELL
PARKING
RESTORED BOATHOUSE
EXPANDED LAGOON
PARKING
PICNIC
PICNIC

STATE ROUTE 147

STREAM

NORTH

0 100 300 500

Figure 7-22 An existing regional park's proposed redevelopment—alternate A.

Figure 7-23   An existing regional park's proposed redevelopment—alternate B.

about historic resources and preservation in the community. Community entertainment is supported by symphony and theater support organizations, each with interest in the park as a location for major public performances.

Other community resources in the area include schools from elementary to high school. The school populations use the park on a scheduled basis for activities such as cross-country meets or performances. The baseball fields have been reduced to inactive status by construction of new fields with bleachers and full services at the high school campus. Other student activities tend to be somewhat more casual. A significant population of teenage cruisers enjoy the park in the evenings (at least parts of it).

In evaluating the two redevelopment proposals (Figures 7-22 and 7-23), it is important to recognize some major guidelines to which the proposals responded. Alternate B (Figure 7-23) responds to the strong concern expressed by a faction of the board about the safety of the park's road system. The existing road system is recognized to have several hazardous areas (Figure 7-20), the result of attempts to accommodate shifts in circulation patterns as new uses grew on the site. The developers of both schemes were aware of the importance of supporting the commercial elements programmed, and consequently both attempt to provide the best possible solution to vehicular circulation, parking, and people movement.

Consider the setting and background, then develop your own thermometer or other device to evaluate the obsolescence of the existing plan and the potential of the new plans. Then evaluate the design proposals in detail. Bear in mind that the plans offered do not give by any means the only answers possible. Try to do more than select a winner and a loser. Evaluate your own suggestions for revisions and additions.

Obsolescence Studies: A Caution

The evaluation of the obsolescence of any site whether for a park or an industrial complex is not a useful exercise if performed in isolation. The study is justifiable only to the extent that it is used as a means of comparing one property to another: *Which is more nearly obsolete?*

Successful development of obsolescence studies will be in direct proportion to the continuing effort by any agency to improve both the quantity and quality of the records it maintains about all its operations. Why bother? Because until such time as agencies find they have unlimited funds, there have to be ways to decide which projects deserve the available funds. This is at least a way to start.

Et Cetera

*I*n any geographical area, it is unlikely that all the people's recreation needs can be met on one site in one park. It is more usual that a number of parks are required. This collection of sites serving the collective need is the *park system*; its planning involves the following steps:

1. Planning begins with an inventory of existing park lands, including acreage, location, and activities provided for. This shows where you are.
2. To determine where you might go, existing acreage is compared against national standards considered to be minimum for the population served. For instance, such standards suggest that a small city or town should have 10 acres of park land for every 1000 people. Thus, a raw goal is established.
3. The next step is to determine where in the district the land with the greatest recreation potential is situated. These parcels are identified through analyses of existing natural and cultural conditions. Then studies concerning population concentrations, future growth directions, and leisure-time interests of affected age, sex, ethnic, and income groups are conducted to provide information which will enable planners to ascertain which pieces of the high-potential land should actually be acquired.
4. Finally, acquisition priorities are spelled out and avenues of financing are investigated.

The product is the *park system plan* (sometimes called *comprehensive plan*), offered as a map showing the location of both the existing and proposed park sites. (See the illustration on page 150 for an example.) Once purchased, each parcel must be given further study to chart its

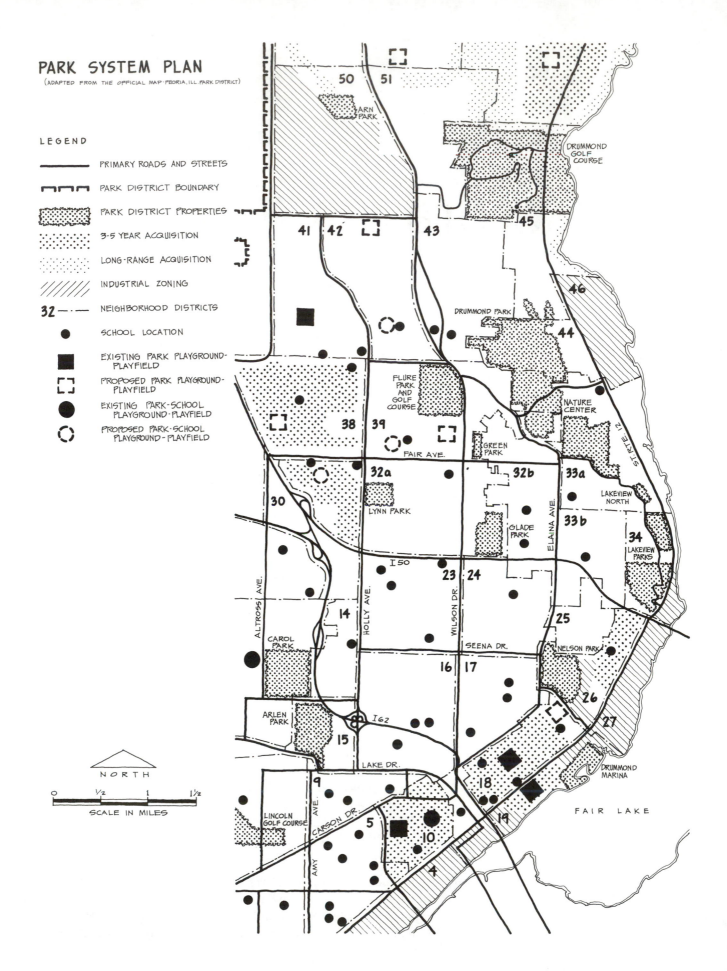

PARK SYSTEM PLAN

(ADAPTED FROM THE OFFICIAL MAP·PEORIA,ILL.PARK DISTRICT)

LEGEND

PRIMARY ROADS AND STREETS

PARK DISTRICT BOUNDARY

PARK DISTRICT PROPERTIES

3-5 YEAR ACQUISITION

LONG-RANGE ACQUISITION

INDUSTRIAL ZONING

32 NEIGHBORHOOD DISTRICTS

● SCHOOL LOCATION

EXISTING PARK PLAYGROUND-PLAYFIELD

PROPOSED PARK PLAYGROUND-PLAYFIELD

EXISTING PARK-SCHOOL PLAYGROUND-PLAYFIELD

PROPOSED PARK-SCHOOL PLAYGROUND-PLAYFIELD

NORTH

0   ½   1   1½

SCALE IN MILES

course of development, but many decisions affecting the success of that development have already been made at the stage of acquisition. If the land is not suited to the activities desired, either program or site will have to be compromised. That is, program units will have to be eliminated because of site restrictions, or the site will have to be fouled up in order to shove in nonconforming facilities.

Park system planning deserves a volume in itself; we cannot even pretend to scratch the surface of the subject here. However, the following recommendations are well within the scope of this brief introduction to design. An expert with a feeling for design and knowledge of development should be a part of the planning team. Ideally, desired uses should be identified before sites are acquired. If this is not possible, *variety* should be a prime criterion ordering the purchase of land. If sites exhibiting a wide range of characteristics are available, there is sure to be a parcel suited to a future need.

When that need arises, design begins. Will it be a quality solution? Remember, you will have to live with the results. So, go on out and have yourself a park.

Appendixes

The following excerpts illustrate the kinds of empirical data and tools available to recreation area designers. You are asked to approach them with the precautions expressed in Chapters 2 and 4 in mind. More extensive tables related to these and other aspects of design are found in many of the books listed in the bibliography.

APPENDIX 1
Selected Park and Activity Size and Facility Standards

Totlot. 2400 to 5000 square feet.
Usually includes: chair swings, sandbox, regular swings, slide, climbing apparatus, wading or spray pool, playhouse, turf area, paved area for wheeled toys, benches.

Neighborhood Playground. 2½ to 10 acres.
Usually includes: play apparatus, turf area, paved court, playfield, storytelling ring, shelter, wading or spray pool, table-game area, picnic center.

Neighborhood Park. 2 to 5 acres.
Usually includes: open lawn, trees, shrubbery, walks, benches, focal point such as ornamental pool or fountains, sandbox, play apparatus, table-game area.

Community Playfield. 15 to 25 acres.
Usually includes: separate sport fields for men and women; courts for tennis, boccie, horseshoes, shuffleboard, and other court games; lawn areas for croquet, archery, and other lawn sports; outdoor swimming pool, band shell, family picnic area, children's playground, running track, day camp center, parking area.

City Park. 100 to 200 acres.
Usually includes: facilities for boating, swimming, picnicking, hiking, field sports, day camp, zoo, arboretum, nature museum.

County Park. 200 acres or more.
Usually includes: preschool play area (3 acres), elementary play area (4 acres), sport fields (15 acres), paved courts (3 acres), multiple-use court (1 acre), family picnic area (30 acres), open area for special events (10 acres), amphitheater (7 acres), natural area (40 acres), parking for 2000 cars (15 acres), day and weekend camping area (25 acres), clubhouse and recreation center (5 acres), maintenance yard (5 acres), landscaped area (15 acres), service roads (20 acres).

Natural Environment Area. 5-acre minimum.
Usually includes: picnic area (8 acres), tent camping area (6 acres), trailer camping area (6 acres), hiking trails, boat access, marina, sightseeing facilities, parking areas.

Nine Hole Golf Course. 75 acres (double for eighteen holes).
Usually includes: fairways, roughs, greens, and tees (43 acres), clubhouse (.25 acre), parking area and service roads (1.75 acres), natural area (20 acres), landscaped area (10 acres).

Lake or Ocean Swimming.
For every 25 linear feet of shoreline: 5000 square feet for sunbathing, 2500 square feet for buffer and picnicking, 1000 square feet of water area for swimming.

Nature Trail. 1 to 2 miles long each.
Fifty people per mile of trail per day.

Rural Hiking Trail.
Forty people per mile of trail per day.

Urban Hiking Trail..
Ninety people per mile of trail per day.

Family Picnic Area within Community.
Sixteen units per acre, each unit consisting of table and cooking facilities. One off-street car space per unit.

Family Picnic Area outside Community. Ninety to one hundred twenty units per area.
Ten to fifteen units per acre, each unit consisting of one table-bench combination with one charcoal-burning stove per two tables; one comfort station per each thirty units serving a 500-foot radius; drinking fountains no further than 150 feet from picnic units; garbage cans in racks near circulation road no further than 150 feet from picnic units, but not near drinking fountain; bulletin board near comfort station.

Campground. Ninety to one hundred twenty units per area.
Four to seven units per acre consisting of one tent area, one table-bench combination, one camp stove, one parking space; one comfort station per each thirty campsites serving a 300-foot radius; drinking fountains, garbage cans, and bulletin board as for picnicking, above.

APPENDIX 2
Recreation Needs Survey

To gather data on which to base long-range plans for facility and program development, the staff of the Madison, Wisconsin School-Community Recreation Department conducted a telephone survey of the community using the questionnaire that follows on pages 156–164.

11/16/81   RESP. PHONE _____

1. (Interviewer: Is call completed?)   <u>Yes</u>   <u>No (To 999)</u>

2. Hello, this is <u>(your name)</u>.   I'm a volunteer calling for the Madison
   Metropolitan School District. Is this <u>(phone no. above)</u>?

              <u>Yes</u>   <u>No (Wrong no.; to 999)</u>

3. The information I have indicates that this number is at a residence within the Madison
   Metropolitan School District. Is that correct?

        <u>Yes</u>   <u>No (To 999)</u>   <u>Don't Know (If can't verify, to 999)</u>

4. (Is telephone no. <u>Odd</u>?   <u>Even?</u> - To Q. 6)

5. We want to give every adult, men and women age 18 and over, a chance to be interviewed
   for this study on community recreation programs sponsored by the school district. At
   odd-numbered telephones, such as yours, an adult man should be the respondent, if a
   man lives there. (May I speak with him)?

        <u>No adult man in household</u>

        <u>Informant is R, or R comes to phone (To Q.8)</u>

        <u>R not available (To Q.9)</u>

        <u>Refused</u> (To 999)

5a. In your home, then, I can speak with an adult woman.

        <u>Informant is R, or R comes to phone. (To Q. 8)</u>

        <u>R not available (To Q. 9)</u>

        <u>Refused</u> (To 999)

6. We want to give every adult, men and women age 18 and over, a chance to be interviewed
   for this study on community recreation programs sponsored by the school district. At
   even-numbered telephones, such as yours, an adult woman should be the respondent, if
   a woman lives there. (May I speak with her?)

        <u>No adult woman in household</u>

        <u>Informant is R, or R comes to phone</u> (To Q. 8)

        <u>R not available</u> (To Q. 9)

        <u>Refused</u> (To 999)

6a. In your home, then, I can speak with an adult man.

   Informant is R, or R comes to phone (To Q. 8)

   R not available (To Q. 9)

   Refused (To 999)

7. (If call back at appointed time) May I speak with (name of designated R)?

   Informant is R, or R comes to phone (To Q. 8)

   R not available (To Q. 9)

   Refused (To 999)

8. The Board of Education and staff of the School-Community Recreation Department need information and opinions in order to set priorities for community recreation programs sponsored by the School District. Your number was selected at random and your individual answers will remain confidential. May I interview you now?

   Yes (Q. 1 on questionnaire)   No   Refused (To 999)

9. When would be the best time to phone (designated R) and whom should we ask for when we call again?

   _____ (If call back, begin with Q. 7).

| R's SEX | APPT? | WHEN TO CALL | | | COMMENTS |
		MO.	DAY	TIME	
	Yes				
	Yes				
	Yes				

999. CALL INFORMATION. DO NOT MAKE MORE THAN SIX CALLS WITHOUT SPECIFIC APPROVAL OF SUPERVISOR.

| INTER-VIEWER | CALL NO. | MO. | DAY | TIME CALL | | RESULT CODE | COMMENTS |
				STARTED	ENDED		
	1						
	2						
	3						
	4						
	5						
	6						

CODE: N/A - No Answer   D - Disconnected or Not in Service
       B   - Busy   I - Interviewed
       CN   - Changed Number   R - Refused
                (Verify Dist. residence)

MADISON METROPOLITAN SCHOOL DISTRICT
SCHOOL-COMMUNITY RECREATION
CITIZEN QUESTIONNAIRE

11/16/81

1. How well informed would you say you are about Madison School-Community Recreation programs? Would you say you are .....

Very Well Informed,	Well Informed,	Not Very Well Informed, or	Not at all Informed?
A	B	C	D

2-10. There are many ways of getting information to people. Through which of the ways that I read would you personally be most likely to see or hear announcements about School-Community Recreation activities?

		Yes	No	(Don't Know)
2.	City-wide newspapers such as State Journal and Capital Times. Would you tend to see recreation announcements in them?	A	B	C
3.	Community or neighborhood newspapers such as put out by neighborhood organizations. Do you read those?	A	B	C
4.	Radio Announcements. Do you tend to hear those? .	A	B	C
5.	Television Announcements?	A	B	C
6.	Direct mailings to your residence?	A	B	C
7.	Announcements distributed to children in school? .	A	B	C
8.	Posters in public buildings?	A	B	C
9.	Posters at shopping centers?	A	B	C
	Any other way you can think of? (Specify)			
10.	_____	A	B	C

11. The School-Community Recreation Department of the Madison School District offers a variety of recreation programs, classes, activities and leagues for children and adults throughout the year. To the best of your knowledge, has any adult member of your household participated in a program sponsored by the School-Community Recreation Department during the past year?

Yes . . . . A

No (To Q. 22) . . . . B

(Don't Know - To Q. 22) C

12-21. Can you tell me what types of programs   -How satisfied would you say the partici-
       adults participated in? (Don't read list;   pant was with the program?
       probe if necessary)

		Yes	Very Satisfied,	Satisfied,	Unsatisfied or	Very Unsatisfied
12.	Sports-league or tournaments .	A	B	C	D	E
13.	Swimming: class or recreation .	A	B	C	D	E
14.	Recreation for the handicapped.	A	B	C	D	E
15.	Senior citizen: club, tour, event	A	B	C	D	E
16.	Class: dance, fitness, cards, etc.	A	B	C	D	E
17.	Sports-open play, practice . .	A	B	C	D	E
18.	Theatre Guild-actor, backstage.	A	B	C	D	E
19.	Madison Community Center: drop-in	A	B	C	D	E
20.	Madison Community Center: club.	A	B	C	D	E
21.	Outdoor, winter-ice skating, Cross-country skiing	A	B	C	D	E

22. How about children or youth in your household; did they participate in any School-
    Community Recreation programs within the past year?

```
                 Yes . . . . . . . . . . . . . . . . . . . . . A
                 No (To Q. 33) . . . . . . . . . . . . . . B
                 No children in household . . . . . . . . C
                 (Don't Know - To Q. 35) . . . . . . . . . D
```

23-32. Can you tell me what types of programs   -How satisfied would you say the partici-
       they participated in? (Don't read list;   pant was with the program?
       probe if necessary).

		Yes	Very Satisfied,	Satisfied,	Unsatisfied or	Very Unsatisfied
23.	Team sports: T-ball, softball, baseball	A	B	C	D	E
24.	Swimming: class or recreation.	A	B	C	D	E
25.	Recreation for the handicapped.	A	B	C	D	E
26.	Summer playground or day camp .	A	B	C	D	E
27.	Stagecoach, Children's Theatre or Art Cart	A	B	C	D	E

		Yes	Very Satisfied,	Satisfied,	Unsatisfied or	Very Unsatisfied
28.	Summer cultural arts class. . . .	A	B	C	D	E
29.	Middle school club or tournament	A	B	C	D	E
30.	High school drop-in night . . .	A	B	C	D	E
31.	Summer tennis instruction . . .	A	B	C	D	E
32.	Outdoor ice skating class . . .	A	B	C	D	E

(To Q. 35)

33-34. Can you tell me why members of your household did not participate in recreation activities sponsored by School-Community Recreation? (Don't read list; probe if necessary. Mark all that apply).

	No children/youth in household	Participate elsewhere	Lack of information	No time	No interest
33.	A	B	C	D	E

	Can't afford it	Too tired	Location bad	Other reasons (Specify)
34.	A	B	C	D _____
				E _____ _____

35-41. We'd like to get a better idea of your total participation in recreation activities. Do you or any member of your household regularly participate (more than twice a month during appropriate season) in a recreation activity offered by ....

		Yes	No
35.	A community social service organization such as YMCA, YWCA, Girl or Boy Scouts, or 4-H?.	A	B
36.	A membership organization such as swim, golf, tennis, racquetball, health or fitness club?	A	B
37.	Commercial recreation outlet such as bowling lanes, movie theatres, electronic game arcade, entertainment or dance establishment?. `.	A	B
38.	Community sports organization such as Little League Baseball, Youth Soccer, Youth Football, Youth Hockey or Youth Swim Team?	A	B
39.	Civic or cultural organization such as Madison Civic Center, Theatre Guild, Civic Repertory, University of Wisconsin theatres, or others?	A	B
40.	Recreation activities offered through churches or synagogues such as fellowship groups, socials and outings?	A	B
41.	Fraternal or service organizations which may sponsor dances, banquets, card parties or other events?. .	A	B

42-43. What makes you and members of your household decide whether or not to participate in recreation programs offered by a public or private agency? (Don't read list; probe if necessary).

	Affordable Cost	Convenient Location	Time/Season It's Offered	Chance to Learn	Like Activity
42.	A	B	C	D	E

	Good organization/Leadership	To be with Friends	Chance for Competition	Other reasons (Specify)
43.	A	B	C	D. _____
				E. _____

44-45. What do you think would be about the right fee to charge for a recreation class in which you would have the opportunity to learn a new skill? Let's say the class would meet for 15 hours over a period of several weeks. Would you be willing to pay ....

44.	More than $10.00?	That's under 75¢ per hour of instruction.	No . . . . A (To Q. 46)
(if yes)	More than $15.00?	That's $1.00 per hour.	No . . . . B
(if yes)	More than $20.00?	(About $1.30 per hour).	No C
(if yes)	More than $25.00?	(About $1.60 per hour).	No . . . . D
(if yes)	More than $30.00?	($2.00 per class hour).	No . . . . E

45.

Yes . . . . . . A

(Don't Know) . . B

Other (Specify)

C _____

46-52. How important do you think it is that the School-Community Recreation Department provides recreation programs for each of the following age groups? We'd like you to choose from among four answer choices for each age group.

For...	Very Important,	Important,	Not Very Important, or	Not at all Important?	(Don't Know)
-Pre-school children, under 5 years old. 46. Is that	A	B	C	D	E
-Elementary children, 5 to 11 years old. 47. Is that	A	B	C	D	E
-Middle school age 48. youth, 12 to 14 years?	A	B	C	D	E

	Very Important,	Important,	Not Very Important, or	Not at all Important?	(Don't Know)
-High school youth, 49. 14 to 18 years?	A	B	C	D	E
-Adults, 18 to 49 50. years. Is that	A	B	C	D	E
-Adults, 50 and over, 51. but still working . . .	A	B	C	D	E
52. Retired adults?	A	B	C	D	E

53-62. The School-Community Recreation Department now offers all of the types of programs I'm going to read. Which programs do you believe should receive continued emphasis?

	Yes	No	(Don't Know)
53. Should swimming programs continue to be emphasized?	A	B	C
54. Sports leagues & tournaments. Should they receive emphasis?.	A	B	C
55. Sports skill classes (tennis, golf, badminton, etc)?	A	B	C
56. Adult education classes (dance, cards, crafts, cooking)? . .	A	B	C
57. Activities for the handicapped?	A	B	C
58. Outdoor education and camping programs?	A	B	C
59. Drop-in or free play sports activities?	A	B	C
60. Physical fitness classes?	A	B	C
61. After-school recreation programs?	A	B	C
62. Cultural arts programs (dance, drama, music)?	A	B	C

63-70. One last opinion question. For each statement I read, please tell me whether you strongly agree, agree, disagree, or strongly disagree. Here is the first statement.

	Strongly Agree,	Agree,	Disagree, or	Strongly Disagree?	(Don't Know)
-It's very important to offer recreation programs to families as a unit. 63. Do you	A	B	C	D	E
-Recreation programs should be planned so that they involve people of different races and nationalities. 64. Do you	A	B	C	D	E
-It's more important to offer a variety of recreation programs in the summer than during other seasons. 65. Do you	A	B	C	D	E

	Strongly Agree,	Agree,	Disagree, or	Strongly Disagree?	(Don't Know)
-In the future it will be _more_ important to offer recreation programs close to where people live than it has been in the past. 66. Do you	A	B	C	D	E
-It's important that various agencies which provide recreation programs cooperate as much as 67. possible with each other. . . .	A	B	C	D	E
-The Madison School District should begin to seek financial help from private organizations and businesses for the School- 68. Community Recreation program. .	A	B	C	D	E
-People should provide their own recreation on weekends without the help of an agency such as the School-Community 69. Recreation Department..	A	B	C	D	E
-Buildings owned by the School District should be made available during non-school times for com- 70. munity recreation use	A	B	C	D	E

71. I'd like to finish by getting some background information. How many people are there currently living in your household?

        A.   1 (To Q. 72)

        B.   2

        C.   3

        D.   4

        E.   5 or more

72. How many, if any, are 17 years of age or younger?

        A.   0   B.   1   C.   2

        D.   3   E.   4 or more

73. How many of your children attend private or parochial schools?

        A.   0   B.   1   C.   2

        D.   3   E.   4 or more

What is your Zip Code? _____ (Record last 2 nos. at top of answer sheet).

What is the closest public elementary school to your residence? (Record at top of answer sheet).

_____   _____

74. (Don't Know) . . . .   A

To the closest year, how many years have you lived in the Madison School District? _____ (Record at top of answer sheet).

What is your present age? _____ (Record at top of answer sheet).

75-76. Was your total family income before taxes in the past year . . . . . .

75.		Less than $5,000?	Yes . . . . A
	(if no)	Between $5,000 and $10,000?	Yes . . . . B
	(if no)	Between $10,000 and $20,000?	Yes C
	(if no)	Between $20,000 and $30,000?	Yes . . . . D
	(if no)	Between $30,000 and $40,000?	Yes . . . . E
76.	(if no)	More than $40,000?	Yes . . . . A
			(Don't Know) . . . . B
			(Refused) C

77. Do you have other comments or opinions you would like to add about public recreation opportunities in the Madison School District?

A. _____

B. _____

C. _____

D. _____

THANK YOU VERY MUCH FOR YOUR COOPERATION.

(Indicate -- but do not ask -- sex of respondent)

78.   Female . . . . A

         Male   . . . . B

APPENDIX 3
Recreation Needs Survey of Community Leaders

To support and focus the community telephone survey data, the staff of the Madison School-Community Recreation Department also prepared and distributed the questionnaire that follows on pages 166–171 to community leaders (including members of Boards of Education and United Way, school principals and administrators, various agency administrators, city council and neighborhood association members, and political representatives).

MADISON METROPOLITAN SCHOOL DISTRICT
SCHOOL-COMMUNITY RECREATION

<u>Recreation Opinion Study</u>

1981

UNLESS INDICATED OTHERWISE, PLEASE CIRCLE ONE ANSWER LETTER FOR EACH QUESTION OR STATEMENT.

1. How well informed would you say you are about School-Community Recreation programs?

Very Well Informed	Well Informed	Not Very Well Informed	Not at all Informed	
A	B	C	D	(1)

2-8. How important do you think it is that the School-Community Recreation Department provides recreation programs for each of the following age groups?

	Very Important	Important	Not Very Important	Not at all Important	(No Opinion)	
-Pre-school children under 5 years old.	A	B	C	D	E	(2)
-Elementary children 5 to 11 years old.	A	B	C	D	E	(3)
-Middle school age youth, 11 to 14 years.	A	B	C	D	E	(4)
-High school youth, 14 to 18 years.	A	B	C	D	E	(5)
-Adults, 18 to 49 years.	A	B	C	D	E	(6)
-Adults 50 and over, but still working.	A	B	C	D	E	(7)
-Retired adults.	A	B	C	D	E	(8)

9-23. The School-Community Recreation Department presently offers a variety of activities within each of the program areas listed below. What <u>degree of emphasis</u> do you believe should be placed on each program area in the next two to five years?

	A Great Deal	Some	Little	None	(No Opinion)	
-Swimming programs	A	B	C	D	E	(9)
-Sports leagues and tournaments.	A	B	C	D	E	(10)
-Sports skill classes (tennis, badminton, golf, etc).	A	B	C	D	E	(11)
-Indoor drop-in or open play sports (basketball, volleyball, etc.).	A	B	C	D	E	(12)
-Indoor drop-in games (pool, ping-pong, cards, etc.)	A	B	C	D	E	(13)
-Adult education classes (dance, cards, crafts, cooking).	A	B	C	D	E	(14)
-Physical fitness classes.	A	B	C	D	E	(15)
-Outdoor drop-in games and sports.	A	B	C	D	E	(16)
-Youth special interest clubs (bowling, chess, computer, etc.).	A	B	C	D	E	(17)
-Educational tours and trips.	A	B	C	D	E	(18)
-Activities for the handicapped.	A	B	C	D	E	(19)
-Outdoor education and camping.	A	B	C	D	E	(20)
-After school recreation.	A	B	C	D	E	(21)
-Cultural arts programs (art, dance, drama, music).	A	B	C	D	E	(22)
-Adult hobby clubs (photo, lapidary, gardening, etc.).	A	B	C	D	E	(23)

24. Fees charged for youth programs sponsored by School-Community Recreation presently cover about 25 percent of direct program costs (leadership, materials, facility use), on the average. What action, if any, do you believe should be taken in regard to youth program fees?

Reduce fees or provide free programs whenever possible . . . . . . A

Raise fees to cover greater percentage of costs. . . . . B   (24)

Retain fees at current level C

(No Opinion) . . . . D

25. Fees charged for adult programs presently cover about 75 percent of direct costs, on the average. What action, if any, should be taken in regard to adult program fees?

Retain fees at current level . . . . A

Reduce fees whenever possible . . . . B   (25)

Raise fees to cover greater percentage of costs C

(No Opinion) . . . . D

26-27. There are many reasons why people may participate in public recreation programs such as those offered by the School-Community Recreation Department. Please indicate below which reasons, if any, you believe should receive increased attention in planning of recreation programs. (Circle one, two, or three reasons only).

Affordable Cost	Neighborhood Locations	Good Leadership	Convenient Times	
A	B	C	D	(26)

Learn New Skill	Participate In Favorite Activity	Good Competition	Meet Friends	
A	B	C	D	(27)

28-34. How much do you agree with each of the following statements?

	Strongly Agree	Agree	Disagree	Strongly Disagree	(No Opinion)	
-The Madison Community Center provides vital recreation services in the downtown area.	A	B	C	D	E	(28)
-Emphasis should be placed on offering programs at schools or other neighborhood locations.	A	B	C	D	E	(29)
-Small groups with special interests should be encouraged to finance their own recreation activities.	A	B	C	D	E	(30)
-Children should learn early that leisure time can provide opportunities for learning and enjoyment.	A	B	C	D	E	(31)
-Public recreation programs should emphasize beginning skills and appreciations over advanced skills.	A	B	C	D	E	(32)

	Strongly Agree	Agree	Disagree	Strongly Disagree	(No Opinion)	
-Attention should be given to developing private financial support for public recreation programs.	A	B	C	D	E	(33)
-Recreation programs should be planned so that they involve people of different races and nationalities.	A	B	C	D	E	(34)

35-45. To assist the School-Community Recreation staff in setting priorities for the next five years, please indicate what level of priority should be set for each of the actions listed below.

	Very High Priority	High Priority	Low Priority	Very Low Priority	(No Opinion)	
-Offering organized recreation programs on weekends.	A	B	C	D	E	(35)
-Offering more daytime classes and activities.	A	B	C	D	E	(36)
-Offering more activities in which families could participate as a group.	A	B	C	D	E	(37)
-Providing daycare services for young children while their parents participate in recreation programs.	A	B	C	D	E	(38)
-Developing cooperative programs with neighborhood based agencies and organizations (community centers, citizens groups).	A	B	C	D	E	(39)
-Developing cooperative programs with community-wide organizations and agencies that offer recreation services (YMCA, youth sports, libraries, etc.).	A	B	D	C	E	(40)
-Expanding the use of volunteers in leadership capacities.	A	B	C	D	E	(41)
-Providing drop-in facilities and activities for people in the downtown area.	A	B	C	D	E	(42)

	Very High Priority	High Priority	Low Priority	Very Low Priority	(No Opinion)	
-Maintaining access to gyms and other facilities even if a school is closed.	A	B	C	D	E	(43)
-Continuing to provide mobile recreation programs such as Stagecoach Theatre and Art Cart.	A	B	C	D	E	(44)
-Providing facilities for recreation groups and clubs to conduct their own activities.	A	B	C	D	E	(45)

46-47.   The map below is divided into ten zip code areas, indicated by the heavy black lines. Which, if any, of these areas of the community do you feel are in need of more extensive recreation services? (Circle as many letters as apply; if "None" or "Don't Know", do not circle any letters).

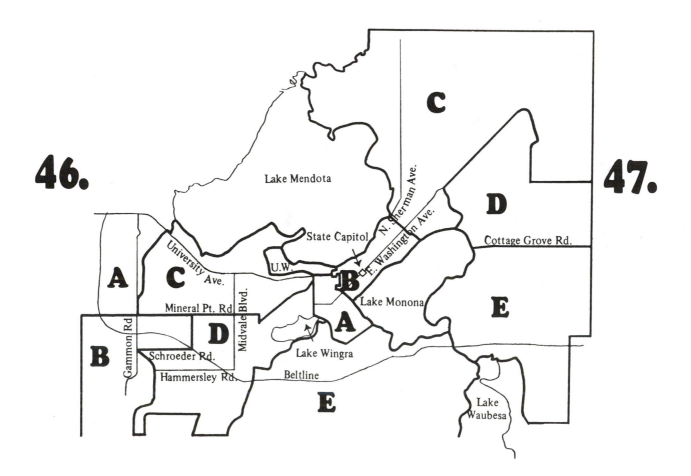

48. How adequate do you believe total recreation opportunities are within the Madison Metropolitan School District, considering the variety of service providers?

Very Adequate	Adequate	Inadequate	Very Inadequate	(No Opinion)	
A	B	C	D	E	(48)

49. Do you have other comments or suggestions regarding recreation services provided by the School-Community Recreation Department?

_____

_____

_____

_____

THANK YOU VERY MUCH FOR YOUR COOPERATION. PLEASE RETURN THE QUESTIONNAIRE IN THE ENVELOPE PROVIDED

APPENDIX 4
Selected Game Area Size Standards

Name	Dimensions of game areas	Use dimensions (linear feet)	Space required (square feet)
Archery	90'–300' in length	50 × 175 (min.)	8,750
	Targets 15' apart	50 × 400 (max.)	20,000
Badminton	17' × 44' (singles)	25 × 60	1,500
	20' × 44' (doubles)	30 × 60	1,800
Baseball	90' diamond	350 × 350 (average with hooded backstop)	122,500
		400 × 400 (without backstop)	160,000
Basketball	42' × 74' (min.)	60 × 100 (average)	6,000
	50' × 94' (max.)		
Boccie	8' × 62'	20 × 80	1,600
Clock Golf	20'–30' diameter	40 × 40	1,600
Croquet	41' × 85'	50 × 95	4,750
Curling	Tees 114' apart	25 × 160	4,000
Field hockey	150' × 270' (min.)	210 × 330 (average)	69,300
	180' × 300' (max.)		
Football	160' × 360'	200 × 420	84,000
Handball	20' × 34'	30 × 45	1,350
Horseshoes	Stakes 40' apart	12 × 52 (min.)	624
Lacrosse	180' × 330' (min.)	225 × 360 (average)	81,000
	210' × 330' (max.)		
Lawn bowling	14' × 110' (1 alley)	130 × 130	16,900
Shuffleboard	6' × 52'	10 × 60	600
Soccer	165' × 300' (min.)	225 × 360 (average)	81,000
	225' × 360' (max.)		
Softball	55' diamond	275 × 275 (min.)	75,625
Tennis	27' × 78' (singles)	50 × 120	6,000
	36' × 78' (doubles)	60 × 120	7,200
Volleyball	30' × 60'	45 × 80	3,600

APPENDIX 5
Selected Game Area Layout Diagrams

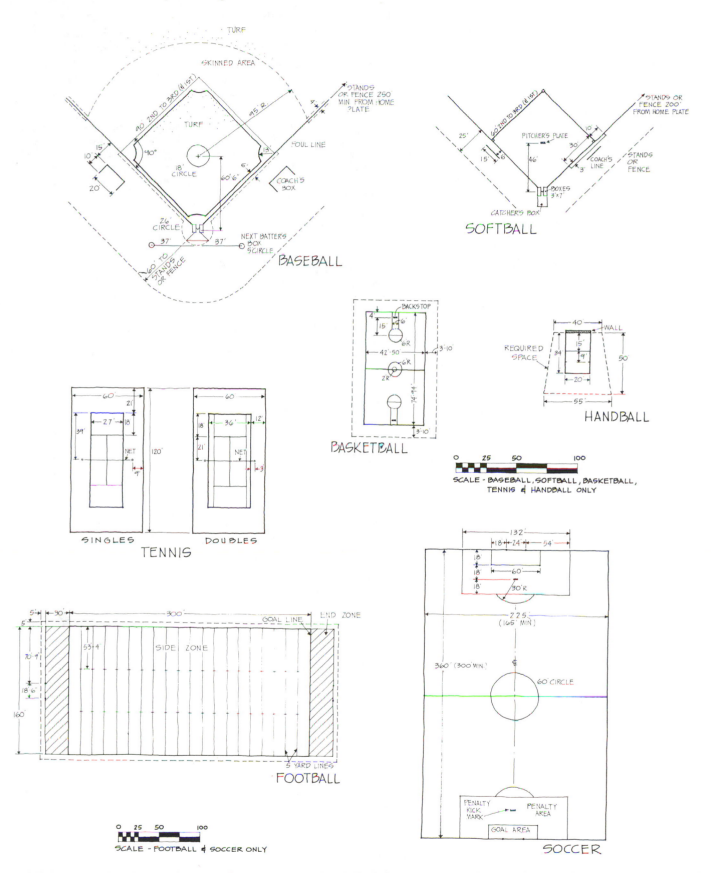

APPENDIX 6
Responses of Selected Trees to Recreation Use

Abstracted from the Southeastern Forest Experiment Station Research Note 171, Asheville, North Carolina, February, 1962, the following represents the results of research conducted on forty-two camping and picnicking sites on the Cherokee, Nantahala, and Pisgah National Forests by the United States Department of Agriculture, Forest Service, Thomas H. Ripley, project director.

Data indicated little or no difference in damage, or in insect and disease problems related to size or dominance of the vegetation. Differences between species, however, were consistently large. The following conifers and hardwoods are listed in order of decreasing ability to withstand the impacts of recreation use, as gauged by disease infection, insect infestation, and decline.

Conifers
1. Shortleaf pine
2. Hemlock
3. White pine
4. Pitch pine
5. Virginia pine

Hardwoods
1. Hickories
2. Persimmon
3. Sycamore
4. White ash
5. Beech
6. Sassafras
7. Buckeye
8. Yellow poplar
9. Dogwood
10. Blackgum
11. Yellow birch
12. Red maple
13. American holly
14. Sourwood
15. Black birch
16. White oaks
17. Black walnut
18. Red oak
19. Black locust
20. Magnolia
21. Black cherry
22. Blue beech

Conifers were clearly more susceptible to disease and insect attack than were hardwoods—with the possible exception of shortleaf pine and hemlock.

APPENDIX 7
Responses of Selected Soil Types to Recreation Use

The following are a few excerpts from *Soil Interpretations for Recreation,* prepared in 1969 by the United States Department of Agriculture, Soil Conservation Service for an Illinois region. The entire table contains ratings for hundreds of soil types.

Similar work has been done by the Soil Conservation Service for other regions, the ratings serving as preliminary information; the user may need to make detailed on-site investigations. Where soil maps or interpretations such as these are not available, the designer must rely even more upon site observations, usually couching the inventory in such general terms as wet soil, fertile soil, or rocky soil, rather than using sophisticated soil-type labels.

Soil Interpretations for Recreation for Major Land Resource Area _____ (Work Sheet)
Degree of Limitations and Soil Features Affecting Use*

Soil type and phase†	Cottages and utility buildings	Intensive campsites	Picnic area	Intensive play areas	Trail and paths	Golf fairways
Ade loamy fine sand:						
0–2% slopes	Moderate (dr, bl)	Moderate (t, dr, bl)	Moderate (t, dr, bl)	Moderate (t, dr, bl)	Moderate (t, bl)	Severe (dr)
2–6% slopes	Moderate (dr, bl)	Moderate (t, dr, bl)	Moderate (t, dr, bl)	Moderate (t, s, dr, bl)	Moderate (t, bl)	Severe (dr)
6–12% slopes	Moderate (dr, bl)	Severe (t, e, s, dr, bl)	Moderate (t, e, s, dr, bl)	Severe (t, e, s, dr, bl)	Moderate (t, e, bl)	Severe (s, dr)
Alvin fine sandy loam:						
2–4% slopes	Slight	Slight	Slight	Moderate	Slight	Slight
4–7% slopes	Slight	Slight	Slight	Moderate (s)	Slight	Slight
7–12% slopes	Moderate (s)	Moderate (s)	Moderate (s)	Severe (s)	Slight	Moderate (s)
12–18% slopes	Severe (s)	Severe (s)	Severe (s)	Severe (s)	Moderate (s)	Severe (s)
18–30% slopes	Severe (s)	Severe (s)	Severe (s)	Severe (s)	Severe (s)	Severe (s)
Andres loam or silt loam:						
0–2% slopes	Moderate (w)	Moderate (w)	Moderate (w)	Moderate (w)	Moderate (w)	Moderate (w)
2–4% slopes	Moderate (w)	Moderate (w)	Moderate (w)	Moderate (s, w)	Moderate (w)	Moderate (w)
Aptakasic silt loam:						
0–2% slopes	Moderate (w)	Moderate (d)	Moderate (d)	Moderate (d)	Moderate (d)	Moderate (d)
Ashkum silty clay loam:						
0–3% slopes	Severe (w, f)	Severe (w, f, t)	Severe (w, f, t)	Severe (w, f, t)	Severe (w, f, t)	Severe (w, f)
Ayr loam, fine sandy loam, or sandy loam:						
0–2% slopes	Slight	Slight	Slight	Slight	Slight	Slight
2–6% slopes	Slight	Slight	Slight	Moderate (s)	Slight	Slight
6–12% slopes	Moderate (s)	Moderate (s)	Moderate (s)	Severe (s)	Slight	Moderate (s)

Aztalan loam:						
0–2% slopes	Moderate (w)	Moderate (w)	Moderate (w)	Moderate (w)	Moderate (w)	Moderate (w)
2–6% slopes	Moderate (w)	Moderate (w)	Moderate (w)	Moderate (s, w)	Moderate (w)	Moderate (w)
Beecher silt loam:						
1–4% slopes	Moderate (w)	Moderate (w, p)	Moderate (w, p)	Moderate (w, p, s)	Moderate (w)	Moderate (w)
4–7% slopes	Moderate (w)	Moderate (w, p)	Moderate (w, p)	Moderate (w, p, s)	Moderate (w)	Moderate (s, w)
Billett sandy loam:						
0–2% slopes	Slight	Slight	Slight	Slight	Slight	Slight to moderate (dr)
2–4% slopes	Slight	Slight	Slight	Moderate (s)	Slight	Slight to moderate (dr)
4–7% slopes	Slight	Slight	Slight	Moderate (s)	Slight	Moderate (s, dr)
7–12% slopes	Moderate (s)	Moderate (s)	Moderate (s)	Severe (s)	Slight	Moderate (s, dr)
Bloomfield fine sand and loamy fine sand:						
0–6% slopes	Moderate (dr, bl, i, s)	Moderate (t, dr, bl, i, s)	Moderate (t, dr, bl, i, s)	Moderate (t, bl, s)	Moderate (t)	Severe (t, dr, i, s)
6–12% slopes	Moderate (dr, bl, i, s)	Moderate (t, dr, bl, i, s)	Moderate (t, dr, bl, i, s)	Severe (t, dr, bl, i, s)	Moderate (t)	Severe (t, dr, i, s)
12–18% slopes	Severe (s, dr, bl, i)	Severe (s, t, dr, bl, i)	Severe (s, t, dr, bl, i)	Severe (t, dr, bl, i, s)	Moderate (s, t)	Severe (t, dr, i, s)
18+%	Severe (s, dr, bl, i)	Severe (s, t, dr, bl, i)	Severe (s, t, dr, bl, i)	Severe (t, dr, bl, i, s)	Severe (s, t)	Severe (t, dr, i, s)
Blount silt loam:						
0–2% slopes	Moderate (w)	Moderate (w, p)	Moderate (w, p)	Moderate (w, p)	Moderate (w)	Moderate (w)
2–6% slopes	Moderate (w)	Moderate (w, p)	Moderate (w, p)	Moderate (w, p, s)	Moderate (w)	Moderate (w)
Brenton silt loam:						
0–2% slopes	Moderate (w)	Moderate (w)	Moderate (w)	Moderate (w)	Moderate (w)	Moderate (w)
2–4% slopes	Moderate (w)	Moderate (w)	Moderate (w)	Moderate (s, w)	Moderate (w)	Moderate (w)
Brooklyn silt loam:						
0–2% slopes	Severe (w, f, d)	Severe (w, f, d)	Severe (w, f, d)	Severe (w, p, f, d)	Severe (w, f)	Severe (w, f, d)
Bryce silty clay loam:						
0–2% slopes	Severe (w, f, d)	Severe (p, w, f, d, t)	Severe (p, w, f, d, t)	Severe (p, w, f, d, t)	Severe (p, w, f, t)	Severe (p, w, f, d, t)
Camden silt loam:						
0–2% slopes	Slight	Slight	Slight	Slight	Slight	Slight
2–4% slopes	Slight	Slight	Slight	Moderate (s)	Slight	Slight
4–7% slopes	Slight	Slight	Slight	Moderate (s)	Slight	Slight
7–12% slopes	Moderate (s)	Moderate (s)	Moderate (s)	Severe (s)	Slight	Moderate (s)
12–18% slopes	Severe (s)	Severe (s)	Severe (s)	Severe (s)	Moderate (s)	Severe (s)
18+% slopes	Severe (s)	Severe (s)	Severe (s)	Severe (s)	Severe (s)	Severe (s)

* Soils are rated on the basis of four classes of soil limitations: *Slight*—relatively free of limitations or limitations are easily overcome; *Moderate*—limitations need to be recognized, but can be overcome with good management and careful design; *Severe*—limitations severe enough to make use questionable; *Very Severe*—extreme measures are needed to overcome the limitations and usage generally is unsound or not practical.

Kind of limitation: b-bedrock depth; d-drainage; e-erosion; f-flooding or ponding; p-permeability; r-rockiness or stony; s-slope; t-texture of surface; w-watertable; i-inherent fertility; dr-drouthy; bl-blowing.

† Only slope phases are shown, unless the interpretations differ by erosion phases.

Sheet ____ of ____

Soil Interpretations for Recreation for Major Land Resource Area ——(Work Sheet) (continued)

Degree of Limitations and Soil Features Affecting Use*

Soil type and phase†	Cottages and utility buildings	Intensive campsites	Picnic area	Intensive play areas	Trail and paths	Golf fairways
Casco loam or silt loam:						
0–2% slopes	Slight (dr)	Slight (dr)	Slight (dr)	Slight (dr)	Slight (dr)	Slight
2–6% slopes	Slight (dr)	Slight (dr)	Slight (dr)	Moderate (s, dr)	Slight (dr)	Slight
6–12% slopes	Moderate (s, dr)	Moderate (s)	Moderate (s, dr)	Severe (s, dr)	Slight (dr)	Moderate (s, dr)
12–30% slopes	Severe (s, dr)	Severe (s)	Severe (s, dr)	Severe (s, dr)	Moderate (s)	Severe (s, dr, e)
Catlin silt loam:						
0–2% slopes	Slight	Slight	Slight	Slight	Slight	Slight
2–6% slopes	Slight	Slight	Slight	Moderate (s)	Slight	Slight
6–12% slopes	Moderate (s)	Moderate (s)	Moderate (s)	Severe (s)	Slight	Moderate (s)
Chalmers silty clay loam:						
0–2% slopes	Severe (w, f, d, t)	Severe (w, f, d, t)	Severe (w, f, d, t)	Severe (w, f, d, t)	Severe (w, f, d, t)	Severe (w, f, d, t)
Channahon silt loam to loam:						
2–4% slopes	Severe (b)	Slight	Slight	Severe (b, s)	Slight	Slight (b)
4–7% slopes	Severe (b)	Slight	Slight	Severe (b, s)	Slight	Moderate (s, b)
Chatsworth silt loam:						
7–12% slopes	Severe (s, e)	Severe (p, e, s)	Severe (e, s, i)	Severe (s, e, p, i)	Moderate (p)	Severe (e, s, i)
12–18% slopes	Severe (s, e)	Severe (p, e, s)	Severe (e, s, i)	Severe (s, e, p, i)	Moderate (p)	Severe (e, s, i)
18–30+% slopes	Severe (s, e)	Severe (p, e, s)	Severe (e, s, i)	Severe (s, e, p, i)	Severe (s)	Severe (e, s, i)
Clarence silty clay loam:						
0–12% slopes, slight and moderate eroded	Moderate (w, d)	Moderate (w, d)	Moderate (w, d)	Moderate (w, p, d, s)	Moderate (w, p)	Moderate (w, p, dr, d)
2–12% slopes, severe eroded	Severe (w, dr)	Severe (t, p, w, dr, d)	Severe (t, p, w, dr, d)	Severe (s, p, w, t, dr, d)	Severe (t, p, w)	Severe (w, dr, d)

Soil / slope	(1)	(2)	(3)	(4)	(5)	(6)	(7)
Colwood silt loam:							
0–3% slopes	Severe (w, d)	Severe (w, d)	Severe (w, d)	Severe (w, d)	Severe (w, d)	Severe (w, d)	Severe (w, d)
Corwin loam or silt loam:							
0–2% slopes	Slight	Slight	Slight	Slight	Slight	Slight	Slight
2–6% slopes	Slight	Slight	Slight	Moderate (s)	Slight	Slight	Slight
6–12% slopes	Moderate (s)	Moderate (s)	Moderate (s)	Severe (s)	Moderate (s)	Slight	Moderate (s)
Dana silt loam:							
0–2% slopes	Slight	Slight	Slight	Slight	Slight	Slight	Slight
2–6% slopes	Slight	Slight	Slight	Moderate (s)	Slight	Slight	Slight
Darroch silt loam or loam:							
0–2% slopes	Moderate (w, d)	Moderate (w, d)	Moderate (w, d)	Moderate (w, d)	Moderate (w, d)	Moderate (w, d)	Moderate (w, d)
Deardurff loam or fine sandy loam:							
0–2% slopes	Slight	Slight	Slight	Slight	Slight	Slight	Slight
2–6% slopes	Slight	Slight	Slight	Moderate (s, dr)	Slight	Slight	Slight
Del Rey silt loam:							
0–4% slopes	Moderate (w)	Moderate (w, p)	Moderate (w, p)	Moderate (w, p, s)	Moderate (w, p)	Moderate (w)	Moderate (w)
Dickinson sandy loam:							
0–2% slopes	Slight	Slight	Slight	Slight	Slight	Slight	Slight
2–6% slopes	Slight	Slight	Slight	Moderate (s, dr)	Slight	Slight	Slight
Dodge silt loam:							
2–7% slopes	Slight	Slight	Slight	Moderate (s)	Slight	Slight	Slight
7–12% slopes	Moderate (s)	Moderate (s)	Moderate (s)	Severe (s)	Moderate (s)	Slight	Moderate (s)
12–30% slopes	Severe (s)	Severe (s)	Severe (s)	Severe (s)	Severe (s)	Moderate (s)	Severe (s)
Dorchester silt loam:							
0–2% slopes	Severe (f, w)	Severe (f, w)	Moderate (f, w)	Severe (f, w)	Moderate (f, w)	Moderate (f, w)	Moderate (f, w)
Dresden loam or silt loam:							
0–2% slopes	Slight	Slight	Slight	Slight	Slight	Slight	Slight
2–4% slopes	Slight	Slight	Slight	Moderate (s)	Slight	Slight	Slight
4–7% slopes	Slight	Slight	Slight	Moderate (s)	Slight	Slight	Slight
Drummer silty clay loam:							
0–2% slopes	Severe (w, f)	Severe (w, f, t)	Severe (w, f, t)	Severe (w, f, t)	Severe (w, f, t)	Severe (w, f, t)	Severe (w, f)

* Soils are rated on the basis of four classes of soil limitations: *Slight* — relatively free of limitations or limitations are easily overcome; *Moderate* — limitations need to be recognized, but can be overcome with good management and careful design; *Severe* — limitations severe enough to make use questionable; *Very Severe* — extreme measures are needed to overcome the limitations and usage generally is unsound or not practical.

Kind of limitation: b-bedrock depth; d-drainage; e-erosion; f-flooding or ponding; p-permeability; r-rockiness or stony; s-slope; t-texture of surface; w-watertable; i-inherent fertility; dr-drouthy; bl-blowing.

† Only slope phases are shown, unless the interpretations differ by erosion phases.

Soil Interpretations for Recreation for Major Land Resource Area ——(Work Sheet) (continued)
Degree of Limitations and Soil Features Affecting Use*

Soil type and phase†	Cottages and utility buildings	Intensive campsites	Picnic area	Intensive play areas	Trail and paths	Golf fairways
Dupage silt loam:						
0–2% slopes	Severe (f, w)	Severe (f, w)	Moderate to severe	Severe (f, w)	Moderate (f, w)	Severe (f, w)
2–4% slopes	Severe (f, w)	Severe (f)	Moderate (f)	Severe (f, s)	Moderate (f)	Moderate (f)
Elliott silt loam or silty clay loam:						
0–2% slopes	Moderate (w)	Moderate (w, p)	Moderate (w, p)	Moderate (w, p)	Moderate (w)	Moderate (w)
2–6% slopes	Moderate (w)	Moderate (w, p)	Moderate (w, p)	Moderate (w, p, s)	Moderate (w)	Moderate (w)
Ellison silt loam:						
0–2% slopes	Slight	Slight	Slight	Slight	Slight	Slight
2–4% slopes	Slight	Slight	Slight	Moderate (s)	Slight	Slight
4–7% slopes	Slight	Slight	Slight	Moderate (s)	Slight	Slight
Elston sandy loam or loam:						
0–2% slopes	Slight (dr)	Slight (dr)	Slight (dr)	Slight (dr)	Slight (dr)	Moderate (s, dr)
2–6% slopes	Slight (dr)	Slight (dr)	Slight (dr)	Moderate (s, dr)	Slight (dr)	Moderate (s, dr)
6–12% slopes	Moderate (s, dr)	Moderate (s)	Moderate (s, dr)	Severe (s, dr)	Slight (dr)	Moderate (s, dr)
Epworth fine sandy loam:						
0–2% slopes	Slight (dr)	Slight (dr)	Slight (dr)	Slight (dr)	Slight	Slight (dr)
2–4% slopes	Slight (dr)	Slight (dr)	Slight (dr)	Moderate (s, bl, dr)	Slight	Slight (dr)
Flanagan silt loam:						
0–2% slopes	Moderate (w)	Moderate (w)	Moderate (w)	Moderate (w)	Moderate (w)	Moderate (w)
2–6% slopes	Moderate (w)	Moderate (w)	Moderate (w)	Moderate (s, w)	Moderate (w)	Moderate (w)
Fox silt loam or loam:						
0–2% slopes	Slight	Slight	Slight	Slight	Slight	Slight
2–6% slopes	Slight	Slight	Slight	Moderate (s)	Slight	Slight
6–12% slopes	Moderate (s)	Moderate (s)	Mode ate (s)	Severe (s)	Slight	Moderate (s)
12–18% slopes	Severe (s)	Severe (s)	Severe (s)	Severe (s)	Moderate (s)	Severe (s)
Frankfort silt loam to silty clay loam:						
2–4% slopes	Moderate (w)	Moderate (p, w)	Moderate (p, w)	Moderate (s, p, w)	Moderate (p, w, s)	Moderate (w, e)
4–7% slopes	Moderate (w)	Moderate (p, w)	Moderate (p, w)	Moderate (s, p, w)	Moderate (p, w, e)	Moderate (s, e, w)

Granby fine sandy loam:						
0–3% slopes	Severe (w, d)	Severe (w, d)	Severe (w, d)	Severe (w, d)	Moderate to severe (w, d)	Severe (w, d)
Grays silt loam:						
2–4% slopes	Slight	Slight	Slight	Moderate (s)	Slight	Slight
Harpster silt loam or loam:						
0–4% slopes	Severe (w, f)	Severe (w, f)	Severe (w, f)	Severe (w, f)	Severe (w, f)	Severe (w, f)
Harpster silty clay or loam:						
0–2% slopes	Severe (w, f)	Severe (w, f)	Severe (w, f)	Severe (w, f)	Severe (w, f)	Severe (w, f)
Harvard silt loam:						
0–2% slopes	Slight	Slight	Slight	Slight	Slight	Slight
2–4% slopes	Slight	Slight	Slight	Moderate (s)	Slight	Slight
4–7% slopes	Slight	Moderate (s)	Slight	Moderate (s)	Slight	Slight
7–12% slopes	Moderate (s)	Moderate (s)	Moderate (s)	Severe (s)	Slight	Moderate (s)
12–18% slopes	Severe (s)	Severe (s)	Severe (s)	Severe (s)	Moderate (s)	Severe (s)
Hebron loam:						
0–2% slopes	Slight	Slight	Slight	Slight	Slight	Slight
2–6% slopes	Slight	Slight	Slight	Moderate (s)	Slight	Slight
6–12% slopes	Moderate (s)	Moderate (s)	Moderate (s)	Severe (s)	Slight	Moderate (s)
Hannepin loam or silt loam:						
4–7% slopes	Slight	Slight	Slight	Moderate (s)	Slight	Slight
7–12% slopes	Moderate (s)	Moderate (s)	Moderate (s)	Severe (s)	Slight	Moderate (s)
12–18% slopes	Severe (s)	Severe (s)	Severe (s)	Severe (s)	Moderate (s)	Severe (s)
18+% slopes	Severe (s)	Severe (s)	Severe (s)	Severe (s)	Severe (s)	Severe (s)
Herbert silt loam:						
0–2% slopes	Moderate (w)	Moderate (w)	Moderate (w)	Moderate (w)	Moderate (w)	Moderate (w)
2–4% slopes	Moderate (w)	Moderate (w)	Moderate (w)	Moderate (s, w)	Moderate (w)	Moderate (w)

Sheet ____ of ____

* Soils are rated on the basis of four classes of soil limitations: *Slight*—relatively free of limitations or limitations are easily overcome; *Moderate*—limitations need to be recognized, but can be overcome with good management and careful design; *Severe*—limitations severe enough to make use questionable; *Very Severe*—extreme measures are needed to overcome the limitations and usage generally is unsound or not practical.

Kind of limitation: b-bedrock depth; d-drainage; e-erosion; f-flooding or ponding; p-permeability; r-rockiness or stony; s-slope; t-texture of surface; w-watertable; i-inherent fertility; dr-drouthy; bl-blowing.

†Only slope phases are shown, unless the interpretations differ by erosion phases.

Bibliography

The numbers in parentheses which follow each citation refer to the chapters in this book which the reference most directly augments. An asterisk (*) indicates that the reference contains information related to the natural resource aspects of park system planning.

Aaron, David, with Bonnie P. Winawer: *Child's Play: A Creative Approach to Playscapes for Today's Children,* Harper & Row, Publishers, Inc., New York, 1965. (2,3)

Allen, Marjorie: *Design for Play,* E. T. Hawn and Company, Ltd., London, 1962. (2,3)

————: *New Playgrounds,* E. T. Hawn and Company, Ltd., London, 1964. (2,3)

————: *Planning for Play,* The M.I.T. Press, Cambridge, Mass., 1968. (2,3)

American Camping Association: *Tent and Trailer Sites,* Bradford Woods, Ind., 1962. (4)

American Society of Landscape Architects: *New Landscapes for Recreation,* Washington, D.C., 1967. (1)

American Society of Landscape Architects Foundation, and U.S. Department of Housing and Urban Development: *Barrier Free Site Design,* U.S. Government Printing Office, Washington, D.C., 1976. (4)

Appleyard, Donald, Kevin Lynch, and John R. Myer: *The View from the Road,* The M.I.T. Press, Cambridge, Mass., 1964. (2)

Ardrey, Robert: *The Territorial Imperative,* Atheneum Publishers, New York, 1966. (2)

Arnold, Serena E.: *Trends in Consolidation of Parks and Recreation: Including Pros and Cons,* American Institute of Park Executives Management Aids Bulletin, no. 41, Wheeling, W.Va., 1964. (1)

Blake, Peter: *God's Own Junkyard: The Planned Deterioration of America's Landscape,* Holt, Rinehart, and Winston, Inc. New York, 1964. (1)

Brown, Joe, and David G. Wright: *Marinas: A Guide to Their Development for Park and Recreation Departments,* American Institute of Park Executives Management Aids Bulletin, no. 54, Wheeling, W.Va., 1965. (4)

Butler, George D.: *Introduction to Community Recreation,* McGraw-Hill Book Company, New York, 1976. (2,4)

————: *Recreation Areas: Their Design and Equipment,* The Ronald Press Company, New York, 1958. (2,4)

————: *Standards for Municipal Recreation Areas,* National Recreation Association, New York, 1962. (2,4)

Callender, John H. (ed): *Time Saver Standards,* McGraw-Hill Book Company, New York, 1982. (2)

Caskey, George B., and David G. Wright: *Coasting and Tobogganing Facilities,* National Recreation and Park Association Management Aids Bulletin, no. 62, Wheeling, W.Va., 1966. (4)

Chaney, Charles A.: *Marinas: Recommendations for Design, Construction, and Maintenance,* National Association of Engine and Boat Manufacturers, New York, 1961. (4)

Clawson, Marion: *Land and Water for Recreation,* Rand McNally & Company, Chicago, 1963. (1)

————: *Land for Americans,* Rand McNally & Company, Chicago, 1965. (1)

Connell, Edward A.: *Lawn Bowling: An Analysis of Public Operations,* American Institute of Park Executives Management Aids Bulletin, no. 10, Wheeling, W.Va., 1961. (4)

Cook, Walter L.: *Manual and Survey for Public Safety for Park and Recreation Departments,* American Institute of Park Executives Management Aids Bulletin, no. 20, Wheeling, W.Va., 1962. (4)

————: *Shooting Ranges: A Survey of and Manual for Park and/or Recreation Departments,* American Institute of Park Executives Management Aids Bulletin, no. 35, Wheeling, W.Va., 1964. (4)

Danford, Howard G.: *Recreation in the American Community,* Harper & Brothers, New York, 1953. (2,4)

Doell, Charles E., and Gerald B. Fitzgerald: *A Brief History of Parks and Recreation in the United States,* The Athletic Institute, Chicago, 1954. (1)

Doell, Charles E., and Louis F. Twardzik: *Elements of Park and Recreation Administration,* Burgess Publishing Company, Minneapolis, Minn., 1979. (1,2,4,6)

Douglass, Robert W.: *Forest Recreation,* Pergamon Press, New York, 1969. (4)

Dubos, René: *So Human an Animal: How We Are Shaped by Surroundings and Events,* Charles Scribner's Sons, New York, 1969. (2,3)

Dulles, Rhea D.: *A History of Recreation,* Meredith Publishing Company, Des Moines, Iowa, 1965. (1)

Eckbo, Garrett: *The Landscape We See,* McGraw-Hill Book Company, New York, 1969. (1,2,3,4,5,6,*)

————: *Urban Landscape Design,* McGraw-Hill Book Company, New York, 1964. (1,2,3,4,5,6)

Ellis, Michael J.: *Why People Play,* Prentice-Hall, Inc., Englewood Cliffs, N.J., 1973. (2)

Ellis, Michael J., and G. J. L. Scholtz: *Activity and Play of Children,* Prentice-Hall Inc., Englewood Cliffs, N.J., 1978. (2)

Fabos, Julius Gy., Gordon T. Milde, and Michael Weinmayer: *Frederick Law Olmsted, Sr.: Founder of Landscape Architecture in America,* University of Massachusetts Press, Amherst, 1968. (1)

Fine, Albert: *Landscape into Cityscape: Frederick Law Olmsted's Plans for a Greater New York,* Cornell University Press, Ithaca, N.Y., 1968. (1)

Flint, Harrison L.: *Landscape Plants for Eastern North America,* Wiley-Interscience, New York, 1983. (4)

Gabrielsen, M. Alexander, and Caswell M. Miles: *Sports and Recreation Facilities for School and Community,* Prentice-Hall, Inc., Englewood Cliffs, N.J., 1958. (4)

Hall, Edward T.: *The Hidden Dimension,* Doubleday & Company, Inc., Garden City, N.Y., 1966. (3)

————: *The Silent Language,* Greenwood Press, Westport, Conn., 1980. (2)

Harvard University Landscape Architecture Research Office: *Three Approaches to Environmental Analysis,* The Conservation Foundation, Washington, D.C., 1967. (6,*)

Hittson, Hamilton, and Paul N. Jones: *Building and Programming Casting Pools,* American Institute of Park Executives Management Aids Bulletin, no. 12, Wheeling, W.Va., 1962. (4)

Holland, Roy (ed.): *Planning and Building the Golf Course,* National Golf Foundation, Inc., Chicago, 1959. (4)

Hopf, Peter S.: *Access for the Handicapped: The Barrier-Free Regulation for Design and Construction in All 50 States,* Van Nostrand Reinhold, New York, 1984. (4)

Jarrell, Temple R.: *Horseshoe Pitching: A Guide to Court Layouts,* National Park and Recreation Association Management Aids Bulletin, no. 71, Wheeling, W.Va., 1967. (4)

Kotter, David H.: "Landscape Design Criteria for Ski Slope Development," master's thesis, University of Illinois, Urbana, 1967. (3,4)

LaGasse, Alfred B.: *Drag Strips, Why, When, and How: A Survey of Public Operations,* American Institute of Park Executives Management Aids Bulletin, no. 19, Wheeling, W.Va., 1962. (4)

————, and Walter L. Cook: *History of Parks and Recreation,* American Institute of Park Executives Management Aids Bulletin, no. 56, Wheeling, W.Va., 1965. (1)

Ledermann, Alfred, and Alfred Trachsel: *Creative Playgrounds and Recreation Centers,* Frederick A. Praeger, Inc., New York, 1968. (2,3)

Lewis, Philip H., Jr., and Associates: *Regional Design for Human Impact,* Thomas Printing and Publishing Company, Ltd., Kaukana, Wis., 1968. (*)

Lynch, Kevin: *Site Planning,* The M.I.T. Press, Cambridge, Mass., 1962. (2,3,4,5,6)

Marshall, Lane L.: *Action by Design,* American Society of Landscape Architects, Washington, D.C., 1983. (1)

McHarg, Ian L.: *Design with Nature,* The Natural History Press, Garden City, N.Y., 1969. (1,2,3,4,6,*)

Moeller, John: *Standards for Outdoor Recreation Areas,* American Society of Planning Officials, Chicago, 1965. (2,4)

Molnar, Donald J.: "Physical Design Criteria for the Landscape Design of Pre-school Play Areas," master's thesis, University of Illinois, Urbana, 1964. (2,3,7)

Mott, William Penn, Jr.: *Creative Playground Equipment,* American Institute of Park Executives Management Aids Bulletin, no. 40, Wheeling, W.Va., 1964. (2)

Mueller, Eva, and Gerald Gurin: *Participation in Outdoor Recreation: Factors Affecting Demand Among American Adults,* Report to the Outdoor Recreation Resources Review Commission, Government Printing Office, Washington, D.C., 1962. (2)

National Facilities Conference: *Planning Facilities for Health, Physical Education, and Recreation,* The Athletic Institute, Chicago, 1962. (2,4,7)

Olgay, Victor: *Design with Climate,* Princeton University Press, Princeton, N.J., 1963. (4)

Park Association of New York, Inc.: *New Parks for New York,* New York, 1963. (1,7)

Pena, William M., with William W. Caudill and John W. Focke: *Problem Seeking,* Cahners Books International, Boston, 1977. (6)

Purdue University, Cooperative Extension Service: *Guidelines for Developing Land for Outdoor Recreational Uses,* West Lafayette, Ind., 1963. (4,6)

Ramsey, Charles G., and Harold R. Sleeper: *Architectural Graphic Standards,* John Wiley & Sons, Inc., New York, 1981. (4)

Ripley, T. H.: *Tree and Shrub Response to Recreation Use,* U.S. Forest Service, Southeastern Forest Experiment Station, Research Note 171, Asheville, N.C., 1962. (4)

Robinette, Gary O. (ed): *Landscape Planning for Energy Conservation,* American Society of Landscape Architects Foundation, Washington, D.C., 1977. (4)

Rombold, Charles C.: *Guidelines for Campground Development,* American Institute of Park Executives Management Aids Bulletin, no. 34, Wheeling, W.Va., 1964. (4)

————: *Natural Ice Skating Surfaces,* American Institute of Park Executives Management Aids Bulletin, no. 37, Wheeling, W.Va., 1964. (4)

————: *Signs and Symbols for Park and Recreation Use,* American Institute of Park Executives Management Aids Bulletin, no. 39, Wheeling, W.Va., 1964. (4)

Rubenstein, Harvey M.: *A Guide to Site and Environmental Planning,* John Wiley & Sons, Inc., New York, 1969. (2,3,4,5,6)

Rutledge, Albert: *A Visual Approach to Park Design,* John Wiley & Sons, Inc., New York, 1985. (2)

Salomon, J. H.: *Campsite Development,* Girl Scouts of the United States of America Council Administrative Series, no. 5B, New York, 1959. (4)

Simonds, John O.: *Earthscape: A Manual of Environmental Planning,* McGraw-Hill Book Company, New York, 1978. (1)

————: *Landscape Architecture: A Manual of Site Planning and Design,* 2nd ed., McGraw-Hill Book Company, New York, 1983. (1,2,3,4,5,6)

Sommer, Robert: *Personal Space: The Behavioral Basis of Design,* Prentice-Hall, Inc., Englewood Cliffs, N.J., 1969. (2)

Stott, Charles C.: *Evaluating Water Based Recreation Facilities and Areas,* National Recreation and Park Association Management Aids Bulletin, no. 70, Wheeling, W.Va., 1967. (4)

Udall, Stewart L.: *The Quiet Crisis,* Holt, Rinehart, and Winston, Inc., New York, 1963. (1)

United States Department of Agriculture, Forest Service: *The American Outdoors: Management for Beauty and Use,* Misc. Publication #1000, 1965. (1,3,4)

United States Department of the Interior, Bureau of Outdoor Recreation: *Outdoor Recreation Space Standards,* 1967. (2,4)

————, National Park Service: *Special Park Uses,* 1961. (2,4)

Van Meter, Jerry R.: *Master Plans for Park Sites,* University of Illinois Cooperative Extension Service, Urbana, 1969. (2,4,6)

Vollmer, Associates: *Parking for Recreation,* American Institute of Park Executives, Wheeling, W.Va., 1965. (4)

Weddle, A. E. (ed.): *Techniques of Landscape Architecture,* William Heinemann, Ltd., London, 1967. (2,3,4,5,6)

Whyte, William H.: *Cluster Development,* American Conservation Association, New York, 1964. (1,*)

————: *The Last Landscape,* Doubleday & Company, Inc., Garden City, N.Y., 1968. (1,*)

————: *The Social Life of Small Urban Spaces,* The Conservation Foundation, Washington, D.C., 1980. (2)

Williams, Wayne R.: *Recreation Places,* Reinhold Publishing Corporation, New York, 1958. (2,3,4)

Wilson, George T.: *Vandalism: How to Stop It,* American Institute of Park Executives Management Aids Bulletin, no. 7, Wheeling, W.Va., 1961. (4)

Wisconsin, State of, Bureau of Recreation: *Recreation Site Evaluation,* Madison, Wis., 1968. (2,4,*)

Wright, David G.: *Public Beaches,* American Institute of Park Executives Management Aids Bulletin, no. 51, Wheeling, W.Va., 1965. (4)

Wyman, Donald: *Shrubs and Vines for American Gardens,* The Macmillan Company, New York, 1969. (4)

————: *Trees for American Gardens,* The Macmillan Company, New York, 1959. (4)

Young Men's Christian Association National Commission on YMCA Camp Layouts, Buildings, and Facilities: *Developing Campsites and Facilities,* Association Press, New York, 1960. (4)

Index

Accessibility:
  federal legislation mandating, 55
  in public places, 55
  ramps for, 39, 55
    maximum slope for, 55
  site modification for, 59
  for wheelchairs, 55
Adaptation of facilities, 10
"Adopt-A-Park" program, 59
Aesthetics, 30, 124
  (*See also* Beauty)
AMAX Coal Company, 61
Amphitheaters, 15, 16, 18, 44
Architect's scale, use of, 88
Automobiles (*see* Circulation systems)

Baseball diamonds, 52, 77, 109–111, 173
  factors affecting design of, 110–111
Beauty, 32, 124
  creating experiences, 36–46
  determining quality, 35, 36, 46, 47, 49
Behavior:
  avoiding circumstances causing injuries,
    77
  challenge, 77
  freedom, 27, 72, 73
  as influencing design, 23–30
  mental exercise, 7
  order, environmental, 35, 48, 124
  pride, 7
  psychological effects of environment, 7
  security, 77
  territorial imperative, 93
  variety, environmental, 36, 43, 47, 124
  (*See also* Space)
Behavioral theory, 26
Benches, 19, 21, 27, 54, 55

Bike racks, spacing, 72
Bikeway, 61
Boat docks, 52, 53
Bodell, Kathleen, 61
Boggy area, use of, 56
*Brief History of Parks and Recreation in the
    United States* (Doell and Fitzgerald),
    3n.
Budget:
  construction, 55, 56
  maintenance, 56
  (*See also* Costs, minimizing)
Budget restrictions, 56
Building boom, 5
Buildings, 15, 18, 44, 61, 126
  new, planning, 60

California state parks, multiple use of
    parking areas in, 63–64
Campgrounds, 51, 52
Caudill Rowlett Scott, programming tech-
    niques of, 92
Central Park, New York City, 1–3
Church, Thomas, 54
Circulation systems, 49, 53, 66, 74, 123,
    125
  artery types of, 74, 123
  orientation points, 76
  parking lots, 16, 18, 20, 53, 122, 123
  roadway design, 21, 53, 61
  vehicular-pedestrian separation, 123
Collaboration with landscape architects:
  behavioral scientists, 24
  building architects, 119
  facility operators, 53
  recreators, 1, 2
Colors (*see* Beauty)

Comfort, user, 54, 55, 77
Commercial elements in design, 142, 147
Computers:
  analysis of maintenance, 58
  analysis of services, 58
  and budget balancing, 57
  cost-saving analysis, 30
  data banks, 12
  data bases, 12
  data management, 104
  data matrix analysis, 104
  decision making and, 12
  ecosystem data, 65
  evaluation of alternatives, 104
  forecasting consequences, 12
  inventory organization, 103
  matrix forms, 12
  simulation, 25
  spreadsheets, 12
Construction budget, 55, 56
Construction costs, minimizing, 44, 56–68
Construction materials selection, 65–68,
    125
Construction plans, 84, 85
Contours, 86–89
  (*See also* Slopes)
Contrast in design, 45
Cost effectiveness, 58
Cost estimation, 30
Costs:
  equipment operation, 57
  and material selection, 66
  minimizing: of construction, 44, 56–68
    of maintenance, 19, 56–72
"Creative" financing, 58

Decision making, 10
  computers and, 12

Demand studies, 23
   purpose of, 23, 51
   questionnaire examples, 155–171
Design process, 82, 91–105, 107
   analysis: site, 97–98
      of use-area relationships, 97
   design concept, 98–102
   inventory of on-site factors, 93–96
   program development, 92–93
   refinement of plan, 102
Design styles:
   contemporary, 4
   English Romantic period, 2
   of Olmsted, 3, 4
Detail plans, 83, 84
DeTurk, Phillip E., 114
Doell, Charles, 3*n.*, 5, 32
Drainage of tile lines, overflow, 56
Drainage patterns, 30, 61, 95
Drinking fountains, 55, 79, 83

Elements of Park and Recreation Administration (Doell), 5*n.*
Elevation(s):
   drawings of, 85
   as height expression, 88
Ellis, Michael J., 22
Enclosure (*see* Space)
Energy conservation, 10, 52, 71
   earth sheltering, 53
   landform, 53
   solar control, 71
   solar design, 53
   solar pool-heating system, 59
   wind control, 71
Engineer's scale, use of, 88
Environmentalists, 5
Equipment costs, 32
Equipment inventory, 32
Experience:
   aesthetic (*see* Beauty)
   recreational, 4, 5, 7

Fees, landscape architectural, 108
Financing:
   "creative," 58
   public and private, 59
Fitness Centers, 59
Fitzgerald, Gerald B., 3*n.*
Flexibility, design, 140
Forest Preserve, Lake County, Illinois, 57
Forms (*see* Beauty)
"Free gift," cost of, 69
Function, 30, 32, 40, 43–45
Functional efficiency, 49–82
   determining quality, 49, 50, 80–82
Funds:
   grants, 9
      for consultants, 9
   and inflation, 9
   for land acquisition, 9
   public, 9
   and recession, 9
Furniture, park, 19, 55, 79, 83, 113
   benches, 19, 21, 27, 54, 55
   drinking fountains, 55, 79, 83
   light fixtures, 19, 83, 113

Furniture, park (*Cont.*):
   sign styles, 21

Game area layout diagrams, selected, 173
Garden hoses, length of, 72
Gradients:
   how indicated, 88, 99
   slope, 88, 94, 95
Grass, 53, 64, 66, 71, 126
   (*See also* Turf)

Hall, Robert T., 27
Handball courts, 18, 172, 173
Historical value, 141
Human needs (*see* Behavior, as influencing design)
Humidity, 52
   (*See also* Design process)

Increased productivity, 10, 12, 13, 55, 62, 141
   in California state parks, 63
   detention basin as amphitheater, 63
   intensifying uses of, 92
   lighting for, 64
   low-density developments, 59
   scheduling for, 63
   specialized vehicles, 63
   turf improvement, 64
Indianapolis Park District, 61
Interpretation, design:
   computer simulations, 25
   models, 25
   sketches, 25
Intuition, designer's, 15, 35, 36, 91
Investment:
   joint private-public ventures, 9
   private, on public lands, 9
Izumita, Ron, 24, 25

Joint ventures with research agencies, 70

Land:
   competition for, 7, 8
   drainage, 61, 94, 95
   shaping, 44, 53, 60, 61, 122
   use of, 9, 15, 17, 18, 60
   use overlap, 62
   (*See also* Contours; Design process)
Landfills, 9
Landscape architect:
   education of, 2, 4, 91
   selecting, 107, 108
   title conception, 1
   (*See also* Collaboration with landscape architects)
Lewis, Todd, 61
Life Cost, 114, 134
Life-cost analysis, 30
Life potential, 138
Light fixtures, 19, 83, 113
Line weights, drawing, 85
Lines (*see* Beauty)
Los Angeles, Skid Row Park in, 24

Maintenance, 53, 56–72, 77
   and pride in a development, 45

Maintenance (*Cont.*):
   productive, 137
   supportive, 137
Maintenance costs, 137–141
   minimizing, 19, 56–72
Marinas, 16
Master plans, 83, 84
Materials, life span of, 10
Materials selection:
   construction, 65–68, 125
   native materials, 66
   plants (*see* Plants)
   sign design, 68
Mining sites:
   depleted, 9
   restoration of strip-mined areas, 61
Models, scale, 85
Mulch, 67
Multiple activity areas, 141
Multiple-use concepts, 10

Natural elements and forces, 15
   (*See also* Design process; Humidity; Plants; Rainfall; Snowfall; Soil; Sun; Water; Wind)
Nature preserve, 56
Nature programs, 57
Nature study areas, 56, 121, 126
Nugent, Timothy, 60

Observation:
   filmmaking techniques for, 26
   and identifying needs, 24
   of play facilities, 24
   of user satisfaction, 12
   of users, 29
Obsolescence, 114, 134
   numerical evaluation of, 141
   relative evaluation of, 147
   "thermometer test," 134
Old School Preserve, Illinois, 57
Olmsted, Frederick Law, 1–4, 7
Open space, use of, 3, 27, 73, 119
Order, environmental, 35–48, 124
   factors affecting, 37–42

Paine, Thomas, School-Park, Urbana, Illinois, 114
Park(s):
   definition of, 4, 5
   design goals for, 8–13
   designer of (*see* Landscape architect)
   planner of (*see* Landscape architect)
   and recreation movement, 2–8
   system for, 3, 80, 149–151
Park departments, 4
Park-school complex, 56
Parking lots, 16, 18, 20, 53, 122, 123
Parkway, 3
Paving, epoxy-bonded, 72
Pena, William, 92, 104
People watching, 26, 54
Personal Space: The Behavioral Basis of Design (Sommer), 27
Perspective drawings, 85
Picnic areas, 18, 19, 52, 53, 67
Plans:
   analyzing, 107–147

Plans (*Cont.*):
    case studies, 113–147
    construction, 85
    creating (*see* Design process)
    detail, 84
    drawing, 85, 86
    interpreting, 25
    master, 83, 84
    planting, 85
    preliminary, 102
    reading, 84–89, 124
    schematic, 84
    site, 83–85
    staging, 84
Planting plans, 85
Plants, 15, 18, 60, 68–71, 79, 174
    limited life span of, 70
    prairie, 57
    (*See also* Design process)
Play theory regarding children, 22
Playgrounds, 19, 21–24, 51, 52, 66, 71, 74,
        77, 120, 125–127
POD Inc., 24
Postconstruction evaluation, 25–26
Prairie plants, 57
Prairie restoration, 57
Preliminary plans, 102
Private developers, 58
Problem Seeking (Pena), 92
Productive maintenance, 137
Productivity, increased (*see* Increased pro-
        ductivity)
Program, checklist of items for, 29
Program elements, value assignment, 96
Programming uses, 92
Public coordinator as liaison between park
        district and neighborhood, 93

Railroads, abandoned rights-of-way of, 9
Rainfall, 15, 53
    (*See also* Design process)
Recreation:
    definition of, 5
    research on, 23, 24
Recreation areas, definition of, 4
Recreation departments, 4
Recreation movement, park and, 2–8
Rehabilitation, 10
Research agencies, 70
Resource decrease, 55
Restoration of strip-mined areas, 61
Ripley, Thomas H., 174
Riverside (Illinois) subdivision, 3
Road system, safety of, 147
Roads (*see* Circulation systems)
Rutledge, Albert J., 22

Safety, 77, 119–121
    of road system, 147

Scale:
    human, 45, 76
    speed, 46
Schematic plans, 84
School-parks, 51
    evaluation of site plan for, 114–127
Section drawings, 85
Security, 27, 60
Sentimental value, 141
Sign design, 68
Sign styles, 21
Silent Language, The (Hall), 27
Site, factors affecting design of (*see* Design
        process; Land, use of)
Site plans, 83–85
Sizes, area, 50–51, 153–155, 172
Ski runs, 53
Skid Row Park, Los Angeles, 24
Slopes:
    as design factors, 18, 53, 122
    how indicated, 86–88, 98
    maintenance of, 71
    orientation of, 32, 53, 125
    (*See also* Contours; Design process;
        Land, shaping)
Snowfall, 53
    (*See also* Design process)
Social gathering spaces, 26, 121
Social Life of Small Urban Spaces, The
        (Whyte), 26
Soesbe, Jerrold, 57
Soil, 18, 62, 175–181
    (*See also* Design process)
Solar energy, 10
    (*See also* Energy conservation)
Solar pool-heating system, 59
Sommer, Robert, 27
Space:
    indoor, psychological effects of, 39–40
    outdoor: functions of, 40–41, 46–47
        psychological effects of, 41–42, 61,
            76
Staging plans, 84
Standards:
    activity, 21, 23, 153–154
    for area sizes, 50–51, 153–154, 172
    for facilities, 21–23, 50–52, 153–154
    of the park system, 149
    quantitative, 22
    as starting points, 28
Step design, 54
String trimmer, 71
Sun, 15, 52–53
    (*See also* Design process)
Supervision of activity, 19, 72–73,
        125
    in high-risk areas, 77
Supportive maintenance, 137
Swamps, 17

Swimming areas, 19, 97–103
Symbols, plan (*see* Plans, reading)

Tennis courts, 18, 52, 61, 62, 126, 172,
        173
Territorial imperative, 93
Textures (*see* Beauty)
Time-Saver Standards (section by Hut-
        macher and Mertes), 22
Toboggan runs, 18, 62, 125
Topography (*see* Contours; Design proc-
        ess; Slopes)
Transition, environmental, 44, 61
Trees, transplanting, 63, 69, 70
"Trees on Wheels" program, 63
Turf, artificial, 64
Turf improvement, sand slit process, 64

Undesirables, discouraging, 78–80
Use, multiple, 10
Use-area relationships, 15–17, 76, 120,
        122
    with site, 17–18, 44, 53, 60, 61, 122
    with surroundings, 16, 80, 121
    (*See also* Design process; Plans, analyz-
        ing)
Usefulness, maintenance evaluation, 138
User needs, determining, 22
    demand studies, 51, 155–171
    design program, 92–93
    (*See also* Behavior, as influencing de-
        sign)
User participation, 25
User satisfaction, 12, 27
User surveys, 12

Value assignment, data, 96
Vandalism, 27
    discouraging, 78–80
Variety, environmental, 7, 36, 38, 43, 45,
        46, 121
Vaux, Calvert, 3
Visual Approach to Park Design, A (Rut-
        ledge), 22, 24, 26

Walkways (*see* Circulation systems)
Water, 15, 17, 18, 53
    (*See also* Design process)
Waterslides, 58, 142
Whistler, James McNeil, 37, 49
Why People Play (Ellis), 22
Whyte, William H., 26
Wind, 15, 53, 121
    (*See also* Design process)
Working drawings (*see* Construction
        plans; Planting plans)

Yosemite Valley, California, 3